The Power of a Promise

Education and Economic Renewal in Kalamazoo

Michelle Miller-Adams

2009

W.E. Upjohn Institute for Employment Research
Kalamazoo, Michigan

Library of Congress Cataloging-in-Publication Data

Miller-Adams, Michelle, 1959-
  The power of a promise : education and economic renewal in Kalamazoo / Michelle
Miller-Adams.
    p. cm.
  ISBN-13: 978-0-88099-339-5 (pbk. : alk. paper)
  ISBN-10: 0-88099-339-1 (pbk : alk. paper)
  ISBN-13: 978-0-88099-340-1 (hardcover : alk. paper)
  ISBN-10: 0-88099-340-5 (hardcover : alk. paper)
  1. High school graduates—Scholarships, fellowships, etc.—Michigan—Kalamazoo.
2. Scholarships—Michigan—Kalamazoo. I. Title.

  LB2338.M53 2008
  378.3'40977417—dc22
                                  2008052863

The facts presented in this study and the observations and viewpoints expressed are
the sole responsibility of the author. They do not necessarily represent positions of
the W.E. Upjohn Institute for Employment Research.

Cover design by Carol A.S. Derks.
Index prepared by Diane Worden.
Printed in the United States of America.
Printed on recycled paper.

"Michelle Miller-Adams captures the truly unique story of the Kalamazoo Promise without losing sight of the universal lessons it offers us. *The Power of a Promise* is essential reading for anyone who wants to understand the future of economic and community development in our country."
–*Governor Jennifer M. Granholm, State of Michigan*

"The Kalamazoo Promise is a fascinating experiment with enormous implications for American education. Will the promise of free tuition inspire students to work harder in school? Will it draw more middle-class families back into the city's public school system, enriching the learning environment for all? Michelle Miller-Adams provides a superb, thoroughly researched, and highly readable account of this closely watched, groundbreaking venture."
–*Richard D. Kahlenberg, senior fellow, The Century Foundation and author of* All Together Now: Creating Middle-Class Schools through Public School Choice

"Across America, economic developers struggle to overcome the disincentives created by low-performance, poverty-impacted school districts. Michelle Miller-Adams offers an insightful first look at the impact of the Kalamazoo Promise in revitalizing a city's declining job market and aging neighborhoods. If 'housing policy is school policy,' the Kalamazoo Promise tests whether 'school policy is housing policy.'"
–*David Rusk, former mayor of Albuquerque and author of* Cities Without Suburbs *and* Inside Game/Outside Game

"Michelle Miller-Adams does a superb job of exploring the political science, economics, sociology, and psychology of the Kalamazoo Promise. Her book begins as an education whodunit and quickly shifts to a policy wonk's dream. As with *The Mystery of Edwin Drood*, the last (and unfinished) work of Charles Dickens, the reader is left with a deliciously tantalizing question. Unlike in Dickens's mystery, however, the Promise question is: In the next 20 years, how will Kalamazoo be able to use its Promise to continue its transformation?"
–*Michael F. Rice, PhD, Superintendent, Kalamazoo Public Schools*

"*The Power of a Promise* captures the dramatic history of the Kalamazoo Promise's first three years and explores the work to be done to contribute to the region's transformation for decades to come. Assessing progress to date, Miller-Adams also gives useful suggestions about what remains to be done. Her book reveals that the success of the Kalamazoo Promise rests not on scholarship dollars alone, but on individual and organizational actions in support of the complementary goals of education and economic development. Having been deeply involved in the work of the Kalamazoo Promise, Miller-Adams portrays a true picture of its vision that, 'Greater Kalamazoo will become a world leader in education, investing in youth to elevate the quality of life for each resident.'"
–*Janice M. Brown, EdD, Executive Director, The Kalamazoo Promise*

The Power of a Promise

Contents

Figures

Tables

Preface

This story began for me at 7:59 a.m. on November 11, 2005, minutes after taking my daughter to preschool in our hometown of Kalamazoo, Michigan. Tuning in to the local public radio station at the top of the hour, I was surprised and a bit puzzled to hear that the superintendent of the Kalamazoo Public Schools (KPS) had announced a new scholarship program that would send all graduates of the school district to college for free. After spending 25 years in higher education, first as a student and then a professor, I knew a fair amount about financial aid, including these two basic facts: almost all scholarships are awarded on the basis of academic merit or financial need, and few cover the entire cost of college. The news seemed too simple and sweeping to be true.

Later that day, the local newspaper offered these specifics: The Kalamazoo Promise would provide scholarships to every KPS graduate who had resided in the district for at least four years. The scholarships could be used at any public college or university in the state, and, depending on how long one had attended KPS, would cover between 65 percent and 100 percent of tuition and mandatory fees. For students who had lived in the district and attended its schools since kindergarten, the full cost of college tuition and fees would be paid by the anonymous donors who had bestowed the Kalamazoo Promise on my community.

It was immediately clear that this program held the potential to transform not just the college-going patterns of Kalamazoo's young people and the personal finances of their parents, but the entire community—indeed, even the region. As an investment in the human capital of every high school graduate of an urban school district, it was unprecedented. As a catalyst for other investments—well, who could tell?

My years in Kalamazoo had been marked by alternating bouts of hope and anxiety as I watched the city and its urban school district struggle against a tide of corporate downsizing and persistent unemployment. Every step forward—a new hospital building or the renovation of the downtown mall—seemed to be followed by a step backward—another plant closing or the next in a series of corporate mergers. As high-paying jobs evaporated, middle-class families left the region, which decreased overall enrollment and led to a growing concentration of poor and minority children in the public schools. As perceptions of the school district deteriorated, many of the middle-class families still living in the city opted to send their children to private or parochial schools, or to move a short distance to a neighboring school district. The cycle fed on itself, with negative perceptions translating into a harsher reality, and the increasing challenges faced by the school district in turn worsening public perceptions of it.

Now this simple gift holds the promise of reversing the cycle. Not only will the scholarships ease the debt burden of middle-income college students and open new doors for low-income youth, they also may help reverse the decline of both the school district and the city of Kalamazoo, a midsized community located halfway between Chicago and Detroit. The Kalamazoo Promise could even become a model of education-based economic renewal for the many other cities across the nation struggling with similar challenges.

A few years ago, I wrote a book about asset-based strategies for fighting poverty. Through my research, I encountered communities and organizations that worked with low-income people in many different settings to help them acquire new human, economic, and social assets and enhance the value of those they already possessed. The Kalamazoo Promise struck me as an asset-building opportunity of unparalleled proportions, opening up avenues for Kalamazoo's young people to increase their human capital; raising the value of residents' economic assets, especially their homes; and strengthening the social fabric. Best of all, it was happening in my own backyard. As a social scientist interested in community asset building, a citizen concerned about the deepening divide between rich and poor in my hometown and beyond, a resident of the KPS district, and the mother of a four-year-old, I could not imagine a more satisfying research topic. And so I embarked on the path that led to this book.

Along the way, I have had exceptional access to and support from individuals throughout the community. Above all, I am grateful for the sponsorship of the W.E. Upjohn Institute for Employment Research, which funded this research, and in particular for the ongoing support of its president, Dr. Randall W. Eberts. The Institute's staff of economists, analysts, and librarians has enriched my research and this book. Special thanks to my colleagues Tim Bartik, George Erickcek, Kevin Hollenbeck, Sarah Klerk, and Bridget Timmeney for their gracious assistance with this project and their invaluable contributions. I would also like to thank my former student and friend Elizabeth Garlow for her research assistance and the publications staff of the Upjohn Institute for their superb editorial and production effort. The insights of urban expert David Rusk and two anonymous reviewers further strengthened this work.

I am also indebted to those individuals throughout Kalamazoo who shared their opinions with me in interviews, and to those who read and commented on portions of this manuscript, including Dr. Janice Brown, Phillip Carra, Pam Kingery, Lee Kirk, and Dr. Michael Rice. The *Kalamazoo Gazette*'s publisher James Stephanek, editor-in-chief Rebecca Pierce, and education reporter Julie Mack deserve extra accolades for the space and energy they have devoted to covering all aspects of the Kalamazoo Promise for their readers. Among the friends who offered personal support for this project and engaged in endless conversation about it, Paula Eckert played a special role. I am grateful once again to have the opportunity to thank my parents, Rachel Galperin and Gerald Miller, for their confidence in me from my earliest years to the present. I have been inspired throughout this research by the growth and development of my daughter, Eliana Adams, who has already benefited from the wonderful array of educational opportunities available in Kalamazoo, and whose life will continue to be enriched by this community's many assets.

Author's note: Updated data and information about the impact of the Kalamazoo Promise is available through the Web site of the W.E. Upjohn Institute for Employment Research at http://www.upjohninstitute.org/promise/index.htm.

Part 1

Origins

1
A Not-So-Simple Gift

The crowd that gathered inside Kalamazoo's Chenery Auditorium on November 15, 2005, was humming with excitement. Hundreds of students, parents, teachers, and administrators had come to celebrate the news that a group of anonymous donors had pledged to provide full college scholarships to every graduate of the Kalamazoo Public Schools (KPS) for decades to come.

KPS superintendent Dr. Janice Brown had announced the scholarship program at a school board meeting a few days earlier with a beaming smile and words that brought many in the audience to tears: "It has been said that Kalamazoo is a very special community. Tonight we have more proof of that than ever before . . . We have a group of donors, [a group] of very, very special people [who] have stepped forward with a willingness to invest in our most important resource—the children, the residents, the parents of KPS."[1]

Outlining the terms of the scholarship, Dr. Brown explained, "It's a very simple concept. Go to school at KPS, graduate from KPS, and in your hands there will be a scholarship in the amount of tuition plus fees [based on] the number of years that you have gone to KPS." She also stressed that the purpose of the program is not simply to enhance access to higher education, saying, "Study after study indicates that an investment in education adds to the quality of our community and the quality of life for all its citizens."

Thus was launched an unprecedented experiment in education-based economic renewal—one that has landed this Michigan city in the national spotlight as communities across the nation seek to emulate some of the program's key principles.

- The Kalamazoo Promise is universally accessible to graduates of KPS. The program differs from most other scholarship programs in that the allocation of funds is based not on merit or need, but on location. Beginning with the graduating class of 2006, every high school graduate who has been enrolled in and resided within the KPS district for at least the previous four years will receive a scholarship to any public university or community college in Michigan. A student who enters kindergarten will find the scholarship waiting when he or she graduates. The program is set up to last in perpetuity, and the donors have committed to giving 13 years' notice to the community in the unlikely event that they ever terminate this scholarship.

- Funding levels are generous. For graduates who have lived in and attended high school in the district for four years, the scholarship covers 65 percent of tuition and mandatory fees, while those who have attended district schools since kindergarten receive 100 percent coverage. For students who fall between these two categories, the proportion of costs covered by the scholarship is prorated, rising 5 percent for each year of attendance. The scholarship pays for up to 130 college credits or a bachelor's degree, whichever comes first.[2]

- Terms of use are extremely flexible. Scholarships can be used to attend any of Michigan's 28 community colleges or 16 public colleges and universities, and students can access their funding any time within 10 years of graduation. To retain their scholarships, students must maintain a 2.0 grade point average (GPA) at their postsecondary institution and make "regular progress" toward a degree.[3] If the GPA drops below 2.0, a student may be reinstated if he or she is able to bring it back to at least a 2.0.

While the concept is indeed simple, its implications are not. The Kalamazoo Promise touches on issues as diverse as regional governance, urban sprawl, and racial segregation. It has been variously described as a scholarship program, an economic development strategy, a boon to the middle class, and a gift to the poor. It has been met with great enthusiasm in most quarters, but also on occasion has elicited suspicion and resentment. It has the potential to unite the region or intensify long-standing divisions between black and white residents, middle- and low-income populations, city and suburb. It may transform the community or leave much unchanged.

This book investigates the origins and initial responses to the Kalamazoo Promise and its relevance as a model for other communities.[4] The Promise is a long-term investment, expected to last for decades; thus, a more thorough assessment of its impact must come at a later date. However, there is a great deal to be learned from examining the reasons why it was created, the structure of the program, and the potential it holds as a catalyst for educational, economic, and social change. Such an analysis is especially important as Kalamazoo and other cities with similar programs grapple with two critical issues: First, how can communities best organize and deploy their resources to maximize the potential benefits of a Promise-type initiative? Second, why should public and private actors beyond the educational system be interested in aligning their activities in support of such an initiative?

There also is a pressing need for accurate information about the early impact of the Kalamazoo Promise. As city after city announces plans for programs inspired by the Kalamazoo Promise, community leaders are turning to Kalamazoo for evidence of success. Changes in school enrollment, graduation rates, and housing prices have all been cited by those planning their own Promise-type programs. Often, however, these data have been taken out of context and their meaning is not always clear.

Even at this early date, it is evident that money alone is insufficient for the Kalamazoo Promise or programs modeled after it to reach their full potential as engines of community transformation. The ingredients mentioned above—a clear conceptual understanding of how such a program can catalyze economic and social change, the engagement of multiple partners and alignment of their efforts around a common goal, and realistic expectations about short- and long-term impact—are also essential. But because it is the financial commitment made by the donors that brought the Kalamazoo Promise into being, it is here that we begin.

A key to making sense of the Kalamazoo Promise is the unusual notion that money is no object. Unlike most college scholarship programs that provide "last dollar" contributions to supplement other financing, such as federal student aid, the Kalamazoo Promise is a "first dollar" scholarship calculated and awarded before any other funding source. There is no complicated application process or assessment of family income (the application form is a single page), and no requirement that students apply for other sources of aid, although this step is encouraged. In fact, early clarifications of program rules reflect the donors' enthusiasm for serving as many students as possible.

When the program was first announced, it was stipulated that Promise funds could only be used for college entrance immediately after graduation and would be available for four years, with deferrals available for military service. Six months later, this requirement was revised to allow students to delay college entry, although it was assumed that the length of the delay would be subtracted from the four years of eligibility—in other words, if a student took a year off before starting college, he or she would only receive three years of the scholarship. Shortly thereafter, the requirement was clarified further to allow eligible students to receive the full four years of tuition any time within 10 years of graduation. As Dr. Brown explains, "We've heard from the donors that this is a four-year scholarship. If someone's life circumstances mean they get a later start on college or they interrupt college, they will still qualify for four years of funding" (Mack 2006a,b).

The repeated easing of restrictions reveals something important about the unique nature of this gift. Most scholarship funds consist of a limited pool of resources with students qualifying or competing to obtain them based on some criteria, whether it is financial need, GPA, or extracurricular accomplishments. The Kalamazoo Promise reverses this relationship: the funds are essentially unlimited, and the challenge is to ensure that they are utilized as widely and fully as possible. As Kalamazoo Promise administrator Robert Jorth says of the donors, whose identities he does not know, "I have been just stunned by their generosity. Every time we've gone back to ask them, it is that they want to give this money out, they want people to take advantage of this. This isn't about trying to narrow it, which I think was the natural inclination of everybody. You'd go to meetings and people would say, 'Do you have to do community service? Do you have to do this? Do you have to do that?' 'No, no, and no.'"[5]

The universality of the Kalamazoo Promise, with scholarships awarded to students regardless of need or merit, circumvents a growing criticism of the current financial aid system—that its main beneficiaries are not those most in need, but rather students from middle-income families who would have gone to college anyway. This argument is grounded in several developments. First, the value of federal grant aid has fallen over time. Thirty years ago, the Pell Grant, the U.S. government's chief tool for assisting low- and moderate-income families with college tuition, covered 72 percent of the cost of attendance at a public four-year institution, while today it covers less than a third of that cost (Kahlenberg 2006a). (In 2006–2007, the maximum Pell Grant of $4,050 had remained unchanged for five years, although by 2008–2009 it had increased to $4,731.) Second, the balance between grant aid that goes mainly to low-income students and loans or tax incentives that tend to benefit middle-class families has shifted. In the early 1980s, grants accounted for 55 percent of student aid and loans accounted for 41 percent, whereas in recent years grants constituted only 38 percent and loans 56 percent of aid. Federal education tax breaks that benefit middle-income families have also expanded dramatically and now rival the Pell Grant program in size (Kahlenberg 2004). Third, while the bulk of financial aid is still made up of need-based grants, these are increasing at a slower pace than merit scholarships. Between 1994 and 2004, for example, grant aid grew by 110 percent, from $18.6 billion to $39.1 billion, while during the same period merit scholarships grew by 508 percent, from $1.2 billion to $7.3 billion (Kahlenberg 2006a). These developments have altered the complexion of student financial aid in the United States and raised questions about whether the nation remains committed to ensuring the affordability of higher education for both lower- and middle-income high school graduates.

While there is nothing inherently wrong with either merit- or need-based aid, each has its weakness as a strategy for expanding access to higher education. Statewide merit-based scholarship programs have a mixed record. One of the best-known, Georgia's HOPE Scholarship Program, has been shown to increase strongly the college attendance rates of middle- and high-income youth, while widening the gap in college attendance between blacks and whites and between students from lower- and higher-income families (Bugler, Henry, and Rubenstein 1999; Dynarski 2000). Similarly, researchers expect the state of Massachusetts' John and Abigail Adams Scholarships to have little impact on broadening college access because so few minority or poor students in the state qualify for the program (Heller 2006a; Goodman 2008). Whether such statewide scholarships reduce or widen disparities in college access by race and income is not a foregone conclusion. It depends on how they are structured. Oklahoma's Promise, for example, a college assistance program created in 1992, reaches most of the state's lower- and middle-income students through its low GPA and high family income cut-offs and has had an impressive effect on college access.

(See Chapter 3 for details on the Oklahoma Promise and other statewide merit aid programs.)

As for need-based programs, they rarely enjoy the broad political support necessary for their maintenance and expansion. In addition to the shrinking Pell Grant, there are many privately funded programs based on need, but they are usually targeted narrowly, whether toward low-income schools (such as the "I Have a Dream" classroom adoption programs) or high-potential individuals (the best-known example is the 20-year, $1 billion Gates Millennium Scholarship program to support outstanding low-income minority students). Most of the beneficiaries of these programs are minority youth, opening the way for the kind of racially based resentment that also characterizes the debate over affirmative action.

Social scientists and policymakers have long recognized that universal, as opposed to income-based, policies tend to enjoy stronger support across the political spectrum. One example is the divergent fates of the Social Security system and the welfare system, with the former proving impervious to change and the latter suffering successive cutbacks since the 1970s. The Kalamazoo Promise is not a government program, but by making scholarships available to all KPS graduates regardless of merit or need, the program avoids these divisive debates and virtually guarantees that there will be broad support for the program, at least within the KPS district.

Who is behind this unusual gift and what motivated them to give? The first part of this question—what the *Kalamazoo Gazette* in 2005 called "This year's best whodunit"—cannot be answered at this time (Jones 2005). In the weeks following the announcement of the program, many people assumed that the identities of the donors would soon become public knowledge, but within a few months it was clear that their anonymity was a critical part of the deal. Apart from Janice Brown, who retired from the office of superintendent in 2007, no one has acknowledged knowing the donors' identities. Even their number remains unclear, with initial reports saying that seven donors are involved and later conjecture that there are fewer. It is not difficult to hypothesize about the identities of at least some of the donors in a city that is home to several families with tremendous wealth: three residents regularly make the *Forbes* list of the world's billionaires.[6] But while local interest in the question has waned, those outside Kalamazoo still seem intrigued. One former community leader dismisses the issue as beside the point: "It's fascinating that we have such a preoccupation with wanting to know. I mean, what are you going to do when you find out? What difference does it make?"[7] Whatever their identities, the donors have conveyed their intention for the Kalamazoo Promise to last in perpetuity. "I am confident that the donors have set up a system to fund the Kalamazoo Promise for many generations to come," says Janice Brown.[8]

The donors' motivations are arguably far more interesting than their identities. Shortly after the Kalamazoo Promise was announced, Dr. Brown recounted a series of private conversations among a group of wealthy individuals concerned about the faltering health of the local and regional economy. The meetings came in the aftermath of a series of plant closings and mergers that had depleted the region's economic base and forced many of its workers to relocate. As downtown real estate developer William Johnston told a *Wall Street Journal* reporter, "One of the conclusions was that a better economy was going to require a healthier Kalamazoo school system" (Boudette 2006). According to Dr. Brown, the donors see the Promise as a way to revitalize their city, and they believe that "equal access to higher education for all creates a powerful incentive that will bring people and employers back to Kalamazoo" (Boudette 2006). The combination of the Kalamazoo Promise's strict residency requirement—to qualify, students must not only have attended and graduated from a district public school but also have lived within the district for a minimum of four years before graduation—and the long-term commitment of funds is a clear reflection of this place-based, economic development goal.

So what will it accomplish? The Kalamazoo Promise is structured to serve as a catalyst for economic, educational, and community change. The offer of fully funded college tuition changes the incentives for a broad range of actors including students, families, school administrators, real estate agents, housing developers, business leaders, entrepreneurs, and public officials. The decisions made in response to these new incentives are likely to lead to a series of outcomes, most of them desirable. While many observers claim with good reason that the Promise is first and foremost intended as an economic development program, others argue that without a clear statement from the donors it is impossible to speak in terms of their goals. In the words of one local observer, "The Kalamazoo Promise is not *about* anything. It's a thing;

a donation. You've had an iceberg land in the middle of the pool. Now you have to find out what it does."[9]

The lack of any public statement by the donors as to their goals has magnified the degree to which the Kalamazoo Promise can be interpreted differently by different groups. The general public and especially parents of school-age children tend to see it first and foremost as a scholarship program, and some of the criticism of the program has come from people whose children and the school districts they attend are left out. Within KPS, administrators believe the Promise will help them transform the district's culture to one where dropping out of high school is not an option and students are prepared to succeed in college. Business leaders, real estate agents, and local government officials focus on the potential impact of the Promise on business investment, economic growth, and community vitality. Some observers view it mainly as an advantage for the city's middle-class homeowners whose property values eventually may rise and whose educational savings accounts are now freed up for other purposes, while others interpret the choice of KPS, an urban school district with a large minority and low-income student population, as a reflection of the donors' desire to give a hand up to the poor. In many respects, the Kalamazoo Promise has contributed to greater unity and a more positive identity for the community, although for some it has intensified long-standing divisions along racial and income lines. There are even debates over the significance of the Promise—is it truly a transformative opportunity, or just an excuse for media hype?

All of these currents of thought and more were played out in the weeks following the announcement of the scholarship program. The immediate reaction to the Promise was startling in its intensity and variety. Above all was the tremendous sense of enthusiasm, excitement, and opportunity. One giddy mother of three KPS students was heard to ask, "Where's a rooftop? I need to shout" (Campbell 2005). Within a few days of the announcement, Superintendent Brown was interviewed on *Good Morning America* and the *Today Show*, and the school district had fielded more than 100 e-mails and calls from parents, many of them from outside the state, interested in moving into the district. Real estate agents, too, were taking calls from families in outlying communities and nearby states, while "College Tuition Qualified" signs produced by the school district sprouted in the yards of homes for sale in the district.

Within days of the announcement, Wayne State University in Detroit had offered a 50 percent discount on its dormitory rates for incoming Kalamazoo Promise recipients. A few hours later, Western Michigan University (WMU), located in Kalamazoo, trumped this offer with four years of free room and board for any 2006 graduate of KPS who received a Promise scholarship. (WMU's 2006–2007 room and board rate was $6,877, while in-state tuition and fees cost $6,866, for a total savings to 2006 graduates attending their local university of more than $50,000 over four years.)[10] Eastern Michigan University and Lake Superior State soon announced offers similar to those of Wayne State. While contributing to the excitement over the program, these schools were motivated chiefly by the goal of increasing enrollment. In a calculus not widely understood, offering discounts to students who arrive with full scholarships in hand can be a boon to college finances. If those same students qualify for any other financial aid—and many coming from KPS do—those resources will help to make up for the discounts. The Michigan Education Trust, the state's prepaid tuition program, quickly revised its rules so that families that had invested in contracts to lock in current tuition rates could cash them in and receive a refund that could be used to pay for room, board, and other expenses.

The district's schools, as well as several local churches, held rallies and information sessions to celebrate the Promise. New college applications were completed and extra dates arranged for admissions tests. The college plans of many seniors were revised as parents debated whether or not going to college out of state remained an option for their children. Opportunities for recovering class credits were expanded to enable more students to graduate on time, and the alternative high school admitted a number of students midyear to make it possible for them to receive their diplomas. At a college fair held at one of the KPS high schools in early December 2005, school representatives noted the greater diversity of the attendees; notably, parents who had never gone to college, and more 9th and 10th graders than in the past (Mack 2005).

While most celebrated, others worried. Concerns were raised about the impact on enrollment at the area's private, parochial, and charter schools. (Kalamazoo's charter schools, Christian schools, and Catholic schools enroll approximately 1,200 students each.) Neighboring public school districts—there are nine districts in Kalamazoo County—expressed wariness about potential enrollment declines, although the superintendent of the Portage Public Schools, Kalamazoo's nearest neighbor and closest competitor, spoke out early, saying, "It's a benefit for the whole county to have any and all districts operating at a strong level."[11] Disappointment was voiced by families whose children were enrolled in KPS but whose residences were outside district boundaries, thereby disqualifying them for the scholarships. (Kalamazoo Public Schools spokesman Alex Lee responded, "This is an incentive for community development. The donors made a gift and put parameters on it. That's it") [Killian 2005a].) In an oft-quoted letter to the editor, a resident of Portage wrote, "I am angered by the Kalamazoo Promise. The Kalamazoo Public Schools has a bad reputation for unsafe learning environments, lower income levels and safety problems. Why use this as an excuse to pay for college degrees?" The writer instead proposed that the funds be used to benefit the "excellent students with bright futures, parents who care, [and] excellent learning environments" of other districts in the county, presumably including her own (Letter to the Editor 2005).

Western Michigan University's free room and board offer was especially controversial, with critics arguing that it was not equitable for a public institution to subsidize costs for a specific geographic group. Moreover, many observed that those receiving the offer—Kalamazoo residents by definition—are arguably the WMU students least in need of free room and board since they have the option of living at home. The university subsequently clarified its policies to underscore that no public funds would be used as part of the offer, but that it would instead draw upon federal need-based aid and unrestricted private gifts (*WMU News* 2005). The policy, while poorly explained, made financial sense for WMU, which had recently experienced sharp enrollment declines, because most of the students receiving the Kalamazoo Promise also qualified for either need-based or merit-based aid that would be applied to their room and board rates. Nevertheless, the public relations fiasco that accompanied the room and board offer hurt the university's standing in the community, and the offer was not renewed (although class of 2006 graduates will continue to receive free room and board for their four years at WMU).

On the economic development front, advocates for the poor and homeless noted the potential for gentrification if investors were to acquire rundown property, convert rental units to owner-occupied homes, or raise rents as the market tightens. At a forum a few days after the Promise announcement, members of the Kalamazoo Homeless Action Network voiced disappointment with the donors' intentions, noting that the money involved in the gift could have housed the city's entire homeless population several times over.[12]

Others made the point that the barriers to college faced by many minority children lie so far beyond the economic realm that there is little in the Promise to benefit them. Arlene Washington, the editor of *Community Voices*, a bimonthly newspaper read widely in the African-American community, asked a question a few days after the announcement of the Promise that was on the minds of many: "Just how is this going to affect the minority community? Our children are falling further behind—dropping out, moving on to alternative schools, not graduating, unable to go to college even if they have the funds . . . How can the Kalamazoo Promise be a reality for all? What is Kalamazoo Public Schools doing to provide the kind of quality education in a manner that at-risk children can be a part of the greater good?"[13]

Attention was not confined to the local press. Newspapers and Web sites around the country reported on the Kalamazoo Promise, with many writers suggesting ways to adapt the idea for their own communities. News coverage was strong throughout Michigan, a state that lags the national average in terms of its percentage of college graduates.[14] While some writers noted the high cost of replicating the Kalamazoo Promise in larger school districts, such as Detroit, others reminded readers of the tremendous wealth that can still be found in many Michigan communities and some of the more cost-effective options for providing college scholarship support. With the state's economy struggling due to the loss of manufacturing jobs, particularly in the auto industry, many articles referenced research showing that a small increase in the state's share of college-educated adults would boost overall economic growth and real earnings.[15]

The most provocative comments could be found on Internet bulletin boards, where writers expressing their amazement and gratitude for the gift were outnumbered by those whose perspectives were more negative. Racial animosity was one theme, as the following exchange suggests: **[Author's note: The following comments are presented exactly as they appear online.]**

▶ It's a wonderful opportunity for many public school kids, however, the majority of kids in K-zoo's public schools are non-white. Since more scholarships go to non-whites, why should they continue to benefit?

▶ Yes you said it. more s--- for the minorities again.!!!!!! WTF. Our govrnment just wants to give them more more and more.... What about us the TRUE AND REAL AMERICANS!!!! True Americans are American Indians and And WHITE PEOPLE!!!!!! We were here first! We found this country. This world is all black this, black that.[16]

Other comments posted online reflected a misunderstanding of the private nature of the gift, with attacks on what was perceived as an unfair government policy.

▶ Why should only the students of the city schools get this benifit!!!!! Are the parents in other districts excluded from this program? Why not every child that lives in Kalamazoo county? Is it because they are not in poverty!!! Some are and alot are close to poverty. Those parents and students that are working are paying taxes to support those familys in the city schools that are in poverty. Lets be real alot of familys choose to be in poverty, thats why Michigan is called the walfare wonder land think about it people![17]

▶ Well guess what will happen now..... Everyone will be flocking to k-zoo public schools so they can get free college. So what happens to the kids in all the small towns? Do you have to be a nonwhite person to get a good education in this damn State. We have two special needs kids who are over coming there disablities. But they need new equipment, more space more everytyhing. We also have three other kids at public schools but because we are white, live in a smaller town then the hell with us right? This government is corupted and completly unfair![18]

Also repeated were some of the negative perceptions of Kalamazoo's public schools that surfaced in the mainstream press:

▶ I think that this is a great opportunity for the people of KPS. However, no self-respecting parent with econminc means are going to pull their children out of Mattawan, Portage, etc. to put their children in KPS- do you know the things that go on in these schools or the people you would subject your children to?[19]

One writer drew a parallel to a scholarship program in Philomath, Oregon (see Chapter 3), where donors threatened to withdraw their funding in protest over the curriculum being taught in the schools, referring to the Kalamazoo Promise donors as a special interest group and asking:

> ▶ How do you prevent the Special Interest Group (SIG) that provides the funds from using their carrot to bring about quantum changes in the curriculum such as "Intelligent Design" for instance? How do you inform [Superintendent Brown] that she now effectively reports to the SIG rather than to the school board? How do you tell the School Board, the teachers and staff that they now serve at the beck and call of the SIG? How do you help the families in Kalamazoo to regard this gift as a gift--one that can be taken away at any time--rather than an entitlement?[20]

These reactions reveal not just the self-interested side of human nature but also highlight one of the central questions about the Kalamazoo Promise: who benefits? The earliest and most direct beneficiaries are those families whose children qualify for full scholarships, but the implications of such a long-term program radiate outward to affect the housing market, the business climate, the city, the school district, and the broader region. Economists believe that any region is only as strong as its urban core. By strengthening the public school district at the center of Kalamazoo County, the Kalamazoo Promise stands to benefit the county as a whole. Even so, this "rising tide lifts all boats" argument is a hard sell for those people who see the world in zero-sum terms—what's good for you must be bad for me—and who measure their gains not in absolute terms but relative to their neighbors.

Whether one views the Kalamazoo Promise as a win-win or a zero-sum endeavor depends as much on one's personal experiences as on the objective realities of the program. Indeed, as the above Internet postings suggest, the negative reaction to the Promise reflects hot-button issues like race or the increasing financial pressures faced by middle-class families and has little to do with the program itself. (Race has figured prominently in Michigan politics in recent years due in part to a November 2006 ballot initiative banning the use of affirmative action by public institutions; voters approved this amendment to the state's constitution by a resounding margin of 58 percent to 42 percent.) However, regardless of outlook, it is undeniable that the Kalamazoo

Promise, by virtue of its design, has the potential to accomplish far more than simply sending more KPS graduates to college. As Carrie Pickett-Erway of the Kalamazoo Community Foundation puts it, "They [the donors] set the bar much higher than anyone was thinking. It gives us an opportunity to let go of our short-term, short-sighted objectives and be more progressive and aggressive in thinking about the future. Somebody went in big, and they picked the right thing because it's connected to everything."[21]

One way to approach the question of how the Kalamazoo Promise is "connected to everything" is to disaggregate its impact into different categories. The long-term nature of the program suggests that it may be most useful to think about impact in terms of the kinds of assets that might be created as a result of this investment. (For more on asset-building strategies for community development, see Miller-Adams [2002].) An asset can be defined simply as something of value, whether tangible or intangible. With the stimulus provided by an unlimited pool of scholarship funds based on residency and available over the long term, the Kalamazoo Promise holds the potential to strengthen three different kinds of assets:

- Human assets (or human capital), including the education, knowledge, and skills that enable individuals to support themselves and their families and that play a crucial role in economic productivity.

- Economic assets, including traditional measures of wealth, such as equity in a home or business, retirement savings, the value of an insurance policy, and a broad range of other financial and real holdings.

- Social assets (or social capital), defined by social scientists as "social networks, norms of reciprocity, mutual assistance, and trustworthiness," that bind communities together and allow individuals to work collectively to improve the quality of their lives (Putnam and Feldstein 2003, p. 2).[22]

Assets and income play different roles in providing security to individuals and families. A central feature of assets is their staying power. Economic assets, such as a home or business, can be passed from parent to child. Human assets, too, give future generations a head start. Educated parents are more likely to read to their children and send them to preschool, while a large body of research shows that the strongest predictor of a child's educational attainment is the educational level of his or her parents.[23] Assets also serve as a cushion against risk. Home equity can be borrowed against if illness strikes or a job is lost, and social capital provides a network of support for families in crisis. Assets have even been shown to have physical and psychological benefits, ranging from greater longevity to higher self-esteem to a reduced incidence of domestic violence.[24] The value of assets is not wealth for its own sake, but the stability, security, and greater degree of self-reliance they bring.

Human assets. The most obvious impact of the Kalamazoo Promise is in the educational sphere where positive outcomes are expected at both the individual student and school district level. Stripped to its essence, the Kalamazoo Promise lowers the cost of postsecondary education to close to zero for those students who continue to live at home, theoretically making it possible for high school graduates at all income levels to obtain additional years of schooling. (There are still opportunity costs for students choosing to attend college rather than work full time, as well as the substantial costs of room and board for those who do not qualify for financial aid and choose not to remain at home—not to mention the ever-rising cost of textbooks.)

Research shows that a college degree substantially increases an individual's lifetime earnings potential. Annual surveys by the National Center for Education Statistics show that between 1980 and 2005, earnings increased as level of education increased, while the gap between those with a bachelor's degree and those with less education widened steadily. In 2005, for example, the $32,800 median salary for all full-time workers ages 25–34 masked a sharp disparity between young workers with different levels of education: $26,800 for those with a high school degree versus $43,100 for those with a bachelor's degree or higher (U.S. Department of Education 2007). There is also some evidence that attending college and earning credits even without completing a degree translates into expanded earning potential (see, for example, Kane and Rouse [1993]). In this sense, an increase in human capital makes possible an increase in economic assets down the road.

As for the school district, the Promise has already reversed KPS's decades-long slide in enrollment, which grew by more than 10 percent in fall 2006 over the previous year, and continued to rise, although at a much smaller rate, in 2007 and 2008. Michigan's educational funding system is unusual in that 100 percent of schools' operational resources come from the state's "foundation grant," which is allocated on a per-pupil basis. Because of this key fact, rising enrollment translates directly into more funds for the district.

The Promise is also expected to reduce the dropout rate and increase the graduation rate. Somewhat more speculative is the idea that its powerful "pull" effect could reverse the trend of middle-class flight from the district and reduce the percentage of low-income children who attend KPS (at last count, 65 percent of students in KPS qualified for the federal free and reduced-price lunch program).[25] This shift could lead to greater socioeconomic integration within schools, a condition thought by many experts to support higher achievement for all.[26] The district may also see a change in the availability of educational services supplied in response to the Kalamazoo Promise: With more students planning to attend college, offerings of college-preparatory courses, advanced placement, and dual enrollment opportunities may be expanded, while lower-achieving students will need to receive added support to graduate and avail themselves of the scholarship.

Finally, the additional years of schooling provided to KPS graduates through the Kalamazoo Promise could also yield higher levels of human capital for the community as a whole in the form of a better-educated workforce. The availability of a pool of skilled workers is a critical factor in attracting business investment to an area.

Economic assets. With its sole focus on providing college scholarships to area youth, it is easy to miss the economic development implications of the Kalamazoo Promise. Nonetheless, the structure of the program suggests that it could serve as a catalyst for economic growth and development in the region. The official Kalamazoo Promise Web site offers this explanation: "The Kalamazoo Promise will create opportunities for individuals who attend Kalamazoo Public Schools and their current and future families. It follows—and studies have shown—that there is a strong correlation between overall academic achievement and a community's economic vitality and quality of life."[27]

Along the same lines, former KPS Superintendent Brown, now executive director of the Kalamazoo Promise, likes to share with audiences what the donors have told her about their motivation: "This is not an educational decision," she reports them saying. "This is an economic development, quality of life, community-building decision."[28] But what does it mean to say that a scholarship program is a tool for economic development, and what kinds of economic assets are created in the process?

Most immediately, the Kalamazoo Promise has an impact on the personal finances of many families. Parents who have saved for their children's college tuition can now use those funds for other purposes, whether retirement, home renovation, or pursuit of an entrepreneurial idea. For others, relief from the burden of paying for their children to attend college opens up new choices, as it has for Linda Van Dis, the mother of three KPS students: "I started talking years ago about how when my kids were in college I'd have to get a full-time job," she says. "I don't have to do that now. I can work part time and be home with my kids until they're all the way through school. I might be ready to work full time, but I don't have to. I have the option."[29] Another profound effect is that students now have the opportunity to graduate from college with much smaller debt burdens.[30] As Ms. Van Dis told her eldest son, "'If we don't have to dip into what your grandmother left you and our little bit of savings, you can come out of college and actually have a little bit of money' . . . It's going to be a whole different future for a lot of these kids if they come out of school without debt." Lolita and Sonita Moss are twin sisters who graduated from Loy Norrix High School with the class of 2006 and used their Promise scholarships to attend the University of Michigan. Lolita Moss, who hopes eventually to get a doctorate in clinical psychology, told the *Kalamazoo Gazette* that the Promise made a huge difference for her parents and herself: "I plan to go to graduate school, and now, with undergraduate paid for, paying for graduate school is all I have to worry about" (Mack 2006c).

Also widely anticipated is a rise in the value of homes within KPS boundaries. Free college tuition—a benefit potentially worth tens of thousands of dollars—creates incentives for families with children to move into the district or opt to remain here. This is expected to bring about a tightening in the slack housing market and reignite an appreciation in home prices that has stalled in recent years. For most families, equity in their homes is their largest financial asset, and any increase in property values will positively affect their overall wealth. There is also the prospect of housing construction that could bring new tax revenue to local governments. Much of this construction, however, is likely to take place outside the urban core in neighboring townships that lie within the school district but have lower tax rates and more space for development.

The initial response of the housing market illustrates the difficulty of projecting the impact of the Kalamazoo Promise. While housing sales and median prices did indeed rise in the months following the announcement of the program, the supply of homes on the market also rose—and at a much faster rate—as owners sought to capitalize on expectations of tightening in the real estate market. The net result was a housing market characterized by even greater oversupply and stagnant prices—an example of an unintended short-term consequence that real estate agents and homeowners hope will reverse itself in the coming years once the current crisis in the national housing market abates (Killian 2006).

Another economic asset for the community is new business investment that could materialize as a result of the Promise. Attracted by the ability to offer the tuition benefit to their employees and the prospect of access to a more educated workforce, business owners may choose to relocate or expand their businesses in Kalamazoo. An early sign of the economic potential of the Promise is increasing construction in the downtown district as occupancy rates rise for office and residential space and local investors place a bet on real estate appreciation. The region's economic development organization, Southwest Michigan First, is using the Kalamazoo Promise as a recruiting tool for new employers and is capitalizing on the national media attention sparked by the program. The Promise is not only a draw for established businesses. Anyone who can work from home or who travels regularly for their job, such as a sales representative, can choose to relocate without finding new employment. Ron Kitchens, the head of Southwest Michigan First, notes: "We have entrepreneurs calling us—a lot of displaced manufacturing workers, management and blue-collar—who are saying, 'My job's evaporated, I'm going to have this severance package and I want to start a company, but if I do that I put my kid's education at risk. So you're telling me that if I move there, you'll pay for my kid's education?' . . . I predict we're going to see a significant number of those individuals come here and invest and start companies. They're taking a risk in starting a company but it minimizes the personal risk to them."[31] Investment and relocation decisions, especially those of large companies, are not made quickly, and it will be a number of years before the full business impact of the Kalamazoo Promise emerges. But economic development officials are hopeful and point to plans announced in 2008 by several companies, both large and small, to expand within the region as a signal of its growing attractiveness to business.

Implicit in most discussions of the economic impact of the Kalamazoo Promise is its potential to reverse the self-perpetuating cycle of middle-class flight from the urban core and the problems it brings, including those in the schools. The president of the Kalamazoo-based W.E. Upjohn Institute for Employment Research, Randall W. Eberts, notes: "Research shows that you must first develop a city core to add economic vitality to a region. I believe the donor group . . . wants to grow Kalamazoo from the inside out" (Killian 2005b). The value of an economically diverse and vibrant central city has been underscored by a spate of recent scholarship, including Richard Florida's (2005) work on how cities can attract and retain the "creative class," and research by David Rusk (1995, 1999) and Myron Orfield (1997) on strategies for containing urban sprawl and minimizing its negative social consequences, including housing and school segregation. (These works and their relevance to the Kalamazoo Promise are discussed in Chapter 3.)

Social assets. It is no surprise that a gift of the magnitude of the Promise would have ramifications for the social fabric of the community. In one sense, the gift is itself a reflection of social capital, as it was connections among the individual donors, their personal ties to the school district and the city, and their philanthropic and economic commitment to the broader community that set the program in motion. But the Kalamazoo Promise also holds the potential to increase the community's stock of social capital through multiple avenues, some more certain than others.

First is what Robert Putnam, the nation's leading authority on social capital, calls the "winning the pennant" effect. The announcement of the Kalamazoo Promise put a spring in the step of many residents, akin to what happens when a local sports team wins a championship. The sense of optimism and excitement that permeated public discussion in the days and weeks after the announcement was especially welcome in a town where bad economic news had become the norm. Second is the substantial impact that higher levels of education have on an individual's and a community's store of social capital. Putnam and John Helliwell have written that, "Education is one of the most important predictors—usually, in fact, the most important predictor—of many forms of political and social engagement—from voting to chairing a local committee to hosting a dinner party to trusting others" (Helliwell and Putnam 1999). Simply by increasing the average level of education of area residents, the Kalamazoo Promise could increase the degree of social engagement. A more difficult question is whether this engagement will build bridges between individuals of different backgrounds—an especially important concern in a community with pronounced divisions by race and class.

Third, the success of the Kalamazoo Promise in meeting its educational and economic objectives depends in large part on the social forces it sets in motion. To date, the Promise has catalyzed an ever-expanding number of groups, initiatives, and networks (both formal and informal), all of them expressions of community support for these objectives. From church-based mentoring and after-school credit recovery programs, to outreach by the local community college, to pro bono services offered by businesses, media companies, and others, the community has mobilized around the Kalamazoo Promise. This process of mobilization has been facilitated by the many networks already in place in Kalamazoo and by the donors' decision to remain anonymous. Without direction from above, the community's leaders and many of its citizens are acutely aware that the success of the Kalamazoo Promise depends on their actions. Anonymity has created a power vacuum that many organizations and individuals are seeking to fill, and it has meant that the process of grappling with the Kalamazoo Promise is a community-wide endeavor with room for many players. However, these efforts thus far have been coordinated only loosely if at all, and many observers believe that a higher degree of cooperation and collaboration is essential.

The asset-building potential of the Kalamazoo Promise, which extends across all three categories of assets, is indeed vast. But formidable challenges are embedded within it as well. The purpose of this book is not just to chronicle the origins and initial response to the program, but to uncover and examine some of these risks and challenges.

Figure 1.1 Map of KPS Boundaries and Surrounding Community

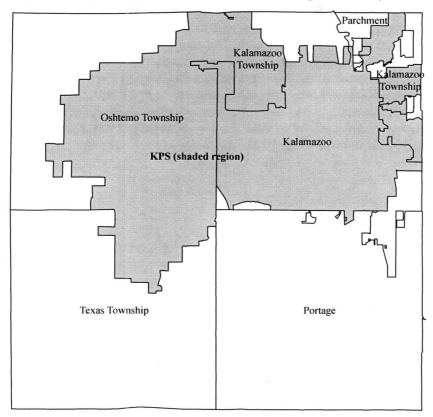

REVITALIZING THE URBAN CORE

The availability of scholarships to every KPS graduate complicates the task of urban revitalization—something that many observers assume is one of the underlying goals of the Kalamazoo Promise. Geographically, slightly over one-half of the school district lies outside the boundaries of the city of Kalamazoo (see Figure 1.1) and, because of limited space for new development in the central city, most of the investment generated by the Kalamazoo Promise is likely to occur in the newer, less dense, and more suburban-like townships that comprise just over half the school district's land and one-quarter of its population. Further complicating matters is a fragmented system of local governance that prevents the city of Kalamazoo from capturing any revenue generated by expansion outside its borders. In addition, two amendments to the Michigan state constitution interact in such a way as to prevent any revenue gains even if property values within the city do appreciate.[32] At the same time, a larger regional population could place an added burden on some city services. All of these factors could deepen rather than alleviate the fiscal crisis already brewing for the city of Kalamazoo.

OVERCOMING DIVISIONS

Compared to neighboring municipalities and Kalamazoo County overall, the city of Kalamazoo has a high concentration of minority and low-income residents, most of them clustered in a few inner-city neighborhoods characterized by limited commercial activity, relatively high crime rates, and decaying housing stock. Despite several decades of desegregation efforts, first through cross-district busing and then through the creation of magnet schools, the district's elementary schools continue to reflect this dual segregation by class and race. As noted earlier, research suggests that socioeconomic integration is among the most powerful tools for raising student achievement. While the Kalamazoo Promise is likely to increase the economic diversity of KPS, it is not clear whether any influx of middle-class families will be robust enough to bring about a truly mixed-income environment—that is, one with a low-income population of less than 50 percent. Also critical is whether socioeconomic integration at the district level will translate into greater diversity within individual elementary schools, or whether it will exacerbate the division between low-income and mixed-income schools that already exists.

There are other divisions that could also be affected by the Promise, including an urban-suburban-rural split, and a lack of integration of the large college student population into the fabric of the city. Even among the city's low-income communities, some are richer in resources than others and are able to organize more effectively to help local youth. And KPS has struggled for years to balance the needs of its less-advantaged youth with those of students capable of accelerated learning. All of these factors raise important distributional questions about who will benefit from the Promise in both relative and absolute terms, and pose a challenge to the community to ensure that the Promise leads to greater unity rather than disunity.

MOBILIZING AND ORGANIZING RESOURCES

The Kalamazoo Promise does not provide any new resources for the schools themselves beyond the increases in state funding that accompany higher enrollment. Former KPS Superintendent Janice Brown repeatedly charged the community to help make real her mantra that "every child is college material." For his part, current superintendent Dr. Michael Rice has vowed that every child will graduate from KPS "college ready." However, the barriers faced by many of the district's students extend well beyond the purview of the schools and include a lack of parental support, an absence of desirable role models, and the punishing effects of poverty. Support services ranging from nutrition programs to mental health services to mentoring are crucial. Even with a considerable outpouring of volunteer energy and a large network of social service agencies, the task of delivering these services in a coordinated manner and raising the money to pay for them remains an overriding priority and one of the community's most daunting tasks.

GROWTH WITHOUT JOBS?

Implicit in the Kalamazoo Promise is the idea that an increase in the supply of educated workers will stimulate a matching response on the demand side, enticing employers to expand or relocate to the community. However, such an increase in demand may not materialize automatically, and without a steady supply of new jobs that require a college education, it is doubtful that families will choose to relocate to Kalamazoo or that college graduates will opt to remain in or move to the community. If the impact of the Kalamazoo Promise is merely a shift of middle-class families from outlying areas into the district, the results will be disappointing from an economic development standpoint—a redistribution of the existing pie rather than its expansion. The Promise in and of itself is probably not a powerful enough incentive to attract major new employers to the region; nevertheless, it is a rallying cry for community engagement and mobilization, and a catalyst for positioning Kalamazoo as an attractive locale for those households and businesses that place a high value on education. By calling into action coalitions of residents, businesses, and organizations working strategically to leverage its potential, the Kalamazoo Promise may emerge as an important new instrument for economic revitalization.

MANAGING EXPECTATIONS

The Kalamazoo Promise is a long-term approach to community revitalization, yet many are eager for quick results. If the short-term benefits of the program are oversold, popular enthusiasm and support within Kalamazoo could wane when they fail to materialize. Outside the region, the dangers of raised expectations are even more acute. Cities considering their own programs modeled on the Promise are looking to Kalamazoo for evidence of success; in the absence of a clear understanding of the long-term nature of such an investment, support for the creation of new programs could fall short. To minimize these risks, it is essential that the broader public understands the long-term strategy behind the Kalamazoo Promise and can assess its impact realistically and over time. A balanced account of the potential results of the Promise is a fundamental first step (and one of the goals of this book), and should be followed by unbiased monitoring and the wide dissemination of results.

As other cities grapple with the task of designing programs modeled on the Kalamazoo Promise, they will undoubtedly face some of these challenges as well as others specific to their communities. But two additional issues deserve attention up front. The first is the political challenge of building support—financial and otherwise—for a program when funding is not provided by anonymous sources. The anonymity of the Kalamazoo Promise donors has minimized debate over the structure of the program and helped catalyze a broad community response. Other communities are unlikely to enjoy the luxury of open-ended funding in perpetuity from donors who have specified the terms of the program and cannot be petitioned to change them. Generating the political will and financial resources necessary for a transformative investment along the lines of the Kalamazoo Promise is a far more complex task when it unfolds under public scrutiny and with the participation of many stakeholders. The second issue is a question that will undoubtedly arise during the planning process: Is the direction of resources toward a scholarship-based economic development program the best use of available funds, or are there alternatives—such as investments in universal prekindergarten education or an integrated system of community support for youth, to name just two—that might have a larger impact on the community?

There will be other challenges that cannot be foreseen today, but a clear understanding of the Kalamazoo Promise concept and the community's initial response to it will help equip Kalamazoo and other communities pursuing similar initiatives to deal with these challenges as they arise.

Notes

1. Dr. Janice Brown, former KPS superintendent, speaking at a school board meeting on November 10, 2005.
2. In-state tuition for 2006–2007 ranged from $1,500 a year for a full-time student at Kalamazoo Valley Community College, to approximately $10,000 a year at the University of Michigan, meaning that the benefit to members of the class of 2006—the first students eligible for the program—is worth as much as $40,000 per child. (Ferris State University's Kendall College of Art and Design was the most expensive option for Promise recipients; its $12,660 annual tuition cost ranked as the highest in-state rate in the nation.)
3. For details of the scholarship program, see http://www.kalamazoopromise.com.
4. As of May 2008, approximately 25 communities in 12 states were at some stage in the process of developing a program modeled on the Kalamazoo Promise. Some communities, including Pittsburgh, Pennsylvania; Denver, Colorado; and El Dorado, Arkansas, had programs up and running, while those in the planning state ranged from industrial towns like Akron, Ohio, and Hammond, Indiana, to rural or resource-based communities like Peoria, Illinois, and Orange, Texas.
5. Author's interview with Robert Jorth, Kalamazoo Promise administrator, July 18, 2006.
6. Two of those on the 2008 Forbes list—Ronda Stryker and her brother Jon Stryker—

are the grandchildren of Stryker Corp.'s founder, while the third—John Brown (no relation to Janice Brown) is the company's former CEO (Forbes.com 2008). For speculation on the donors' identities, see Boudette (2006) and Jones (2005).

7. Private communication with the author from community leader, January 31, 2006.

8. Author's interview with Dr. Janice Brown, March 25, 2008.

9. Michael Scriven, consultant, The Evaluation Center, Western Michigan University, public comment, June 8, 2006.

10. Tuition, fees, and room-and-board rates can be found at http://www.wmich.edu (accessed March 3, 2009).

11. Peter McFarlane, then superintendent of Portage Public Schools, quoted in Chourey (2005).

12. Author's notes from forum with Kalamazoo Homeless Action Network members at Kalamazoo College, November 15, 2005.

13. E-mail message from Arlene Washington, editor of *Community Voices*, to Mayor Hannah McKinney, November 14, 2005.

14. The Lt. Governor's Commission on Higher Education & Economic Growth (the Cherry Commission) reported that only 29 percent of Michigan adults have an associate's or higher degree, while only 22 percent have a bachelor's degree or higher, both rates below the national average and well behind those of leading states. (Cherry Commission 2004)

15. The Cherry Commission concluded that a 5 percent increase in the share of college-educated adults would boost overall economic growth by 2.5 percent over 10 years, and the real wages of all Michigan residents by 5.5 percent (Cherry Commission 2004).

16. Exchange posted on a forum at http://www.woodtv.com, November 12, 2005.

17. Comment posted on a forum at http://www.woodtv.com, November 11, 2005.

18. Exchange posted on a forum at http://www.woodtv.com, November 26, 2005.

19. Comment posted on mlive.com, November 14, 2005.

20. Comment posted on WoodTV forum, November 16, 2005.

21. Author's interview with Carrie Pickett-Erway, Kalamazoo Community Foundation, February 16, 2006.

22. The definitive work on social capital is Putnam (2000). For stories of specific social capital-building efforts, see Putnam and Feldstein (2003).

23. For a review of this literature, see Haveman and Wolfe (1995).

24. For a review of this literature, see Page-Adams and Sherraden (1996).

25. Fall 2007 data provided by Kalamazoo Public Schools.

26. On the benefits of socioeconomic school integration, see work by Richard Kahlenberg and others at http://www.equaleducation.org.

27. Kalamazoo Promise Web site FAQ, accessed through https://www.kalamazoopromise.com.

28. Comments by former KPS Superintendent Janice Brown at Kalamazoo Communities In Schools (KCIS) Community Partners Meeting, February 8, 2006.

29. Author's interview with Linda Van Dis, KPS parent, February 9, 2006.

30. The Center for Economic and Policy Research reports that nearly two-thirds of students attending a four-year public college or university take on student loans while they are in school, and that the average indebted graduating senior in 2004 was $17,600 in debt on graduation day. See Boushey (2005).
31. Author's interview with Ron Kitchens, chief executive officer, Southwest Michigan First, March 29, 2006.
32. The Headlee Amendment, ratified in 1978, limited the growth of property tax revenue by controlling how a local government's maximum authorized millage rate is calculated. When growth on existing property in a community appreciates at a rate faster than inflation, the local government must "roll back" its maximum authorized millage rate so that the increase in property tax revenue does not exceed inflation. In March 1994, Proposal A created a new methodology to determine property values for tax purposes with the introduction of taxable value. Taxable value on an individual property cannot increase by more than the lesser of inflation or 5 percent annually until a property is sold or transferred regardless of how quickly existing property values may be growing. The interaction of these two laws has severely constrained any upside growth in local tax revenues. For more information, see Audia and Buckley (2003).

2
What Came Before

Why did the donors behind the Kalamazoo Promise believe there was the need for such a program in their community, and why did they choose this particular approach? An examination of the region's economic and social history sheds some light on both questions. But there is an equally compelling reason for surveying the history of Kalamazoo: The proliferation of programs modeled on the Promise suggests that many other communities see in Kalamazoo a reflection of their current predicament and a possible solution to it. Indeed, southwest Michigan has been affected by most of the large-scale social forces that shaped the nation in the twentieth century.

In the late 1800s, Kalamazoo's economy shifted from an agricultural to a manufacturing foundation. Production contracted during the 1930s and rebounded during World War II. Growth continued into the 1950s, as the creation of the interstate highway system, rise of the suburbs, and general prosperity led to an expansion of the auto industry and related manufacturing activities. But, as in the rest of the nation, the "affluent society" described by John Kenneth Galbraith in 1958 hid both poverty and racial tension and, in the 1960s, the civil rights movement came to Kalamazoo, challenging the community's social structure and ushering in the kind of urban unrest (albeit on a small scale) witnessed across the nation. The conflict played out in the schools, with a court-ordered desegregation plan, mandatory busing, and "white flight" in the late 1960s and 1970s. The black–white and urban–suburban divisions that characterize Kalamazoo today date from this era. In the 1980s and 1990s, the region's leading industries confronted globalization and technological change, and Kalamazoo began a wrenching transformation that included plant closings, mergers, job losses, and rising poverty, especially within the urban core. By 2005, the city's poverty rate for families stood at 17.6 percent—almost twice the national average and almost three times the rate for the rest of Kalamazoo County.[1]

In some ways, Kalamazoo was more fortunate than many of the other communities affected by similar trends. Its economy was relatively diverse, with reliance on multiple industries rather than a single corporation (as in nearby Battle Creek, where the Kellogg Company has long held the key to the community's financial health). The economic blows were also cushioned by a large philanthropic sector that has devoted substantial resources to both economic revitalization and social well-being. (In Battle Creek, the W.K. Kellogg Foundation plays a similar role.)

But Kalamazoo also faces special challenges, especially a system of local governance in which metropolitan regions are comprised of very small jurisdictions, each with its own governing body, public officials, and property tax rate. Kalamazoo County, with a population of approximately 240,000, encompasses 24 local jurisdictions grouped into nine separate school districts, making it the fifth-most fragmented metropolitan area in Michigan, one of the states most conducive to such a "little box" system.[2] This arrangement has made it easy for residents to leave the central city and its urban schools behind by relocating only a few miles in any direction, lowering their tax rates and keeping their jobs while sending their children to schools that are largely white and middle class. One indicator of these demographic trends is a 20 percent decrease in the population of the city of Kalamazoo from 1970 to 2007, at the same time that the county's population grew by 19 percent.[3] As it has in other cities, such a jurisdictional system also has intensified the process of suburbanization and facilitated a growing concentration of minority and low-income families in the urban core and the public schools (see Table 2.1).

The rise and decline of Kalamazoo is a familiar story, and familiar solutions have been tried. Experts have touted the benefits of regional cooperation and unified governance. Tax abatements have been offered to companies threatening to move out, and incentives offered to those considering a move in. Bidding wars have erupted between neighboring cities and even states (the Indiana border is only 40 miles away). Downtown revitalization has been pursued, and successive regional economic development entities have taken the lead in wooing businesses and jobs. Sporadic efforts have been made to integrate the large population of college students, numbering more than 35,000, into the community. An emerging life sciences industry has been identified by some as the solution to Kalamazoo's woes, and the city's educational, arts, and cultural organizations have been marketed as powerful attractions for new resi-

Table 2.1 Population Trends, 1970–2007

	1970	1980	1990	2000	2007
KPS enrollment[a]	17,285	13,280	12,584	11,245	11,378
% African American	17[a]	30	36	44	48
City of Kalamazoo pop.	85,555	79,722	80,277	77,145	71,441
% African American	10	15.6	18.8	20.6	20.8
Kalamazoo County pop.	201,550	212,378	223,411	238,603	244,153
% African American	4.8	7.5	8.7	9.7	9.9

NOTE: School enrollment numbers from Kalamazoo Public Schools' September 2007 head count (rounded to nearest percentage point)
[a] Data for 1970 are not broken down by race; this number represents all minority students.
SOURCE: U.S. Census Bureau, American Community Survey.

dents. Yet the economic downturn has continued, with some indicators approaching what urban expert David Rusk has called "the point of no return" for urban areas (Rusk 1995).

One interpretation of the Kalamazoo Promise is that the city and the school district have declined together and that their revival will require attention to both sectors. In this sense, the Kalamazoo Promise is much more than a scholarship program; it is a potentially powerful tool to shift Kalamazoo away from the tipping point of urban decay and set it on a virtuous cycle of school improvement, population growth, and economic revitalization. To understand how this might happen, it is helpful to have a mental map of the community and some knowledge of its history.

A TEXTUAL TOUR

A tour of Kalamazoo might begin at Bronson Park (see Figure 2.1) in the heart of downtown—what a recent magazine article called "a town center straight out of the 1930s," ringed by churches, city hall, and the Civic Theatre (O'Brien 2006).

A short walk brings one to the Kalamazoo Mall, the nation's first outdoor pedestrian mall, constructed in 1959. Lined with family-owned businesses (there are no chain stores in downtown Kalamazoo apart

Figure 2.1 Kalamazoo City Map

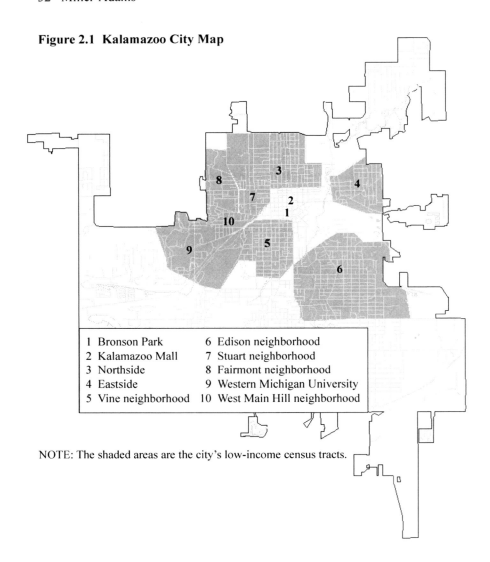

1	Bronson Park	6	Edison neighborhood
2	Kalamazoo Mall	7	Stuart neighborhood
3	Northside	8	Fairmont neighborhood
4	Eastside	9	Western Michigan University
5	Vine neighborhood	10	West Main Hill neighborhood

NOTE: The shaded areas are the city's low-income census tracts.

from fast-food franchises), the street's fortunes declined when the first enclosed malls were built in the 1970s. To increase commercial traffic, a road was carved through the Kalamazoo Mall in 1998, accompanied by heated sidewalks to melt the snow, benches, and new historic markers. Stores have opened, stores have closed, and despite myriad efforts to entice people downtown, until recently one could stroll down the street most days at noon and see only a handful of local office workers making their way to lunch.

But downtown Kalamazoo is a neighborhood in flux. In 2007, 9 businesses closed in the downtown district while 14 opened, and 79 percent of the available office space in the area is rented.[4] Downtown foot traffic is increasing, while monthly "art hops" and other special events draw large crowds. One block beyond the mall is a 14-screen movie theater with loft-style condominiums above it that opened in 2006. The first downtown cinema in 20 years, it is a development that city planners and local businesses hope will attract college students and other young people and support the mini-renaissance under way in the surrounding streets. In 2007, *Urban Land* magazine named downtown Kalamazoo one of the nation's top 10 downtown turnaround stories, putting it in the company of much larger cities like Memphis, Philadelphia, and San Francisco (Nyren 2007).

Moving north across the railroad tracks, the renovated buildings, coffeehouses, and microbreweries give way to a no-man's-land of shuttered factories, vacant lots, and the occasional light manufacturing operation. There are no amenities and virtually no pedestrians. The Kalamazoo River borders this abandoned landscape, once home to heavy industry and several junkyards, much of which is now designated a brownfield site. The city of Kalamazoo is working to develop the riverfront, and while clean-up costs are formidable, a range of federal and municipal resources exist to make such an effort possible.

A few blocks away is the heart of the Northside, a largely African American neighborhood and one of the city's low-income census tracts. Here, street life centers on the area's many churches, the newly renovated train and bus station, and two nearby homeless shelters. The neighborhood also has a high concentration of social service providers, a mixed blessing for those who are working to encourage retail activity. Economic development efforts led by local residents have yielded modest but meaningful gains—a supermarket, a pizza franchise, and some small businesses—but the commercial center is confined to a few blocks. There are two magnet elementary schools in the neighborhood—Lincoln International Studies School, until recently the home of a highly regarded dual-language immersion program, and Northglade Montessori School, one of the few Montessori-certified public schools in the United States. Despite these unique attributes, designed to draw students from across the district, both schools still enroll a high percentage of minority and low-income students.[5]

The Northside neighborhood became home to Kalamazoo's African American population after World War II, when the explosion of manufacturing industries enticed many Southern black families to move north in search of jobs. Those who came to Kalamazoo settled in this older, formerly Dutch neighborhood where housing prices were low and properties were not covered by the restrictive covenants that banned nonwhite residents, as was the case in the city's newer neighborhoods. (Federal mortgage-lending policies intensified patterns of segregation in Kalamazoo as they did elsewhere, with the Federal Housing Administration refusing to insure mortgages for blacks in white neighborhoods and vice versa.)[6] As white residents moved out at a faster rate than black residents moved in, the population began to shrink, and when restrictive lending practices were banned, middle-class African Americans left as well. Between the 1970 and the 1990 censuses, the Northside's overall population fell and the percentage of the black population rose. In 2000, 81 percent of the neighborhood's 5,776 residents were African American, and the poverty rate for the neighborhood stood at 37 percent.[7]

The city's other low-income neighborhoods are more racially mixed, and each has its challenges. The Eastside is a neighborhood of 2,610 cut off from the rest of the city by a highway bypass, railroad tracks, and a major artery. Its physical isolation means that many longtime Kalamazoo residents have never even driven through the area, where almost one-third of the population lives in poverty. The area is hilly and in places has an almost rural feel. There are fewer churches and community organizations here, and little commercial activity. Plans are under way for the construction of a youth center in the neighborhood, in part because of concerns over the lack of after-school or summer activities for Eastside youth, but financial resources are limited.

To the south of downtown is the Vine neighborhood, one of the oldest in Kalamazoo. Here, owner-occupied homes vie for space with rental housing for students from the nearby college and university. Vine actually has the city's highest poverty rate—41.5 percent—but many of these are the "college-student poor" living in apartments or large homes divided into multiple living quarters. The relationship between long-term residents and the more transient student population can be strained, and homeowners complain about widespread building code violations by absentee landlords. Vine Street School, which housed KPS's alternative-education programs through 2005, sat shuttered at the center of the neighborhood until a new dual-language elementary school opened there in 2008. The adjacent Old Central High School building—home to the highly regarded Kalamazoo Area Math and Science Center—also is in active use, and its gem of an auditorium has recently undergone a multimillion-dollar restoration effort.

The Edison neighborhood, to the southeast of downtown, is the largest low-income census tract in the city, with over 8,000 residents. Edison was the location of the city's minuscule red-light district, complete with topless dance club and adult bookstore, until organizing efforts by community members forced these businesses to relocate. Now a variety of revitalization efforts are under way. Edison is home to much of the city's Hispanic community (Hispanics officially make up 4.8 percent of the population, according to the most recent U.S. census estimate,[8] but that number may be unduly low in light of the undocumented population—for example, Hispanic students accounted for 9.5 percent of KPS enrollment in 2007–2008)[9] and the major street through the neighborhood boasts a Mexican grocery, bakery, and several small retail stores. Two of KPS's magnet elementary schools are here, Washington Writers' Academy and Edison Environmental Science Academy, both enrolling a largely poor, minority population, and serving as important hubs for the surrounding community.

The city's final low-income census tract encompasses the Stuart and Fairmont neighborhoods, adjacent to each other and just to the west of downtown. The Stuart neighborhood includes the city's largest collection of Victorian houses, most built in the 1870s and 1880s. During the twentieth century, these homes were gradually converted to multifamily rental units, but in 1976 the area was designated a local historic district and new owners have returned many residences to their original character. The oldest elementary school still in operation is located here, now called the Woodward School for Technology and Research.

Together, the city of Kalamazoo's low-income neighborhoods account for 36.5 percent of its total population (Kalamazoo County Health
and Community Services 2006). They are also home to most of the
region's minority population, as well as much of its violent crime and
what many consider to be nascent gang activity.

Plenty of middle-income families choose to live in Kalamazoo; indeed, some of the region's most desirable housing stock is located within
city boundaries. In family-oriented neighborhoods like Westnedge Hill,
Winchell, and Milwood, parents load up on enough candy on Hallow-
een to satisfy the several hundred children likely to ring their doorbells.
Each of these neighborhoods has a local elementary school that helps
anchor the community; Winchell Elementary was the first to reach its
maximum enrollment the year after the Kalamazoo Promise was announced. The West Main Hill neighborhood is anchored by Kalamazoo
College on one side and WMU on the other, and contains some of the
most diverse housing stock in the city. The most elegant street in the
city may be Long Road, just up the hill from the Vine neighborhood,
with 20 or so homes that would not be out of place in the nicer reaches
of Beverly Hills.

But many more middle- and upper-income families have opted for
newer housing in Portage to the south or Oshtemo and Texas Township
to the west, due in part to lower tax rates outside the city proper. The
wealthiest among them have built sprawling new homes on the area's
outlying lakes or in rural areas. With the construction of the two high-
ways that intersect in Kalamazoo—I-94 that links Chicago and Detroit,
and U.S. 131 running north to Grand Rapids and south to Indiana—the
commercial and residential focus of the community shifted away from
downtown. This is where the big box stores and major chains have continued to locate, with commercial activity spreading ever further away
from the center. These areas are overwhelmingly white and nonpoor, a
demographic makeup also reflected in the public schools. (See Table
2.2 to compare the characteristics of the two largest school districts in
the county—KPS and Portage Public Schools.)

The urban core retains many of the region's most important amenities: educational institutions, including WMU (along with its entertainment and athletic venues), Kalamazoo College, and the downtown campus of Kalamazoo Valley Community College (KVCC); the art museum,
public library, symphony, and other cultural institutions; churches and

Table 2.2 School Characteristics, 2007

	Kalamazoo Public Schools	Portage Public Schools
Enrollment	11,684	8,889
Minority enrollment (%)	60.1	14.6
Economically disadvantaged	65.0	20.0[a]
Reading proficiency (%)	64.4	90.4
Math proficiency (%)	54.3	85.4

[a] Data provided by Portage Public Schools.
SOURCE: Standard & Poor's SchoolData Direct.

parks; a public swimming pool, the fairground, and a newly developed downtown festival site; and restaurants and businesses. Because of the nonprofit status of many of these entities, close to 50 percent of the property in the city of Kalamazoo is tax exempt—a fact that has had negative implications for public finances and limits the potential impact of Kalamazoo Promise–related development on city coffers.[10]

Even for those who live within its borders, Kalamazoo remains a city of communities that often seem separate and unequal. Robert Putnam, a Harvard University professor and expert on social capital who has visited the town several times, reports being surprised by the extent of what he calls the "donut effect"—a poor and black urban core ringed by middle-class and largely white neighborhoods. The president of Kalamazoo College, Eileen Wilson-Oyelaran, commented shortly after her arrival in town on what she perceived as the physical separation between the black and white populations. Dr. Wilson-Oyelaran, who is African American, compared Kalamazoo to her previous hometown of Winston-Salem, where "You will find successful people of color all over the town . . . In Kalamazoo, the community appears much more racially isolated. It sometimes feels as if the black community is cordoned off."[11]

There are other divides as well, as is evident to anyone who lives in Kalamazoo and wonders where WMU's 25,000 students go when they are not in class. They are seldom seen downtown, in part because the university is physically separated from the business district by a four-lane thoroughfare and a set of railroad tracks, and in part because, until recently, few central city businesses have made a concerted effort to cater to the student population. The town-gown relationship is notably different from Ann Arbor, where the transition from the University of Michigan's main campus to the surrounding business district is virtually seamless, with students streaming off campus between classes and at the end of the day to eat at downtown restaurants, drink at downtown coffeehouses, shop at downtown bookstores, and dance at downtown clubs.

It is difficult to decide where a tour of the city might end—perhaps heading even farther south or west, where farmland is increasingly giving way to Wal-Marts, new housing tracts, and other commercial development. Or we can return to the southeast corner of Bronson Park, where the city's past, present, and future meet. Across the street stands the Park Club, a private dining club established in 1904 and still catering to the city's elite. On the opposite corner is the glass-walled Kalamazoo Public Library. Constructed in 1959 and extensively remodeled in 1996, it was named National Library of the Year in 2002. On the fourth corner, a new office tower was completed in 2007, home to one of the area's largest law firms and a step toward the downtown revitalization that many hope will be one of the outcomes of the Kalamazoo Promise.

ECONOMIC EBB AND FLOW

While Native Americans from the Potawatomi tribe had inhabited the area since the 1600s, the first white settlers arrived in Kalamazoo County in 1828. Titus Bronson came the following year and purchased the land where downtown Kalamazoo is now located. In 1831, he and his brother-in-law registered their land with the county, naming it the "Village of Bronson." Five years later, the town's name was changed to Kalamazoo.[12] (Historians speculate that Bronson had by then alienated many of his fellow settlers with his outspoken views on politics and denunciations of alcohol, tobacco, dancing, and card playing [Kekic 1984].) By the late nineteenth century, Kalamazoo had become known as "Celery City" because of the rich, mucky soil and the many Dutch immigrants who cultivated a sweeter, paler variety of celery than is eaten today. Celery fields covered the region and, by 1871, the amount of celery shipped from Kalamazoo by rail made the city the second most active freight center in Michigan after Detroit. The town regularly named a "Celery Queen," and local farmers were known to board trains as they stopped in Kalamazoo to sell celery to the passengers. More significant for the local economy, the celery industry spawned a variety of patent medicines based on the supposed purifying and aphrodisiac qualities of the plant. While some of the producers of these medicines were charlatans, others were respected members of the community and legitimate drug manufacturers.

As late as 1939 there were still more than 1,000 acres of celery beds under cultivation in the area. But the celery business declined as growers failed to adapt to new techniques, competition from other areas increased, and the proliferation of paper mills lowered the water table. By 1985, there was only one celery farmer left in the area, and by the end of the century there were none. Agriculture, however, remains a part of the local economy, farmers having converted to new crops, especially bedding plants. Kalamazoo is home to the nation's largest bedding plant cooperative and the outskirts of town are dotted with greenhouses (Peppel 2005).

Ever since Glenn Miller's recording of "I've Got A Gal In Kalamazoo" occupied the number-one Billboard Records spot for eight weeks in 1942, Kalamazoo has been best known as home to "that freckle-faced kid." But the city's economic claim to fame is the variety of industries that thrived here over the centuries. Local historian Peter J. Schmitt wrote that "much of Kalamazoo's history is the story of talented inventors and businessmen who recognized a need, developed a solution, and marketed a product" (Massie and Schmitt 1998, p. 8)—a deceptively simple strategy that could bring Kalamazoo renewed economic success in the twenty-first century.

Kalamazoo may seem out of the way today, tucked into the southwest corner of Michigan, but its location on a railroad line equidistant from Chicago and Detroit, and access to labor (largely in the form of immigrants) and natural resources (including plentiful lumber and the Kalamazoo River) positioned it well for the industrial age. By the early twentieth century, 272 factories produced a remarkable range of goods for the national market. Among these was the Gibson Mandolin-Guitar Manufacturing Company, incorporated in 1904 and headquartered in the city until 1981. The Gibson plant closed three years later, but several of its craftsmen opted to remain locally based, accounting for the surprisingly large number of guitar makers in the area. Other manufacturers included the American Playing Card Company, which produced up to 18,000 decks of cards daily; Henderson-Ames, which made uniforms and regalia; the Kalamazoo Stove Company, which closed its doors in the 1950s; the Kalamazoo Corset Company, which at one time produced 1.5 million corsets a year; and Checker Motors, which built its famous yellow cabs in Kalamazoo from 1923 until 1982.

The area's two most important products by far were paper and pharmaceuticals.[13] The first paper mill opened in 1866, and by the 1930s more paper was produced in Kalamazoo's 15 mills than anywhere else in the world. The industry thrived thanks to a steady supply of immigrant labor; the railroad, which provided access to nearby markets; and the Kalamazoo River, relied on by the mills for production and disposal of their by-products. By midcentury, the paper industry accounted for approximately 32 percent of the combined sales of all industries in the area and 24 percent of residents' total personal income (Smith 1958). The decline of the industry beginning in the 1970s was hastened by technological change, foreign competition, and environmental concerns. (Paper production is notorious for the pollutants it generates, and the Kalamazoo River—designated a superfund site because of the presence of toxins in its fish, sediment, and surface water—is still recovering from the industry's impact even after 30 years of clean water legislation.) Thousands of semiskilled workers lost their jobs as the plants closed, five in 2000 alone, and since then local governments have struggled to procure the resources to demolish the old mill sites, rid them of toxic substances, and find new uses for them.

The city's dominant employer for much of the twentieth century was the Upjohn Company. The firm was established in Kalamazoo in 1886 as the Upjohn Pill and Granule Company by Dr. William E. Upjohn, a graduate of the University of Michigan Medical School, and his three brothers. Their invention of the first easily dissolvable pill spawned a company that grew into a worldwide provider of pharmaceutical, agricultural, and chemical products. By the 1950s, the Upjohn Company had become one of the nation's top pharmaceutical manufacturers, and by the mid-1960s, it was Kalamazoo's largest employer. In 1978, the company's annual sales surpassed $1 billion for the first time, and in 1980, 6,400 workers were employed locally. In 1995, the Upjohn Company was swept up in the ongoing agglomeration of pharmaceutical firms into ever-larger entities when it merged with the Swedish company Pharmacia, headquartered in Stockholm. Neither party wanted the new headquarters to be located in the other firm's hometown, so the headquarters of what was now the world's ninth-largest pharmaceutical firm was established in Windsor, England, where a skeletal staff of 30 supervised global operations. Over the next two years, Kalamazoo lost more than 1,000 local jobs, and in 1998 the headquarters of the U.S. operation relocated to Peapack, New Jersey, close to the nation's other major pharmaceutical firms. In 2000, Pharmacia & Upjohn merged with Monsanto (attracted by its G.D. Searle pharmaceuticals unit) and was renamed simply Pharmacia. A short two years later, Pfizer Inc. announced a $60 million deal to purchase Pharmacia, and the following year all research activity was moved out of Kalamazoo, translating into an additional 1,200 jobs lost in the county. In contrast to earlier layoffs when the paper mills and a large auto plant shut down, many of the Pfizer-related job losses were well-paying positions held by highly educated workers, and their departure hurt not only the employment picture of the region but also its tax base and housing market. In January 2007, Pfizer announced plans to close its human-drug-testing operation in Kalamazoo by 2008, eliminating another 250 jobs downtown, although a large manufacturing plant in Portage and the veterinary research operation remain in place. The Upjohn Company's fate cut into the budgets of many nonprofit organizations, as the firm had been Kalamazoo's leading corporate philanthropist for decades and a generous supporter of the community's arts and cultural organizations.

Kalamazoo lost a second corporate headquarters when First of America Bank Corporation was acquired by National City Bank of Cleveland in 1998. Many of First of America's 3,200 Kalamazoo jobs, including hundreds of well-paying executive positions, were eliminated or relocated to Ohio, and the renovated downtown buildings in which First of America's employees had worked still stand largely vacant.[14]

While Checker Motors cut back production in the 1970s, the automobile industry had a continuing regional presence in the form of General Motors' Fisher Body stamping plant located just outside the city of Kalamazoo.[15] The plant employed almost 4,000 skilled laborers when it opened in 1965. Retrenchment in the auto industry led to successive waves of layoffs and the ultimate closure of the two-million square foot facility in 1999. Another source of steady employment for blue-collar workers had been lost, and the massive plant was converted to an industrial park that is not yet fully occupied.

One homegrown company has bucked these trends, becoming one of the country's most profitable firms. Beginning in the 1930s, Dr. Homer Stryker, an orthopedic surgeon practicing in Kalamazoo, developed a series of products to serve his patients, including a turning frame for hospital beds and an oscillating saw to remove casts. These inventions, which were first marketed in the 1940s, launched the Stryker Corporation. Today, Stryker is one of the world's leading medical device companies. With over $6 billion in sales in 2007, the company is best known among investors for its regular double-digit increases in annual profits (*Fortune 500* 2008). A newly constructed 70,000-square-foot facility suggests that Stryker will remain headquartered in Kalamazoo, even though most of its 15,000 workers are located outside the region.

The continued presence of firms like Stryker and Pfizer, two major hospitals, a research university, and the availability of venture capital have helped position the region as a potential center for the life sciences industry. The Southwest Michigan Innovation Center, a public–private collaboration initiated in 2002, has served as a source of support for start-up companies in this field, many of them founded by scientists who once worked for Pfizer. A major expansion by the regionally based preclinical drug testing company MPI Research, announced in 2008, has lent credence to the viability of this life science–based strategy (see Chapter 6 for details).

As this survey suggests, Kalamazoo's economy in its heyday offered employment to workers with a broad range of skills and a home to entrepreneurs whose inventions formed the basis for highly successful companies. These firms and their employees contributed not only to the economy but also to the area's quality of life through their community involvement and philanthropic giving. The mergers and acquisitions of the 1980s and 1990s and the larger forces of economic restructuring that led to a decline in manufacturing thus hurt both Kalamazoo's job market and its social fabric, as many families chose to relocate while others turned to lower-paying jobs.

Its many years of economic prosperity did endow Kalamazoo with medical, educational, cultural, and philanthropic institutions that have helped buffer the negative effects of change. Borgess Medical Center and Bronson Methodist Hospital, both located in the urban core, are the second- and fourth-largest employers, respectively, in the region.[16] Educational institutions, including Kalamazoo College, a private liberal arts college founded in 1833; WMU, a public university founded in 1903; and KVCC, founded in 1966; draw thousands of young people to Kalamazoo each year from around the state and the nation. High-profile cultural events, such as the biennial Gilmore International Keyboard Festival, attract music lovers from well beyond southwest Michigan, while many local events and festivals bring thousands of people down-town each summer to eat, drink, and dance. A well-endowed group of foundations, as well as a strong United Way, make up a diverse philan-thropic and nonprofit community focused on local needs. These assets, however, have left untouched many of the region's critical problems, such as the decline of manufacturing industry, flight from the urban core, and racial segregation in the housing market and the schools, all of which have increased strains on the public education system.

THE EVOLUTION OF EDUCATION

For most of the nineteenth century, public education for Kalama-zoo's children was limited to tax-funded "common" schools, the rough equivalent of today's elementary schools. The first schoolhouse opened in 1833 and also served as a temporary church and courthouse. By 1848, four schools were in operation, including a brick schoolhouse that cost $606 to build. Initially, the schools operated separately, but they were soon consolidated into a single district by legislative act. The community also decided upon the construction of a Union School to serve the entire village of Kalamazoo, and in 1858 a districtwide school was built on a five-acre site near the present location of Old Central High School, at a cost of $45,000. A separate school served the community's African American children from 1861 to 1872, when the district was officially integrated.[17] By 1876, enrollment had climbed to 2,000 students, although census figures show that there were more than 3,000 children of school age in the district. Also by this time, individual elementary schools had been established and the Union School became a high school.

The dual purpose of the high school was to prepare a select group of students for higher education and to give everyone else the more advanced vocational skills they would need to find employment within a changing economy. In the 1850s, a state law had been passed allowing school districts with more than 200 children to elect school boards that could set up high schools funded by local taxes, provided that the district's citizens voted in favor of the proposal. Kalamazoo Union High School operated with only minor opposition until 1873, when three prominent property owners filed a suit challenging the school board's right to fund the high school through local taxes. The grounds for the lawsuit were that Kalamazoo's residents had never voted to establish the high school and that the decision instead had been made by the school board acting on its own. One of the plaintiffs in the case was Charles E. Stuart, a former U.S. Senator from Michigan. Stuart, like others of his time, believed that a common school education was sufficient for most children and that any additional schooling should be paid for privately. His opponents argued that universal high school was an essential measure for bridging the gap between common school and university, and should be accessible to all. The case was decided by the Circuit Court in favor of the school board and appealed to the Michigan Supreme Court. Justice Thomas M. Cooley, former dean of the University of Michigan Law School, upheld the decision of the Circuit Court and in the Kalamazoo School Case decision of 1874 put to rest the question of public financial support for high schools in Michigan. This landmark case served as one of the precedents for legal challenges to universal high school elsewhere and had an important effect on the number of high schools in the state, which increased dramatically in the 20 years following the decision.[18]

Initially, these high schools were attended only by the children of wealthy and middle-class families. Michigan was among the first states in the nation to pass (in 1871) a compulsory school attendance law, and by 1890 this law required youth ages 8–14 to attend four months of school each year. In the 1880s, a child labor law had been enacted at the state level, placing some restrictions on working conditions for young people. But as long as jobs (especially those in the relatively high-paying manufacturing sector) did not require a high school education, the only children attending Kalamazoo's high school were those whose parents could afford for them not to work. As a result, the school's initial emphasis was on collegiate preparation, as these students were also likely candidates for higher education. (Beginning in 1899, at least 60 percent of the high school's graduates went on for further study [Bennett 1956]). After 1910, due to changes in the economic conditions of the community and the needs of business, the high school's emphasis on "practical education" through manual training and vocational courses grew in importance.[19] As the relative demand for white-collar workers in manufacturing rose in the early twentieth century, and blue-collar jobs began to require and reward formal schooling, the financial returns to a young person from each year of schooling grew, and high school attendance became the norm among most social classes. National trends mirrored those in Michigan; in 1910, the rate of enrollment in secondary schools had been only 18 percent nationwide, but by the 1940s it had risen to 71 percent (Goldin and Katz 1997, p. 27).

Another factor that affected rates of high school attendance and graduation across the nation was a state's commitment to fund its colleges, since public support served as a powerful incentive for young people to graduate from high school and continue their education (Goldin and Katz 1997). The University of Michigan, founded in 1817, was one of the first public universities in the United States and the recipient of the most generous level of state financing.[20] It remains the most prestigious school in Michigan, whether public or private, but is only part of a varied postsecondary landscape. Michigan State University, established by the state legislature in 1855, served as the prototype for 72 land-grant institutions later established under the federal Morrill Act. Eastern, Western, Central, and Northern Michigan Universities were established between 1849 and 1903 as two-year teacher training schools, while Wayne State University was founded in 1868 as a medical school. All are now large research universities. The near quadrupling of the nation's higher education enrollment rates from 1940 to 1970 was facilitated by the addition of other public four-year institutions and a network of community colleges, currently numbering 29 in Michigan, as well as the GI Bill of 1944 that paid for veterans to attend college.

Despite its diversity, Michigan's system of higher education has suffered in recent years. The state's college enrollment rates have declined faster than the national average (by 7 percent, compared to a national decline of 2 percent, between 1992 and 2006), and access to affordable higher education has been curtailed by stagnant wages, tuition increases, and limited investments in need-based financial aid (National Center for Public Policy and Higher Education 2006). The state's ongoing struggle to adapt to the declining fortunes of the manufacturing sector, especially automobiles, has set in motion a vicious circle of lower tax revenues, budget cutting, reduced funding for higher education, tuition increases, and declining enrollment that will be difficult to reverse.

CIVIL RIGHTS AND THE SCHOOLS

The evolution of Kalamazoo's public school system was profoundly shaped by a second major court decision—the school desegregation order of 1971. The issues that KPS faces today have their roots in the years leading up to and following this judicial battle. And, as with the evolution of its economy, Kalamazoo mirrored national trends in race relations and their impact on public education.

Kalamazoo was hardly a pioneer in the fight for civil rights. It wasn't until 1955 that KPS hired its first black teacher, and minority representation among teachers and administrators remained low, even as the black population of the district grew in the 1960s and 1970s. At WMU, student housing was segregated throughout the 1950s—if a black student and a white student wanted to room together, they each had to submit a written request as well as a letter of consent from their parents (WMU Library). Even so, by the early 1960s, race relations had become a regular topic of campus dialogue, and in this context Dr. Martin Luther King was invited to speak at the university in December 1963. In his address, attended by an estimated 2,000 people, he stressed the need for Congress to pass the civil rights bill before it at that time, claiming the need for legislative changes even if they did little to change attitudes; in King's words, "After laws are passed the heart can then be persuaded to change its feelings" (*Western Herald* 1963).

That same year, Northside residents picketed the Dutch-owned Van Avery Drugstore located in the neighborhood, claiming that its owners refused to hire a black clerk even though nearly half their customers were black. After three weeks of picketing and negotiations, a settlement was reached with the local chapter of the NAACP. This event marked the beginning of civil rights activism in Kalamazoo and raised public awareness that something needed to be done to address the problems of the Northside neighborhood, as well as the larger issues of de facto housing and school segregation in Kalamazoo.

In 1966, 11 years after the 1954 *Brown v. Board of Education* Supreme Court decision, state officials in Michigan called on all school districts to develop plans to balance their schools racially. In 1968, a committee of citizens was designated by the school district to draft such a plan. At the time, Kalamazoo's schools were highly segregated, with 91 percent of all black public elementary school students attending five schools on the Northside, out of the district's 19 public elementary schools. Fourteen elementary schools had minority enrollments of less than 10 percent, and 5 of these schools enrolled no minority students. In addition, 96 percent of all black junior high school students attended three of the district's five junior highs, while 93 percent of all black high school students were enrolled at Kalamazoo Central High School. The newer of the district's two high schools, Loy Norrix, had been built in 1961 at the very edge of the school district—land actually had to be annexed from Portage to construct the school—in an area with virtually no black population. While the school was open to anyone in the district, students had to provide their own transportation, effectively placing it out of reach for low-income black students from the Northside. In 1969, Kalamazoo Central's student body was 20 percent black, while Loy Norrix's was less than 2 percent black.

Edward P. Thompson, a lawyer and member of the school board at the time, was later asked to reflect on the desegregation period in a speech to a local business club. Thompson was a member of the "old" board that ultimately came to support desegregation, and his comments provide valuable insight into changing attitudes about race in Kalamazoo, especially among the elite. He wrote: "Before the racial confrontations I was sympathetic to the demands of blacks without being involved . . . I, like other members of the school board, believed that our local black population did not have these [civil rights] complaints, but we soon found out that they did . . . Kalamazoo always tried to be fair and progressive with regard to the black community, but that was the judgment of a white community still shackled by old attitudes and assumptions about blacks" (Thompson n.d.).

The Citizens' Racial Balance Committee announced its plan in 1969, and opposition formed almost immediately. The plan called for a gradual process of educating the public about racial segregation, increasing the proportion of black professionals in the schools, reorganizing the district, and ultimately busing elementary school students to achieve racial balance by the 1971 school year. The committee argued that its plan would not only bring the schools into compliance with the law, but also help overcome the achievement gap between middle-class and low-income children, both black and white.

The years leading up to the desegregation order had been tumultuous. The students entering Kalamazoo Central High School each autumn came from highly segregated elementary and junior high schools, and racial tension flared regularly. One of the earliest disputes occurred in 1967 over the racial integration of the all-white cheerleading squad, which had been mandated by the school board. In 1968, the high school closed for 10 days due to fighting on school grounds. In 1970, black students boycotted Kalamazoo Central and three junior high schools amid accusations of institutional racism. A junior high school principal stated that at one point as many as 20 race-related fights per day were occurring in his school, which was 40 percent minority at that time (U.S. Commission on Civil Rights 1977).

In January 1971, the school board voted to proceed with the citizens' committee's desegregation plan, a vote strengthened a few months later when the U.S. Supreme Court upheld the use of mandatory busing to achieve integration. The spring of 1971 saw intense public debate over the issue, with one meeting in May drawing 2,100 attendees, 130 of whom spoke during a four-hour session. A month later, the district's voters rejected a millage (bond) proposal by a 2–1 margin and on the same ballot voted to elect two antibusing candidates to the school board, eliminating the majority in favor of busing and putting the desegregation plan on hold. In August 1971, the NAACP filed a lawsuit seeking an injunction to reinstate the busing plan. With the injunction upheld, busing went ahead in September 1971. It took two years for the case to work its way through the courts, but in fall 1973, after a six-week trial, U.S. District Judge Noel P. Fox ruled in favor of the NAACP in *Oliver v. Kalamazoo Board of Education* and imposed a long-term desegregation plan. His opinion states that "the board had by its actions and inactions 'followed a purposeful pattern of racial discrimination by creating and maintaining segregated schools.'" The newly constituted school board voted 6–1 to appeal, but the appeal was rejected by the

Sixth U.S. Circuit Court of Appeals in 1974 and the Supreme Court in 1975 (Mah 1991).

The U.S. Commission on Civil Rights tracked the Kalamazoo case as 1 of 29 studies of communities around the nation that had experience with desegregation. It found that the elementary schools had become markedly less segregated in the five years following the court order. By 1976, with the closure of five largely white schools (due to a rapid decline in enrollment) and cross-district busing, the highest concentration of minority students in any one elementary school was 54 percent and there were no all-white schools (the smallest minority proportion in any school was 14 percent). The two high schools had been balanced racially, with a minority population of 25 percent at Kalamazoo Central and 22 percent at Loy Norrix. These changes occurred at a time when the minority population of the district was growing overall, in part as a result of the busing order as well as the racial unrest that had preceded and accompanied it. Most "white flight" out of the district took place in the years immediately before and after the desegregation order, with white enrollment falling by 8.5 percent between 1968 and 1978 and by 15 percent between 1970 and 1973 (U.S. Commission on Civil Rights 1977). Another of the primary goals of the desegregation order was to increase the percentage of minority teachers, which rose from 7 percent in 1970 to 12 percent in 1976 (U.S. Commission on Civil Rights 1977); this stood at 17.3 percent for the 2007–2008 school year.[21]

An equally important finding of the commission's report was a rapid decline in the level of interracial violence among students in the years following the desegregation order. As one principal explained at the time, "Before elementary school desegregation, students came to this junior high unaware of other races and the trouble began quickly. Now, with every incoming class there is less and less tension between blacks and whites, since each succeeding class has been in a desegregated setting for a longer time than the preceding class" (U.S. Commission on Civil Rights 1977).

In 1991, following a series of federal court decisions that made mandatory busing unenforceable, *Oliver v. Kalamazoo Board of Education* was amended to allow the district to meet its desegregation goals through a magnet school system that had resulted from the most recent redistricting.

The desegregation battle coincided with a long slide in enrollment in KPS. District enrollment declined from its high point of 18,054 in 1970–1971 to 13,752 a decade later. The downward trend was exacerbated by the end of the baby boom (1946–1964), which had inflated the number of school-age children throughout the nation. But enrollment continued to fall through the 1990s and into the new millennium, contracting to a low point of 10,187 in 2004. The decline in enrollment among white children was especially pronounced, with 14,285 enrolled in KPS in 1970 as opposed to only 4,133 in 2000. The percentage of black children in the public schools rose from 16 percent in 1970 to 44 percent in 2000, far outpacing the rate of increase in the city's African American population, which grew from 10 percent of total population in 1970 to 20 percent in 2000. The Hispanic population of the city and the school district also rose.[22] These shifts had something to do with local demographics—in particular, the growing number of Kalamazoo residents without school-age children—but they also reflected flight from the area's urban core. While the population of the city of Kalamazoo declined by 15 percent between 1970 and 2005, the population of Kalamazoo County rose by more than 5 percent over the same period. In other words, people moving to the region or choosing to remain within it opted increasingly to locate outside the urban core and its school district.

Especially after the passage of Proposal A in 1994, school finances suffered since virtually all of KPS's operating budget now came from the state's foundation grant, which is based on enrollment numbers.[23] Between 1999 and 2005 alone, more than $19 million was cut from the KPS budget, involving reductions in positions and programs, the closing of several school buildings, and the partial privatization of custodial and grounds services.[24] One response to these financial pressures has been greater involvement in the schools by social service and community organizations, many of them coordinated through the private nonprofit Kalamazoo Communities In Schools. Another is the occasional philanthropic gift to support special programs sometimes funded by anonymous donors. The Kalamazoo Promise fits into this pattern of private support for public institutions and draws attention to the resiliency and innovation of the community's philanthropic and nonprofit sectors.

A GIVING SPIRIT

Kalamazoo has a long tradition of local philanthropy and civic engagement. A number of individuals who made their wealth in Kalamazoo have chosen to reinvest much of it locally, as have their descendants. The Upjohn family, which dates its local connection to 1835, is the best-known example. As the Upjohn Company became increasingly successful, W.E. became one of the community's leading philanthropists, helping to create Bronson Methodist Hospital, the Civic Auditorium, and the Kalamazoo Community Foundation, and providing an endowment that led to the establishment of the W.E. Upjohn Institute for Employment Research. After W.E.'s death in 1932, the Upjohn Company continued to play a central role in the philanthropic life of the community, creating the Kalamazoo Area Mathematics and Science Center to develop scientific talent among youth across the county, and serving as a powerful force behind the ambitious annual campaigns of the Greater Kalamazoo United Way (GKUW). Many of W.E.'s heirs still live in the community and contribute to community life as board members and donors to Kalamazoo educational, cultural, and social service organizations.

Over the years, several generations of Upjohns intermarried with members of another leading family, the Gilmores. The Gilmores, too, had earned their fortune in Kalamazoo, in their case by opening a dry goods store on Burdick Street in 1881 that grew into Gilmore's Department Store. The store served as one of the anchors of downtown until it closed in 1999, and the family played an important role in strengthening the city's center as a commercial and cultural destination. The youngest of the three Gilmore brothers, Irving S. Gilmore, was known throughout the community for his generosity, often granted anonymously. His formal giving focused on the arts and human services, and in 1972 the Irving S. Gilmore Foundation was established. The foundation has invested more than $100 million in the community over the years, although in a mark of respect for Gilmore's memory, organizations receiving grants from the foundation are not allowed to disclose the amount. Notable among the programs supported by the foundation is the Irving S. Gilmore International Keyboard Festival, which every two years brings the world's leading pianists to Kalamazoo for several weeks of performances and every four years chooses a Gilmore Artist to receive one of the world's most prestigious and largest piano performance awards. The foundation was also pivotal in transforming another shuttered department store on the Kalamazoo Mall into the Epic Center, where many of the region's arts and cultural organizations are based. In 2007, when Michigan's budget crisis forced a moratorium on payments to arts organizations from the state arts council, the foundation stepped in and provided the missing funds to ensure that local arts organizations could continue with the projects they had already planned; Kalamazoo was the only community in the state where such private funding was forthcoming.

A third family to play an important role in the community's philanthropic life is the Strykers. Two of Dr. Homer Stryker's three grandchildren, both of them exceptionally wealthy, still live in Kalamazoo.[25] Ronda Stryker serves on the board of Kalamazoo College and operates a foundation with her husband, William D. Johnston. Johnston is chairman and president of the Greenleaf Companies, owner of (among other investments) the Radisson Plaza Hotel, a 650,000-square-foot hotel and convention center in the heart of downtown Kalamazoo. Ronda Stryker's brother, architect and national political activist Jon Stryker, founded and is the sole donor to the Arcus Foundation, the main mission of which is the advancement of social justice inclusive of sexual orientation, gender identity, and race. Jon Stryker has also contributed to the resurgence of downtown Kalamazoo with an award-winning historic preservation project that converted the city's abandoned railroad depot into a home for his foundation and other community nonprofits.

Not all of Kalamazoo's philanthropists are business owners or their heirs. The chemist who set up the Upjohn Company's first formal research laboratory, along with his wife, established the F.W. and Elsie L. Heyl Science Scholarship Fund in 1972. The coveted Heyl Scholarships go to academically high-achieving graduates of KPS and cover the full cost of attending Kalamazoo College (close to $40,000 a year for 2008–2009). The awards also support graduate study at WMU's School of Nursing and at Yale University. More than 400 KPS graduates have received Heyl Scholarships.

Personal wealth and civic-mindedness have interacted in Kalamazoo to create a community rich in philanthropic institutions. Many of these trace their origins to wealthy individuals, but their continued vitality rests on a tradition of philanthropy that extends throughout the community. The GKUW is a prime example. In 2007, the organization ranked 72nd out of more than 1,350 United Way communities nationwide in dollars raised annually and was the third-largest United Way in Michigan, despite the fact that the county has only the seventh-largest population. The GKUW, with its 43 local member agencies, serves not only as a critical source of funds for social service organizations but also a focal point of networking and information sharing among organizations.

The Kalamazoo Community Foundation is also an exceptionally large and healthy institution relative to the size of the community. Established in 1925 with an initial investment of Upjohn Company stock worth $1,000, today the foundation has assets of $295 million and distributed $16.3 million in grants in 2007.

This philanthropic culture underpins an arts community that is unusually large, diverse, and financially healthy relative to the size of the population. The Kalamazoo Symphony Orchestra, founded in 1921, has grown into the third-largest professional orchestra in Michigan, supported by an endowment that gives it a degree of financial stability virtually unheard of in the cash-strapped world of symphony orchestras. The Kalamazoo Institute of Arts, founded in 1923, also has a healthy endowment and a multimillion-dollar budget. The area's theater companies, modern dance company, chamber music organization, and contemporary music ensemble have all been recognized nationally in their respective fields, and the community supports not one but two performance organizations devoted to the music of J.S. Bach.

Kalamazoo's civic-mindedness is not confined to the philanthropic sector. In a Harvard University survey of social capital in 40 communities nationwide, Kalamazoo respondents scored highest (and well above the average) on informal socializing, diversity of friendships, associational involvement (including participation in a wide variety of groups), and giving and volunteering (Saguaro Seminar 2001). Multiple service organizations, many of them founded in the early twentieth century, remain active, including the Rotary Club (founded in 1914), the Kiwanis Club (1917), the League of Women Voters (1920), and the Junior League (originally the Service Club, founded in 1928).

Perhaps even more significant than the variety of institutions that characterizes civic involvement and cultural life in Kalamazoo is the degree to which they are linked to each other. Networks play an important role in facilitating communication and collective action among groups with similar missions. Most of the community's major social service organizations are members of the GKUW, which operates a variety of programs in addition to its annual fund-raising campaign. One of these is the Kalamazoo Youth Development Network (KYDNET), which brings together about 80 local organizations focused on the needs of young people. Its monthly "Action Fridays" regularly draw representatives from several dozen organizations, ranging from the Boys and Girls Club to the Great Lakes PeaceJam to the Kalamazoo County Juvenile Home.

The Northside Ministerial Alliance fulfills a similar networking function, with weekly meetings that draw not only church leaders but also representatives from the public schools, the police department, city government, and others to discuss issues facing the Northside neighborhood and the African American community more generally. A broader group of religious organizations are connected through Interfaith Strategy for Action and Advocacy in the Community (ISAAC), a network devoted to advancing social justice through a congregation-based organizing model.[26] As in other communities, neighborhood associations, business groups, and parent-teacher organizations of varying cohesiveness dot the landscape.

One network that is critical to the success of the Kalamazoo Promise is Kalamazoo Communities In Schools (KCIS). Formed in 2003 from the merger of three existing student support organizations, KCIS brings together major service providers, school officials, community volunteers, business leaders, and citizens to focus on the needs of students enrolled in KPS. Among its activities, KCIS helps facilitate student access to services, such as dental care or mental health counseling, and coordinates many of the community's tutoring, mentoring, and afterschool programs. The Kalamazoo Promise unleashed a flood of volunteer energy and added urgency to KCIS's mission of supporting student success. Kalamazoo Communities In Schools, which relies on private and philanthropic resources for its funding, is struggling to build its capacity to meet these needs. An ambitious capital campaign launched in 2007 is likely to strengthen KCIS's effectiveness in supporting the goals of the Kalamazoo Promise.

Kalamazoo is already a community rich in social capital, as exemplified by its networks, the propensity of citizens to join groups, local philanthropic resources, and an overall high level of education (a critical determinant of social capital). But, as in many communities, it has been far easier to create and maintain social capital of the "bonding" or inward-looking variety, in which networks link people who are similar in crucial respects, than the "bridging" or outward-looking kind, where networks transcend different groups and interests. Putnam and Feldstein (2003) liken the former to "sociological Super Glue" and the latter to WD-40, and stress that both types are crucially important: "A society that has only bonding social capital will look like Belfast or Bosnia—segregated into mutually hostile camps" (pp. 2–3).

In practice, it can be difficult to distinguish between these two types of social capital. A single network can play both a bonding and a bridging function—for example, the member agencies of the Greater Kalamazoo United Way share an emphasis on social services and a regional focus but represent different constituencies and missions. The agencies that participate in KYDNET are all committed to serving youth, but the group's networking function is expressly designed to facilitate information sharing and partnerships among different kinds of organizations. Given the community's racially polarized history, one of the most pressing questions for Kalamazoo is the extent to which networks bridge racial divides. The Northside Ministerial Alliance brings together the leaders of multiple churches, most led by African American ministers, with representatives of the broader community, including police officers and school officials. ISAAC's congregation-based organizing approach represents bonding among those with a religious affiliation but provides a forum for the bridging of black and white congregations. Some of the best examples of bridging social capital in Kalamazoo, as in other communities, are found in tutoring or mentoring programs, such as Big Brothers Big Sisters, that are designed explicitly to bring together individuals from different generations and often different socioeconomic groups.

The Kalamazoo Promise has the potential to strengthen the community's stores of social capital through several avenues. The first of these is an increase in residents' average level of education whether through increased high school graduation rates, higher college attendance and completion rates, or the attraction of better-educated workers, since the propensity to form networks of trust and reciprocity increases in line with educational attainment. The second is an expansion in the activities of community- and faith-based organizations in the city's poorest neighborhoods intent on supporting disadvantaged youth with the resources they need to benefit from the Promise. Since the scholarship program was announced, these organizations have presented information fairs, held rallies, provided assistance with financial aid applications, and offered tutoring and family support programs. A third avenue is the proliferation and expansion of mentoring programs that focus specifically on bringing students together with adults who can help them navigate the transition from high school to college. Fourth, the increased engagement of parents in the schools, whether as volunteers or advocates for their children, is another crucial element in creating social capital that bridges the schools and the broader community. (Teachers report that the proportion of parents of all income groups attending their children's teacher-parent conferences rose markedly after the Kalamazoo Promise was announced.) Finally, the intensive efforts of community leaders and grassroots organizations to align their work around the goals of the Kalamazoo Promise (discussed in Chapter 4) has led to a surge in communication and sometimes even collaboration across different organizations—a positive sign in a community that has remained fragmented by class, race, and neighborhood despite its wealth of social capital.

The issues facing the community in November 2005 were multifaceted: a wrenching economic transformation from manufacturing to something as yet unknown; a school district grappling with shrinking enrollment, fewer resources, and needier students; a community where networks abound and social capital is high, yet where divisions persist; and a scholarship program that many believe is the answer to all of these problems. The next chapter examines the Kalamazoo Promise within the broader context of college financial aid and economic development strategies in order to understand how the program might help address these critical challenges—not only in Kalamazoo but in communities around the nation that confront many of the same issues.

Notes

1. The poverty rate for individuals in the city of Kalamazoo was 30.2 percent in 2005—more than twice the national average—but the large proportion of college students in the community tends to inflate this number; a more accurate assessment is provided by the family poverty rate (U.S. Census Bureau 2006).
2. As measured by the Metropolitan Power Diffusion Index (MPDI) developed by David Y. Miller and calculated by David Rusk based on 1992 data.
3. U.S. Census Bureau data from 1970 and 2000; U.S. Census Bureau estimate for 2005.
4. See the "State of the Downtown Address, 2008," available for download from http://www.central-city.net/download.
5. According to data provided by KPS, in 2006–2007, Lincoln International Studies School had a minority population of 90 percent and a free and reduced-price lunch population of 87 percent, and Northglade Montessori School had a minority population of 86 percent and a free- and reduced-price lunch population of 72 percent.
6. For an excellent treatment of the role of federal housing and lending policy in creating segregated cities, see Sugrue (1996).
7. Census 2000 Summary File 3 (SF3)–Sample Data, Detailed Tables P1, P6, P53, P87.
8. Fact Sheet: Kalamazoo, American Community Survey 2007, U.S. Census.
9. Data provided by KPS.
10. 32.28 percent of the city's land area is strictly exempt property; 13.31 percent is roads; and 3.68 percent is part of special collections districts (City of Kalamazoo Assessor's Office 2008).
11. Author's interview with Eileen Wilson-Oyelaran, Kalamazoo College president, March 30, 2006.
12. The word Kalamazoo, which probably comes from the language of the Potawatomi Indians who lived in the area, has a long and ambiguous history, with meanings that range from "boiling pot" to "mirage" to "reflecting river." See Rzepczynski (1998).
13. For more on the history of Kalamazoo businesses, visit the Local History Collection of the Kalamazoo Public Library online at http://www.kpl.gov/collections/LocalHistory/AllAbout/default.aspx.
14. The bank has never released the exact number of layoffs or transfers resulting from this acquisition.
15. Checker Motors still produces auto parts in Kalamazoo, although the last Checker Cab was manufactured in 1982.
16. Borgess Medical Center was established in 1889 by leaders of the Catholic Church. Bronson Methodist Hospital, originally called the Kalamazoo Hospital, was founded in 1904. For a list of the region's largest employers, see the Web site of the Kalamazoo Regional Chamber of Commerce: http://www.kazoochamber.com.
17. This paragraph draws on Dunbar (1969).

18. The number of high schools in the state rose from 107 in the early 1870s to 278 by 1890 (Timmerman 2000, 2005).

19. Some of the subjects taught at Central High School during these years were geometry, algebra, band and orchestra, physical education, and zoology. In 1905, the school's menagerie, established for the benefit of the zoology classes, contained a rooster, a "Bayer," a coon, a crane, and a wolf (Bennett 1956, p. 17).

20. This was unusual for the time. Willis Dunbar (1955, p. 308) writes, "In Michigan, as nowhere else in the nation, the resources of a State were concentrated upon the building up of one great State institution of higher learning, rather than being dissipated and divided among a large number of small, weak, struggling, faction-ridden institutions."

21. Data provided by KPS.

22. According to the U.S. Census Bureau, in 2007, the Hispanic/Latino population of the city of Kalamazoo stood at 4.8 percent; however, Hispanic students accounted for 9.5 percent of KPS enrollment for 2007, according to KPS.

23. The foundation grant for KPS was $7,733 per full-time enrolled student for 2007–2008. In an effort to equalize the disparities in funding between school districts across the state, Proposal A shifted public school financing from local property taxes to a per-pupil foundation grant related directly to enrollment numbers. For more information, see Summers-Coty (2007).

24. "Budget Reductions, Kalamazoo Public Schools," provided by the office of the Deputy Superintendent for Business, Communications, and Operations, November 1, 2006.

25. Forbes's 2008 ranking listed Ronda Stryker with $3.0 billion in assets and Jon Stryker with $2.1 billion (Forbes.com 2008).

26. The Interfaith Strategy for Action and Advocacy in the Community is an affiliate of the national Gamaliel Foundation, "a network of grassroots, interfaith, interracial, multi-issue organizations working together to create a more just and more democratic society." See http://www.gamaliel.org.

3
The Kalamazoo Promise in Context

When the Kalamazoo Promise was announced, it was widely heralded as the only program of its kind. Skeptics have asked if this is indeed the case, noting a mind-boggling array of scholarship programs, from the $1 billion Gates Millennium Scholars program for minority students to statewide merit scholarship programs, such as the Georgia HOPE Scholarship Program, to scholarships for recipients with specific characteristics, such as athletic or artistic talent or a particular ethnic background.

Indeed, the Kalamazoo Promise is unique in terms of its scope and cost, but its place-based, economic development–oriented model has at least one forerunner. In 1959, in the small town of Philomath, Oregon, members of a wealthy timber family set up a foundation to pay for college for all graduates of the local high school.[1] The donors, Rex and Ethel Clemens, were motivated by concern about the economic future of Philomath and jobs for its residents in light of the decline of the timber industry already on the horizon. The scholarship would cover the full amount of tuition for four years at Oregon State University, although students could use the money to attend any institution, public or private. Initially, to qualify for the scholarship one needed only to graduate from the local high school and be admitted to college.

With the stimulus provided by the scholarship money, the college attendance rate for students at Philomath High School rose from almost zero in 1959 to its current level of about 70 percent. In 1993, with the area growing rapidly, the foundation introduced a residency requirement of eight years to ensure that the scholarship would benefit only long-term residents. Other requirements added along the way included full-time college attendance and random drug testing.

The design of the Kalamazoo Promise resembles the Clemens Foundation program in several important respects. The scholarships will help the community adapt to a changing economic environment, they are available to all graduates of the school district regardless of financial need or academic achievement (as the Philomath program was

59

until recently), and they are limited to relatively long-term residents of a geographically bounded area. But there is an important difference. The donors who created the Kalamazoo Promise chose to remain anonymous, while the donors in Philomath were anything but. Allied to the area's logging industry, their interests were at odds with the cultural and political currents that emerged in the Pacific Northwest beginning in the 1970s, especially the growing influence of the environmental movement. Tension between the timber industry and environmentalists has divided communities in many of the region's small towns ever since, and not surprisingly the schools became one of the arenas in which this struggle has played out.[2]

In 2002, troubled by what they saw as antitimber bias in the Philomath High School curriculum (especially the teaching of environmental science), the foundation's board members, led by descendants of the Clemens family, asked the district to fire the school board, the high school principal, and the superintendent, who had recently come to the district from Chicago. The district refused and the foundation suspended the scholarship program. Soon after, both the superintendent and principal resigned. The scholarships were then reinstated with the proviso that students must apply for the program and have either a family background in the timber industry or be involved in clubs or school programs that reflect "American values," such as 4-H or Boy Scouts. "We are not going to use timber dollars to send the professors' kids, the physicians' kids, the teachers' kids to school, because they are the ones helping to shut down the timber industry, with environmental donations to Greenpeace. They support those people who are killing us," said Steve Lowther, a board member and nephew of the original donors (Associated Press 2002).

In practice, most students still receive the scholarships; in 2005, for example, the Clemens Foundation granted $1.6 million in scholarships to 600 graduates—almost the entire senior class of Philomath High School. However, new controversies have emerged, and in 2006, the foundation prevented scholarship recipients from using their money to attend Oregon State University because of concerns over the university's participation in a regional environmental sustainability program and what was seen as lax discipline of university athletes.

The Philomath story is a powerful reminder of the benefits and limitations of private philanthropy. Since its inception, the Clemens Foundation has paid for the college tuition of thousands of local residents, fundamentally altering their future opportunities and the nature of the community. But when the trustees of a private foundation decide to change its rules, as they did in Philomath, they are well within their rights, regardless of how others may feel.[3]

The Kalamazoo Promise, too, originated as a private gift, and as such its funds are ultimately controlled by the donors. While the donors have issued no public statements about their intentions, the structure of the program signals the essential elements of their thinking. A long-term, open-ended investment in the human capital of Kalamazoo's youth will help prepare students for the twenty-first century economy while making the region more attractive to businesses and residents that value education. With this intervention, a virtuous circle of higher educational attainment and job creation could be set in motion, positioning the Greater Kalamazoo region and its urban core for success in an increasingly competitive economic environment. The simplicity and power of this vision, as well as the essentially unlimited pool of money that backs it up, are widely recognized as the chief strengths of the program, but donor anonymity has proven advantageous as well for reasons discussed in Chapter 4.

A REVOLUTIONARY IDEA

The Kalamazoo Promise arrived on the scene at an auspicious moment. For decades, policymakers at the federal, state, and local levels have experimented with diverse approaches to stimulating local economic development and increasing access to higher education. At the turn of the twenty-first century, both challenges seemed more pressing than ever. Cities, especially those in the industrial regions of the Northeast and Midwest, have struggled to maintain their economic vitality in the face of job loss, population decline, and the hollowing out of the urban core. At the same time, the changing nature of employment in the United States and increased global competition has led many to conclude that higher education is essential in today's economy. The Kalamazoo Promise represents an unprecedented joining of these two agendas and suggests that the best strategies for increasing educational attainment and promoting economic development may be one and the same.

In *The World Is Flat*, one of the best-selling books of 2005 and 2006, Thomas Friedman (2005) argues that barriers to international competition have been virtually obliterated. The "flat" world of the twenty-first century is one in which manufacturing will continue to move offshore (to countries like China), and large portions of the service sector will be outsourced to English-speaking developing countries (like India). While wealth in this hyperglobal economy will expand thanks to trade and technology, it will shift toward those with high skills, leaving low-skilled workers behind. Among the guidance Friedman offers policy-makers seeking to respond to this challenge is to make postsecondary education compulsory and increase government funding for it—a strategy that would benefit the United States in two ways: "One is that it produces more people with the skills to claim higher-value-added work in the new niches. And two, it shrinks the pool of people able to do lower-skilled work, from road maintenance to home repair to Starbucks. By shrinking the pool of lower-skilled workers, we help to stabilize their wages (provided we control immigration), because there are fewer people available to do those jobs" (p. 289).

The American middle class was formed in the first half of the twentieth century through a similar strategy: expanded access to higher education and employment opportunities that paid decent wages to workers without a college degree. In the economy of the twenty-first century, however, only those with access to higher education will get their slice of the pie, while Americans without such access will get less and less.

Former U.S. Senator and 2008 presidential candidate John Edwards agrees: "We decided as a nation that we're going to make public education K-12 available to all kids . . . Well, in today's world, that's just not enough. Higher education is absolutely crucial to being successful, and not just important for the individual kids involved and their families. It's important for America, because . . . colleges are the places where we ensure that America is competitive" (Selingo 2006).

While there is broad agreement on the need to train a larger proportion of Americans for high-wage, high-value-added work, it is less clear how to do so. Some advocate public funding for pre-K through 16 education, but this may be unrealistic in the near term. Tuition costs are rising, financial aid is failing to keep pace, and racial and income gaps in college attendance and completion rates persist. Even if postsecondary education were more accessible financially, not everyone would benefit because the nation's K-12 system, despite the lofty goals of "No Child Left Behind," does indeed leave many behind. Gaps between middle-class and poor children in grade-to-grade progress, dropout rates, and high school graduation continue even in the face of national standards and a plethora of school reform experiments.

The economic decline of many urban areas adds to the challenge of educating Americans for the twenty-first century workforce. As jobs and workers exit (whether due to layoffs, transfers, or a move to the suburbs), inner-city school districts are left with high concentrations of poor children, many with needs that extend well beyond the classroom. Urban centers and older suburbs have become depopulated and poorer, with residential and commercial energy shifting to the ever-expanding margin, bringing with it problems of sprawl and congestion.

In the face of these trends, cities have pursued economic development strategies centered on the revitalization of downtown districts, the attraction of businesses through subsidies and tax rebates, and public investment in amenities such as sports arenas or commercial complexes. But these policies are expensive, and they often involve cutbacks in other areas of public spending, including education.

The Kalamazoo Promise offers a welcome change from this landscape of trade-offs and hard choices. If the goals of educational attainment and economic development are indeed linked, perhaps they can be solved with the same set of tools. The tool being demonstrated in Kalamazoo is a large, private, and long-term investment in the educational attainment of local youth. This investment can be likened to a pebble thrown into a pond whose ripples spread outward to encompass the entire surface (the size and duration of the donors' commitment may make a boulder a better analogy). The availability of full college scholarships for a sizeable proportion of the community's young people over a several-decade period has ramifications for both the educational and the economic spheres. These may include population growth in the school district (including the attraction and retention of middle-class families), greater socioeconomic integration in neighborhoods and schools, more financial resources and a cultural change in the schools, growing demand for quality-of-life amenities in the urban core, the stabilization of the real estate market, new residents drawn to a community that values education, and employers attracted by the availability of a skilled workforce.

The power of this vision, as well as the scope of the donors' gesture, sparked a level of media exposure that Kalamazoo had never before experienced and a level of scrutiny that raises the stakes for success. Feature articles in all of the nation's major newspapers, a segment on the *CBS Evening News*, coverage on the *Today Show* and *Good Morning America*—nothing in the city's history had attracted such widespread attention. Even more telling was the response of other communities. One year after the program was announced a dozen communities had launched or were planning programs modeled on the Kalamazoo Promise. By its second anniversary, that number had doubled, and in the spring of 2008, new programs were being announced almost weekly. In June 2008, more than 200 representatives of about 80 communities attended the inaugural conference of PromiseNet, a national network devoted to sharing experiences and information among communities that are establishing Promise-type programs.

The Kalamazoo Promise also attracted the attention of philanthropic organizations, such as the W.K. Kellogg Foundation, which provided a grant to support data collection and community mobilization efforts, and national research organizations, including the U.S. Department of Education, which funded an early evaluation of the program.[4] Academics, too, paid attention, developing research projects to assess varied aspects of the program.

One of the most revealing of these academic endeavors came in a session devoted to the Kalamazoo Promise at the annual Association for the Study of Higher Education (ASHE) in November 2006. Most scholars on the ASHE panel were deeply critical of the program. Their comments reflect a basic misunderstanding of the Kalamazoo Promise—and, by extension, programs modeled on it—but also insight into the differences between the Kalamazoo Promise and most scholarship programs.

In a paper prepared for the panel, Alicia Dowd of the University of Southern California argues that the Kalamazoo Promise emphasizes economic development over principles of equal access to higher education (Dowd 2008). This is a fair assessment, but one that the panelists in their meeting seemed not to accept as legitimate. One concern expressed was that the Kalamazoo Promise would benefit middle-class

students more than low-income students since the former are more likely to go to four-year-colleges that cost more and the latter already have
access to need-based aid. According to Robert Shireman of the Project
on Student Debt, "Any time you have a program that takes a universal
approach to tuition assistance you're going to provide three times as
much benefit to rich students as to low-income students" (Mack 2006d).
In a similar vein, Michael Olivas of the University of Houston argued
that while the program is technically race-neutral, in reality it is biased
against black residents since one of its presumed goals is to keep white
families from leaving the district (Mack 2006d).

Timothy J. Bartik, a senior economist at the W.E. Upjohn Institute,
takes issue with both of those points, noting that the question of whether the program is sufficiently targeted toward the poor or minorities
can be raised about any program with universal access, including free
public high school or kindergarten (arguments such as these were, in
fact, made against these innovations at the time). Similar charges have
been leveled at other universal programs like Social Security. "What the
critics miss is that from a political and social point of view programs
targeted only for the poor tend to lack sufficient political support to ever
be well funded, or to ever be sufficiently attended so that the quality
is maintained," writes Bartik.[5] At the same time, there is ample documentation that the availability of financial aid nationally has shifted
away from low-income students (who rely mainly on grant aid) and
toward middle-income families that can benefit from tax breaks and
have enough income to pay off student loans. In choosing to focus their
philanthropy on KPS, the donors ensured that the low-income students
who make up 65 percent of the district's enrollment, many of them minorities, would have the opportunity to attend college for free without
having to meet any academic merit threshold. Another important element of the Kalamazoo Promise, and one not noted by the panelists, is
that it can be utilized by undocumented immigrants, unlike most scholarships and virtually every source of public financial aid.

A second concern voiced by the ASHE panelists was that the Kalamazoo Promise would contribute to gentrification, increasing housing
values to the point where low-income residents are priced out of the
housing market. This argument revealed a profound lack of awareness
of the realities of the housing market in Kalamazoo and many other older cities throughout the Northeast, Midwest, and South. The problem in

these locales is not that housing prices are too high but that they are too low. When housing values are depressed and there is no opportunity for appreciation, residents lack the incentive to maintain or improve their homes, and outsiders have no reason to locate in or near the urban core. Neighborhoods slip into disrepair and the cycle of downward pressure on value continues. While concerns about gentrification are legitimate, especially in the nation's largest cities, where housing is barely afford-able for the middle class (and, perhaps not coincidentally, where most of the panelists live), there are communities in every state that would benefit from a program that puts some upward pressure on housing val-ues. Also, as Bartik puts it, "The argument about the Promise pricing people out of the housing market could be made against any policy that improves the quality of life in Kalamazoo. If we want to lower rents for poor people in Kalamazoo, I know a surefire way to do it: allow crime to increase and school quality to deteriorate" (Mack 2006e). The panelists also worried about rising property taxes forcing poor people out the city, seemingly unaware that property taxes in Michigan have been capped through a variety of legislative actions and that the schools receive their operating funds from the state, not through property tax assessments.

A third concern in the ASHE session was related to the nature of the gift itself, with panelists questioning whether the Kalamazoo Promise had undermined democratic participation in the public schools. Alicia Dowd's argument, that the program "usurps the democratic process" is difficult to understand. The scholarship funds are quite clearly a pri-vate philanthropic gesture, similar to thousands of other scholarship programs and subject to the same regulations imposed by the Internal Revenue Service for the awarding of 501(c)(3) tax-exempt status. Kal-amazoo Public Schools and the broader community could have chosen to reject it, but the idea that the donors should have engaged the com-munity in debate about "how to allocate the available funds among stu-dents according to various definitions of need and merit" (Dowd 2006, p. 10) misses the point. It is in fact the unexpected, anonymous, and unrestricted nature of the Kalamazoo Promise that has made it such a powerful catalyst for change within the community.

THE KALAMAZOO PROMISE AS A SCHOLARSHIP PROGRAM

The college aid universe has changed greatly over the past several decades in response to four broad trends. First, the cost of college tuition has risen across the board at rates that far outpace inflation. In 2007–2008, the average cost of tuition and fees at public, four-year U.S. institutions rose 6.6 percent over the previous year, compared to an annual inflation rate of 1.5 percent. The cost of attending a public two-year institution increased by 4.2 percent over the same period, while average tuition at private four-year colleges rose by 6.3 percent.[6] Over the previous decade, published tuition and fees rose at an average rate of 4.4 percent per year after inflation at public four-year colleges, 1.5 percent per year at public two-year colleges, and 2.9 percent per year at private four-year colleges (College Board 2007a).

Second, financial aid has failed to keep pace with the rising cost of tuition. Financial aid makes an important contribution to college affordability, with the actual price paid by students averaging well below the "sticker price." (Full-time students receive on average about $3,600 of aid per year in the form of grants and tax benefits at public four-year colleges, $2,040 at public two-year colleges, and $9,300 at private four-year colleges [College Board 2007a].) In addition, tuition and fees represent only a portion of education-related expenses; at the University of Michigan, for example, tuition and fees for 2008–2009 cost $11,037 for in-state freshmen and sophomores, while room and board cost $8,590 and books cost approximately $1,048 per year (University of Michigan n.d.). Federal grants in particular have lagged the rise in costs. The federal Pell Grant is still an important source of aid, but even the maximum covers a much smaller proportion of total college costs than it did in the past—32 percent at a public four-year college in 2006–2007, down from 52 percent in 1986–1987 (College Board 2007b, p. 2). While Pell Grant funding in 2006–2007 was 73 percent higher in real terms than it was a decade earlier, the maximum amount provided to an individual student was unchanged between 2003 and 2007, and the average Pell Grant for 2006–2007 was $2,494—the lowest level since 2000–2001. (The higher expenditures reflect an increase in the number of students receiving Pell Grants—5.2 million in 2006–2007 compared to 3.7 million in 1996–1997 [College Board 2007b].)

Third, loans account for an increasing proportion of college financing relative to grant aid. Total undergraduate funding in 2006–2007 was divided almost evenly between grants (46 percent) and loans (49 percent)—a marked shift from the predominance of grant aid prior to the 1990s. Nearly two-thirds of college graduates now leave school with some debt, up from less than half in 1993, and among those with loans the average debt has jumped from $9,250 in 1993 to roughly $21,100 in 2006, a 58 percent increase after adjusting for inflation. Pell Grant recipients (an indicator of modest family income) are more likely to have student loans and to borrow more than other students.[7] The average amount borrowed (in real terms) has increased for students at every income level since 1992–1993 (College Board 2007b, p. 13). Parents, too, have increased their indebtedness on behalf of dependent children, with the number of parents taking PLUS loans increasing 92 percent between 1996 and 2006, and the average loan size increasing 39 percent in real terms (College Board 2007b, p. 11).

Fourth, there has been a shift in emphasis from aid based on financial need to that awarded for merit, especially at the institutional and state levels. Between 1995–1996 and 2003–2004, merit-based aid granted by colleges and universities grew by 212 percent while need-based aid rose by 47 percent. Merit grants awarded by colleges constituted 54 percent of all aid in 2003–2004, up from 35 percent just eight years earlier. Public spending has moved in the same direction. During the 1980s and into the early 1990s, state funds awarded without regard to financial need amounted to less than 10 percent of total state aid but, beginning in 1994, this proportion rose steadily to the point where today one in four state dollars is awarded without regard to need (Heller 2006b).

Scholarship programs can be categorized in a number of ways, two of the most important of which are the source of funds and the program's goals. Traditionally, grants from the federal government intended to make higher education more affordable have been the chief source of financial aid for low-income students. Federal involvement in broadening college access has an illustrious history. The GI Bill of 1944 paid for vocational training for 8 million World War II veterans and sent 2 million more to college. The program was generous, including monthly stipends as well as full tuition coverage. The GI Bill democratized America's system of higher education, which had previously been restricted to the elite or the exceptionally talented, and helped set off an economic boom when millions of educated veterans entered the workforce. Today's main federal program, the Pell Grant, has its roots in the Higher Education Act of 1965, an important element of the War on Poverty initiated by the administration of President Lyndon B. Johnson. This legislation established federal scholarships for needy undergraduates and government insurance of private loans to students. Through amendments to the act in 1972, the Basic Opportunity Grant was created to provide a "floor" for an undergraduate's financial aid package to which other aid would be added. The Basic Grant also introduced the concept of "portability," offering low-income students funding that could be used at any institution as opposed to a grant from a particular college or university. In 1980, the Basic Grant was renamed the Pell Grant in honor of Rhode Island's senior senator at the time, Claiborne Pell.

During the 1970s, both funding and eligibility expanded, but the Reagan-era deficits and cutbacks in social spending of the 1980s led to tightened requirements and stagnant funding. (When President Ronald Reagan took office in 1980, the maximum Pell Grant covered 69 percent of the cost of attendance at a four-year public institution; when he left office eight years later, the proportion had declined to 47 percent [King 2000, p. 8, Table 1]). Ongoing budgetary pressures and the rising cost of the Pell Grant program due to increased eligibility led to a further decline in its value, while federal policy increasingly emphasized aid to middle-income students delivered mainly through tax benefits and subsidized student loans.

While federal aid has shrunk, statewide merit programs have proliferated (although they still account for a much smaller proportion of total grants than those based on need). Between 1990 and 2006, 14 states introduced broad merit scholarship programs available to all residents who meet certain criteria, usually involving a minimum grade point average (GPA) requirement of 3.0 in high school and sometimes a minimum score on a college-entrance exam. A minimum college GPA is also required for scholarship renewal. The scholarships, which are awarded to students regardless of family income, are paid for out of general funds, lottery revenue, or in some cases money from tobacco litigation settlements. States have identified three main policy objectives for such programs: increasing college access and attainment, rewarding or encouraging academic achievement in high school and college, and keeping the best students from attending college out of state.[8]

In a series of papers on the impact of merit-based aid programs, Susan Dynarski of Harvard University finds that such programs substantially increase the college attendance rate while shifting students from two-year programs toward four-year colleges. She also finds that by reducing costs, merit-based programs improve college completion rates, especially for women (Dynarski 1999, 2000, 2002, 2005). Studies of the Georgia HOPE Scholarship Program, one of the nation's oldest and most thoroughly evaluated programs, suggest that the HOPE scholarship has affected where students choose to go to college, with more Georgia students opting to remain in state, but that the scholarship funds have gone mainly to students who would have enrolled in college anyway (Cornwell et al. 2006). Other research shows that, depending on the eligibility criteria, merit aid programs can disproportionately benefit middle-income students over low-income students, and white over minority students. For example, a study of the John and Abigail Adams Scholarship program in Massachusetts, eligibility for which is based solely on student performance in the statewide 10th grade English and math tests, shows that there has been little benefit to poor or minority students in the state (Heller 2006a). Another study of the Adams Scholarship finds that the increase in the public college attendance rate brought about by the program was due almost entirely to students already bound for college opting to attend public rather than private schools (Goodman 2007).

On the other hand, merit programs can be an important tool for broadening college access depending on how they are structured. Oklahoma's Higher Learning and Access Program operates the statewide Oklahoma Promise scholarship program. Its relatively low high school GPA cutoff (2.5, as opposed to the more typical 3.0) and high-income cutoff (families with incomes of up to $100,000 at the time the student starts college are now eligible) means that it has the potential to enroll a greater proportion of the state's high school students than other merit-based programs.[9] An early commitment process in which students are recruited for the program in 7th and 8th grade and must sign up for it no later than 10th grade provides an incentive for students to complete high school. Students enrolled in the program tend to have above-average GPAs, ACT scores, college-going rates, college persistence, and degree completion rates, although questions remain about whether these achievements are the result of participation in the program or whether it is the higher-achieving students who are enrolling (as is the case in other statewide merit programs). The motivation for the program, which cost taxpayers $33.8 million in 2006–2007, is to boost college graduation rates in a state where only one in five residents has a college degree. In 2006–2007, the program passed the $100 million mark in terms of scholarships awarded, and Oklahoma has improved from 47th to 42nd place among the 50 states in terms of its six-year college graduation rate (National Center for Higher Education Management Systems n.d.).

Michigan, too, has a merit scholarship program, although the criteria for qualifying are much more stringent than in Oklahoma. The original Michigan Merit Award program, in place for the high school graduating classes of 2000 to 2006, was based on a student's performance on a series of standardized tests. Renamed the Michigan Promise Scholarship in 2006, the program now offers more funding (up to $4,000 instead of $3,000) and is available to all students who have taken the Michigan Merit Exam while in high school, have completed two years of postsecondary education, and have a cumulative college GPA of 2.5. Coming two years into a student's postsecondary education, the award is designed as an incentive for additional years of schooling. This is an important consideration in light of Michigan's low rates of college attendance and completion and the state's current economic challenges, but it does nothing to address the needs of students who do not have the resources (monetary or otherwise) to attend college in the first place.

Another important source of financial assistance is institutional aid granted by colleges and universities, whether public or private, out of their own resources. These funds come either from donations or tuition revenue designated for scholarship purposes, and are used to create a more diverse student body or recruit students with specific attributes, such as athletic or academic talent.[10] Institutional aid is usually comprised of some combination of private and public funding, but the privately funded scholarship field extends well beyond that provided by colleges themselves. In 2003–2004, 1,276,000 undergraduates received private scholarships (excluding aid from the government, employers, and colleges) amounting to a total of $2.53 billion (U.S. Department of Education 2005). FastWeb, one of the many scholarship search engines available on the Internet, includes in its database 1.3 million scholarships worth over $3 billion. Some of these are small, contributing only a fraction of a student's overall costs, while others provide a full ride. The largest privately funded effort is the Bill & Melinda Gates Foundation's Millennium Scholars program, designed to increase access to higher education for talented minority students. The foundation has committed $1 billion to support 20,000 scholarships over a 20-year period; low-income students of color with high GPAs and demonstrated leadership skills apply for the scholarship when they reach the 12th grade.

Other programs that seek to increase college access for disadvantaged groups have taken a different approach, enlisting students at an earlier age and providing them with various types of support before high school graduation to ensure that they are prepared for success in college. One example is the Kauffman Scholars program, established in 2003 with a $70 million endowment from the Kansas City–based Ewing Marion Kauffman Foundation and serving 200 students per year from the Kansas City area. Participants enroll in the program in 7th grade and receive academic support, life coaching, college and career planning, and ultimately scholarship assistance. Programs such as this one differ from traditional competitive scholarship programs in that they identify potential recipients before they reach high school, and participation is based on potential success rather than past achievement. The Legacy Scholars program in Battle Creek, Michigan, funded through a $4 million endowment contributed by the W.K. Kellogg Foundation in honor of its 75th anniversary in 2005, is modeled along similar lines. Originally structured to serve 500 6th grade students each year based on nominations by teachers, parents, pastors, and other community members, the program was expanded in 2006 to cover every 6th grade student in the two local public school districts. (This change was motivated in part by a reluctance to participate by families who resisted the "at-risk" designation that the Legacy Scholars program was initially designed to address.) The program provides multifaceted support services to youth and families throughout their middle- and high school years, as well as last-dollar scholarships for students to attend the local community college.

Still other initiatives begin even earlier. Under the "I Have a Dream" model, an individual sponsor adopts a single early elementary class or grade level and works with that cohort of children and their families through high school with the support of a project coordinator. The long-term commitment of mentoring, tutoring, enrichment, and tuition assistance is designed to motivate and empower children from low-income communities to set high educational and career goals. The premise is that if children grow up knowing they will have the resources to attend college and are surrounded by a group of peers and adults who expect them to do so, they will plan accordingly.[11] (The expectation of a cultural change in the schools as a result of the Kalamazoo Promise is based on a similar premise.) Early intervention programs such as this one draw on a substantial body of research showing that investments in an individual's human capital generate the highest returns when they occur at a young age. Among those to make this argument most forcefully is James J. Heckman, the University of Chicago professor and Nobel Prize–winning economist, who has quantified the economic and social benefits of early investments in children's cognitive and noncognitive skills (Heckman and Masterov 2007). In 2007, Brookings Institution scholars Jens Ludwig and Isabel Sawhill released a proposal for helping every child achieve success in school by age 10 (Sawhill and Ludwig 2007), and evidence for the long-term economic benefits of universal, high-quality preschool continues to mount.[12]

One of the criticisms leveled at the Kalamazoo Promise is that it neglects this critical element of student support by channeling all the donors' resources into the scholarships themselves. A local resident may have overstated the case when she wrote, "I would think that the visionaries of this golden egg would instead invest their money in providing the foundation for the college-bound student instead of the prize at the end of a rocky and subpar journey" (McLeod [2005]), but it is true that the Kalamazoo Promise in and of itself does nothing to increase the resources needed to ensure student success. As a result, some community members voiced concern early on that in a district where large numbers of low-income and minority students fail to graduate from high school, the scholarship program would be most likely to benefit those students planning to attend college in any case.

But the Kalamazoo Promise has something going for it that almost no other scholarship program does: it is available to all high school graduates in the district, regardless of academic performance, income, race, or any other criteria. The universal availability of scholarships (provided KPS graduates have met the four-year attendance and residency requirement) is critical to understanding the potential of the Kalamazoo Promise as a catalyst for community transformation. Among the vast array of college scholarship programs, scholarships like this are exceedingly rare. Apart from the Philomath example cited earlier, there are two other universal-access programs that warrant mention. The first is an unusual federally funded program in Washington, D.C. that expands higher education choices for college-bound residents of the district. The DC Tuition Assistance Grant (DC TAG) is available to all high school graduates residing in the District of Columbia regardless of financial need or merit, and covers the difference between in-state and out-of-state tuition and fees at any public college or university in the nation. The program's main purpose is to expand the range of choices for college-bound residents of the district, but it has also helped to retain the district's middle-income population, something that many hope the Kalamazoo Promise will do as well. Since DC TAG was launched in the 2000–2001 school year, the college enrollment rate of District of Columbia's Public Schools graduates has doubled (although the graduation rate remains lower than the national average for low-income, minority districts). Eleanor Holmes Norton, the District of Columbia's delegate in the House of Representatives, has underscored DC TAG's wide appeal, saying, "It's hard to find a program that is more popular in the District among all groups of people. It has gotten the same reception in our wealthy neighborhoods as in our poorest" (Files 2006). In this case, the availability of generous scholarship funding with few strings attached seems to have increased substantially not only the choice of where, but also of whether to go to college on the part of many district youth (Kane 2007), while its universality has secured broad public support.

A second example of a universal-access program that has had a positive impact on college attendance rates is one initiated by former Senator John Edwards in Greene County, North Carolina, a rural area in which only 8 percent of the population has a bachelor's degree or higher, compared to the U.S. average of 24 percent (U.S. Census Bureau 2000). Beginning with the class of 2006, the program, funded by a foundation established by Senator Edwards, provides all graduates of Greene Central High School with scholarships covering in-state tuition, fees, and books for the first year of college at any of the state's 16 public universities or 58 community colleges.[13] Any high school graduate who has resided in North Carolina for at least three years is eligible, provided he or she maintains a 2.0 GPA in college and commits at least 10 hours a week either to a work-study job or community service. Despite providing only a single year of last-dollar funding, the program has had striking results. In a setting where historically only 25 percent of high school graduates have gone on to postsecondary education, more than 80 percent of graduating seniors from the Greene Central class of 2006 applied to college, with 86 students ultimately receiving more than $300,000 in aid. Of these, 72 students completed their freshman year. The program was extended to the class of 2007, with 105 students attending college as of fall 2007 and another $300,000 in scholarships scheduled to be disbursed.[14]

The College for Everyone story suggests that while money is important, it is far from the only—or even the primary—barrier to postsecondary education for many individuals, especially those from homes where college attendance is not the norm. Two factors, apart from the scholarship funds, seem to account for the early positive results of this program. The first is a cultural change within Greene County High School that predated the introduction of College for Everyone and was in fact the reason it was selected as a pilot site for the program. The community's educational and civic leaders, recognizing the importance of postsecondary education in a radically transformed economy, had aligned their activities around this goal, actively encouraging local students to consider college and receiving a major federal grant in support of this effort. The second element is a comprehensive college preparation program provided to every senior at Greene Central High School. The nationally known college preparation firm College Summit was hired to train teachers and advisers to provide students with the information they need to successfully navigate the high school-to-college transition. About one-third of the incoming senior class in 2006 attended summer programs at two state universities where they wrote their college application essays and began work on their financial aid application forms. In the first week of class, these students served as peer leaders who, along with their teachers, helped other seniors begin these same activities. Every senior is enrolled in a class called "Senior Navigator"; as an incentive for completing their college preparation tasks, those seniors who are up to date with their work are taken on a college tour with all expenses paid by the school. In a demonstration of the power of peers, in October 2006, only 10 students were eligible for the tour. By December, 30 students participated, and by March, 55 students had joined the group. Over the summer, students from the class of 2006 who attended college (whether successfully or not) returned to the community to share their experiences and insights with a new crop of seniors.

The early results of the College for Everyone program provide powerful ammunition for the idea that it is not just about the money—that the college-going support and cultural change that permeates Greene County High School is at least as important as the promise of a single year of funding. And what happens after that first year? The conclusion of those involved with the program and outside observers is that once students understand the college application process and availability of financial aid, once they have had success in applying to and being accepted to college, and once they have made the transition and spent a year as a college student, the barriers to continued attendance come down, even in the absence of full scholarships.[15]

Apart from these few examples of place-based, universal scholarship programs, the Kalamazoo Promise has few precursors and none of a similar scope. Many more such programs are on the horizon today because of the powerful demonstration effect provided by the Kalamazoo Promise on communities around the nation. Closer to home, the program had an impact on state policy, with Governor Jennifer Granholm proposing a plan for replicating the program throughout Michigan. The legislation would establish "Promise Zones," public/private partnerships that tap future state revenue to fund scholarships in high-poverty communities, provided matching local resources are invested as well.[16] In unveiling her plan, the governor underscored the linkage between education and economic development, saying that "economists and experts across the country agree that education is the single most effective strategy for stoking a state's economic growth." And she charged the legislature to invest more in the state's educational infrastructure, quoting Bill Gates as saying that twenty-first-century businesses are far more sensitive to the quality of talent in a given location than they are to tax incentives. "These twenty-first-century CEOs will tell you," Granholm continued, "no business wants to come to a state that is making deep cuts in schools when their future business success depends on having access to skilled workers" (Granholm 2007). While Michigan Promise Zones were billed mainly as a program to increase student access to higher education, their structure and the current state of the Michigan economy leave little doubt that their ultimate purpose is local economic development.

THE KALAMAZOO PROMISE AS AN ECONOMIC DEVELOPMENT STRATEGY

Place-based economic development is nothing new. For half a century, cities, regions, and states have pursued strategies to increase the number of jobs available for residents, expand the tax base, and improve the quality of life. Since their large-scale adoption in the 1960s, local economic development policies have passed through three stages: Until the early 1980s, the focus was on strengthening a community's infrastructure to increase its appeal to outside investors. From the 1980s to the mid-1990s, the emphasis was on customized aid for specific businesses and industries, including the creation of business incubators, start-up support, and technical assistance. Beginning in the late 1990s, communities began to adopt more holistic approaches intended to make the entire business environment more hospitable. Greater support for the development of business clusters, an emphasis on workforce development and education, the creation of public/private partnerships, and attention to quality of life indicators are elements of this effort (World Bank n.d.). As shown in Chapter 2, Kalamazoo's economic development efforts broadly followed this trajectory, from the construction of the downtown pedestrian mall in 1959 to the comprehensive, cluster-based strategy advocated 50 years later.

The World Bank has categorized local economic development efforts as follows, with communities choosing to pursue some or all of these elements:

- ensuring that the local investment climate is functional for local businesses
- supporting small and medium-sized enterprises
- encouraging the formation of new enterprises
- attracting external investment

- investing in physical ("hard") infrastructure
- investing in soft infrastructure (educational and workforce development, institutional support systems, and regulatory issues)
- supporting the growth of particular clusters of businesses
- targeting particular parts of the city for regeneration or growth
- supporting informal and newly emerging businesses
- targeting certain disadvantaged groups (World Bank n.d.).

Kalamazoo's economic development efforts encompass the entire list and are carried out by multiple entities, some with overlapping responsibilities. These include:

- Southwest Michigan First, a nonprofit organization that receives both public and private funding. Southwest Michigan First focuses on business recruitment and retention at the regional level. Its creation in 1999 marked an important shift from economic development being the responsibility of local governmental agencies to a regional and private sector–led approach (Johnson 2005).
- Southwest Michigan Innovation Center (SMIC), an incubator and business accelerator that provides start-up assistance to bioscience companies. Located in the WMU Business Technology and Research Park, SMIC's tenants have access to state-of-the-art, advanced lab facilities, as well as the opportunity to share essential business services with other firms.
- The Kalamazoo County Chamber of Commerce, a membership organization that offers a variety of programs and partnerships to assist businesses and the Kalamazoo County Convention and Visitor's Bureau, with responsibility for marketing the community as a conference venue and tourist destination.
- The city of Kalamazoo and city of Portage each with its own economic development department charged with promoting growth within the cities' boundaries. In Kalamazoo, these efforts have focused on brownfield redevelopment, the downtown district, and neighborhood revitalization.

- Downtown Kalamazoo Inc. (DKI), the development agency for the downtown area, founded in 1989 and funded in part by revenues from a tax increment financing district.

- KVCC, offering vocational education and associate's degrees in a wide range of fields and operating the Michigan Technical Education Center (M-TEC), a training center built with state and private funding. M-TEC works in partnership with local and state economic development agencies to offer employer-driven, customized training to support the workforce needs of companies in the region.

- Neighborhood organizations, such as the Northside Association for Community Development and the Vine Neighborhood Association, which focus on the commercial and residential revitalization of low-income neighborhoods.

As is the case for other issue areas, this multiplicity of organizations reflects a wealth of institutional assets at the same time that it poses a challenge for coordination and integration.

The Kalamazoo Promise provides a common goal and vision in this fragmented landscape and one in keeping with the latest thinking in economic development that emphasizes human capital and quality of life as critical factors in keeping businesses connected to a community. Firms have become more footloose in recent years thanks to lower costs of transportation and communication and the shift from manufacturing to service provision; as a result, recruitment and retention efforts are easiest in a city that is home to the kind of workers businesses value. As Adam Smith put it 200 years ago, "a man is of all sorts of luggage the most difficult to be transported" (Smith 1776).[17]

A Michigan-based consultant writing shortly after the Kalamazoo Promise was announced recognized this important shift from past economic development approaches to a human capital–centered strategy:

> Communities facing hard times have traditionally focused on such things as new public buildings, business parks, and the like as a means of enticing new employers and new residents to a community. Temporary tax breaks and incentives have also been tried frequently. Success has been limited. The Promise is different. The enticement of new residents to the community to take advantage of funding of their children's college educations is a strong one. Giv-

en tight labor markets across the nation, new companies are also likely to consider Kalamazoo as a place to do business as they see a rising population. The lure of more and more college graduates in the local labor force in coming years is also a powerful incentive to locate a business in Kalamazoo. (Thredgold 2007)

By situating education at the center of the community's economic development strategy, the Kalamazoo Promise emphasizes the value of human capital and provides a tangible incentive for its creation.

Education, Productivity, and Economic Growth

Assuming that economic development is the underlying goal of the Kalamazoo Promise (a reasonable assumption given its structure and likely outcomes), why are college scholarships the cornerstone of the program? The short answer is that education is possibly the most important factor in a community's economic success. The longer answer rests on the premise, found throughout the economics literature, that education has the very real potential to increase an individual's productivity and that productivity is in turn the key to economic growth. In Chapter 1, the Kalamazoo Promise is characterized as an initiative with the potential to increase the economic, social, and human capital of the Greater Kalamazoo region. Human capital can be defined as "the stock of skills that people are endowed with or acquire through investment in training and education, and which renders them more productive in their work" (Johnes 2006). Most economists believe that the greater an individual's human capital, the more productive he or she will be as a worker. This is what underpins the wider range of job choice and higher earnings of the skilled or educated worker.

But the benefits of education do not accrue only to the individual. The logic of capitalism requires that businesses seek to maximize productivity. One of the chief mechanisms for doing this is to assemble a well-trained and productive workforce. Because access to such a workforce is critical to business success, cities or regions rich in workers with high human capital are among the most appealing places for businesses to locate.

Edward L. Glaeser of Harvard University and Albert Saiz of the University of Pennsylvania are among the many economists who have explored the connection between workers' skills and regional economic growth (Glaeser and Saiz 2003). They find that, apart from climate, (which, along with immigration, is the most important driver of metropolitan population growth in the United States), "skill composition may be the most powerful predictor of urban growth. This is both a boon to the skilled cities that have done spectacularly over the past two decades and a curse to the cities with less skilled workers that have suffered an almost unstoppable urban decline" (p. 42). Glaeser and Saiz argue that human capital matters most in potentially declining places. Skills are most valuable in these settings because they help cities adapt and change in response to negative economic shocks. This finding has clear implications for urban policy: "City growth can be promoted with strategies that increase the level of local human capital" (p. 43), including the provision of quality public schools. A high-quality educational system plays two roles, attracting educated workers to a community while producing more of them through graduation and access to higher education.

The Kalamazoo Promise and programs modeled on it are good examples of this dual dynamic. The availability of scholarships creates an incentive for workers and businesses who value education to move to or remain within the community. At the same time, it increases pressure on the public school district to educate and graduate students who are prepared to pursue some kind of postsecondary education. Over time, these two paths should converge to yield a more highly skilled local workforce.

Elaborating on the education-economy connection, Glaeser and Christopher R. Berry of the University of Chicago show that regions with skilled workforces ("smart" regions) experience higher rates of population and income growth than those without these assets (Glaeser and Berry 2006). Their research finds that regions where more than 25 percent of the population had college degrees in 1980 saw their population surge by 45 percent on average over the subsequent 20 years, while low-skilled metropolitan areas (those where fewer than 10 percent of adults had college degrees in 1980) grew on average by just 13 percent. In addition, even unskilled workers located in the "smart cities" earned significantly more than their counterparts in metropolitan areas with lower levels of educational attainment. And the gap in educational attainment between skilled and less-skilled areas has accelerated. One possible reason for the widening gap is that entrepreneurs of the past tended to hire large numbers of unskilled workers (think Henry Ford), whereas today's most successful businesses rely on highly educated workers (think Bill Gates). In a virtuous circle in which smart places are getting smarter, regions with an initial advantage in human capital are better able to attract employers who provide jobs for workers with high levels of skills and education.

Other research has shown that an increase in a metropolitan area's concentration of college-educated residents has a positive effect on employment growth (Shapiro 2006), while cross-national comparisons suggest that the educational level of the population is an important factor in a country's competitiveness in the global economy. Within a community, the presence of institutions of higher education can also contribute to economic growth. Even if the direct impact on growth is debatable (Federal Reserve Bank of Chicago 2007), universities play a critical role in workforce development and as a resource for businesses seeking to develop or apply new technologies. Kalamazoo's Business Technology and Research Park, which shares a campus with WMU's College of Engineering and Applied Sciences, is an example of the kind of collaboration that can emerge in a community that is home to a research university. Higher education institutions also serve as an amenity for those who live near them. College sports, cultural events, recreational facilities, and continuing education are among the benefits provided by such institutions. In Kalamazoo, for example, one of the community's two major fine arts facilities is located on the campus of WMU, while WMU, Kalamazoo College, and Kalamazoo Valley Community College (KVCC) offer programming for adults and youth that ranges from traveling Broadway shows and hockey lessons to evening language classes and dance performances.

The Demand Side: Strategies for Job Creation

The research summarized in the previous section focuses on how the existence of an educated workforce is connected to better economic performance. But educated workers do not move to or remain in a region if they can't find jobs. Turning from the supply to the demand side of the equation, how have local economic development authorities sought to attract and retain those employers with an interest in hiring educated workers? In other words, where will the jobs for these more productive workers come from?

In the Greater Kalamazoo region, the business recruitment and retention function falls largely to Southwest Michigan First. With the longtime presence of the Upjohn Company and Western Michigan University, Kalamazoo has long fit the profile of a smart city as Glaeser and Berry (2006) define it; residents of Kalamazoo and Portage, the county's two largest municipalities, far outpace both the state of Michigan and the nation in terms of the percentage of the population with at least four years of college (see Table 3.1). The gap is even larger at the master's and doctorate levels.

In an effort to retain the region's intellectual and financial capital in the aftermath of corporate downsizing (especially the loss of the Upjohn/Pharmacia/Pfizer headquarters and research divisions), Southwest Michigan First has pursued a regional cluster strategy that focuses on the life sciences. The identification and pursuit of this strategy, which dates from the late 1990s, reflected the conviction that Kalamazoo's 125-year legacy of life science innovation represented an asset that could translate into long-term economic growth.

Industry clusters are geographic concentrations of interconnected firms that share common markets, technologies, and labor pools, and that are often linked by buyer-seller relationships (Citizens Research Council 2007b, p. 6).[18] The role of clusters in economic development has received growing attention in recent years as a way for regions to build on their unique strengths rather than trying to imitate the paths of other successful communities. A cluster strategy also brings economies of scale, allowing economic development authorities to focus

Table 3.1 Educational Attainment—Residents with Four Years or More of College (%)

	1970	1980	1990	2000
City of Kalamazoo	17.0	26.8	29.8	32.8
City of Portage	16.9	25.5	31.3	36.9
State of Michigan	9.4	7.2	17.3	21.8
United States	11.0	17.0	21.3	26.0

NOTE: All numbers are for population age 25 and above.
SOURCE: U.S. Census Bureau.

their resources not on individual firms but on groups of firms and the support they need in terms of skills, technology, financing, training, infrastructure, communications, and the regulatory climate (Economic Development Administration 1997). Cluster-based economic development activities include facilitating consortiums and research of value to an industry, developing and providing customized training, providing physical infrastructure, and offering incentives to attract and grow firms in the cluster.

Cluster strategies are often conceived of at the regional level. In west Michigan, for example, Southwest Michigan First has joined forces with the economic development authority of Grand Rapids, 50 miles away, to pursue the life science field together. The leaders of this effort envision a "mega-metropolitan area" encompassing much of west and southwest Michigan, akin to North Carolina's "research triangle"—a stellar example of a successful cluster strategy. Already, close to 200 pharmaceutical, medical device, biomedical, and health service companies are listed on the Web sites of both organizations under the heading Western Michigan Life Science Companies.[19]

A crucial aspect of regional economic development is connecting businesses to sources of capital. In Kalamazoo, the Bank Consortium for Innovation brings together local financial institutions to provide information and financial coaching to companies, expand the capital market for entrepreneurs and firms that are diversifying, and serve as a link between traditional lending and growing venture capital activity. There are also several venture capital funds that are devoted to providing resources for local companies with promising discoveries in the life sciences field, as well as an "angel network" that provides investments of between $250,000 and $1 million and mentoring to start-up businesses.

Many of the economic development resources in the Kalamazoo region have gone into retaining those scientists who lost their jobs in the pharmaceuticals industry in the 1990s and attracting investment in related fields. But overreliance on an industry cluster can have its dangers, as the decline of the Detroit-based automotive industry has shown, and some question whether the life science field is the best choice for the region given the many other areas around the country pursuing a similar goal. In the case of Kalamazoo, the region's relatively diverse industrial base seems to have shielded it from the kind of sharp downturn experienced in single-industry towns, such as Flint, or even the Detroit area. Accordingly, efforts are also in place to preserve that diversity by building on past success in manufacturing; attracting new kinds of businesses, such as call centers, to the region; and developing a supportive environment for entrepreneurship of all kinds.

Strengthening the Urban Core

The economic development strategies outlined above are critical in attracting high value-added employers to a region, but the Kalamazoo Promise scholarship program is offered specifically to students in the urban school district that lies at the region's core. Accordingly, community leaders included both regional economic development and the revitalization of the core city among the four strategic priorities they devised when thinking about how to leverage the Kalamazoo Promise most effectively (see Chapter 4).

Why did the donors select as the target of their generosity a shrinking urban school district that serves a student body made up mainly of low-income and minority children? Most likely, this choice reflects a growing understanding that a region is only as strong as its core. As Dreier, Mollenkopf, and Swanstrom (2001, p. 25) write, "Regional economies are integrated wholes, with different parts of the metropolitan area specializing in different economic functions . . . Older central cities continue to provide large pools of private assets, accumulated knowledge, sophisticated skills, cultural resources, and social networks." There is also a new recognition of the economic and environmental costs of urban sprawl, which is arguably more expensive than other, more compact forms of development (Burchell et al. 2005).

While a few of the nation's largest cities have remained vital, most urban areas lost population, wealth, and influence during the past several decades. In his insightful account of the decline of Detroit, University of Pennsylvania historian and sociologist Thomas J. Sugrue identifies three forces that he argues accounted for the urban crisis in metropolitan areas across the nation: the flight of jobs, especially the unionized manufacturing jobs that characterized the post–World War II urban economy; the persistence of workplace discrimination; and racial segregation in housing that led to an uneven distribution of power and resources in metropolitan areas. It is worth quoting from Sugrue (1996, pp. xvii–xviii) at some length about the current state of the urban American landscape and particularly the role of race in shaping it:

> Despite more than half a century of civil rights activism and changing racial attitudes, American cities (particularly the old industrial centers of the Northeast and Midwest) remain deeply divided by race. Poverty rates among people of color in major American cities are staggeringly high. Vast tracts of urban land lie pockmarked with boarded-up buildings, abandoned houses, and rubble-strewn lots. At the same time, hundreds of thousands of acres of marshland, meadow, farm, and forest on the periphery of major metropolitan areas get gobbled up each year for vast tracts of new housing, shopping malls, and office parks. City governments struggle with shrinking tax bases and ever-increasing demands on public services, while wealthy suburban municipalities enjoy strong property tax revenues, excellent public services, and superb schools.

Others have shown in more detail how this landscape emerged. In *Metropolitics*, Myron Orfield (1997, p. 16) traces the decline of once vibrant, middle-class neighborhoods in the urban center into tracts of concentrated poverty through what he calls the "vacancy chain":

> A household move to a new unit at the periphery creates a vacancy at the old address, to be filled by another household, which leaves a vacancy at its old address, and so on. Building new housing at the periphery sets in motion vacancy chains reaching far back into the city's central core. Thus the more rapid peripheral growth of middle-class sectors leaves excess housing and low demand at the center of its vacancy chain. As demand declines, so too does price, opening up opportunities for the region's poor people . . . As these [central] neighborhoods grow poor, social and economic decline accelerate, pushing the middle class out while the vacancy chain simultaneously pulls these residents outward . . . Ironically, as the various economic classes leave central-city areas, all the social and economic changes that occur in the core of their sectoral housing markets eventually follow them through the vacancy chains out into the suburbs.

With unemployment, racial segregation, and single-parent homes coming to dominate the older, poorer neighborhoods, residents grow increasingly isolated from middle-class society and the private economy. "Individuals, particularly children, are deprived of local successful role models and connections to opportunity outside the neighborhood" (Orfield 1997, p. 18). Crime is the last resort in such communities.

Theoretically, public schools work against this dynamic, providing equal opportunity to all and serving as a way out for children from distressed homes and communities. In reality, however, schools take on the characteristics of the neighborhoods that surround them and perpetuate the cycle of decline. "It is the rapid increase of poor children in local schools . . . that sounds the first warning of imminent middle-class flight" (Orfield 1997, p. 38). David Rusk, the former mayor of Albuquerque and an authority on urban affairs, has demonstrated in a variety of studies that housing segregation almost always equates with school segregation. The concentrated poverty found in most urban school districts, which maps closely with race, is a mirror of the segregated neighborhoods created by middle-class flight. These neighborhoods are home to high-poverty schools that struggle to retain quality teachers, grapple with their students' poverty-related behavioral problems, and almost always earn low scores on standardized tests. The reverse side of this neighborhood-school dynamic is that when neighborhoods become more diverse in terms of family income, so do their schools, with benefits for all students (see "Socioeconomic Integration in the Schools").

Another challenge for urban areas and one that is especially pressing in Kalamazoo is the high degree of local government fragmentation discussed in Chapter 2. Rusk and Orfield both advocate regional integration as a way of overcoming the inefficiencies that result from multiple governing jurisdictions in a single geographic area. The chief remedy for the linked problems of declining core cities, deindustrialization and urban sprawl, according to Rusk, is for a city's boundaries to be flexible enough for it to capture the growth in population and tax base that occurs in the suburbs. "For a city's population to grow, the city must be 'elastic,' and if a city is not growing it is shrinking," writes Rusk (1995, p. 9). Michigan is a state where local governments hold a relatively high degree of power, and Kalamazoo County is very much a "little box" system where multiple jurisdictions bump up against each other on all sides. These factors make it difficult to envision the solutions proposed by Rusk and Orfield, such as annexation of neighboring municipalities, consolidation of government functions, or even joint planning on a regional scale.

Socioeconomic Integration in the Schools

This section draws on extensive research on socioeconomic school integration carried out by Richard D. Kahlenberg of The Century Foundation. See, in particular, Kahlenberg (2006b). For a complete list of Century Foundation publications on the topic, see http://www.equaleducation.org.

Greater socioeconomic diversity in the Kalamazoo Public Schools is one of the most important potential outcomes of the Kalamazoo Promise. Since the 1970s, a combination of middle-class flight and structural economic change has led to a steady increase in the proportion of low-income children enrolled in the Kalamazoo Public Schools. The Kalamazoo Promise provides new incentives for middle-class families to move into the district and is also expected to stem the outward movement of the district's existing middle-class population. There is solid evidence to suggest that if these trends lead to the creation of mixed-income schools, student achievement across the board will rise.

The literature on socioeconomic school integration defines a school as mixed-income, or middle class, when fewer than 50 percent of its students qualify for the federally subsidized lunch program. When the Kalamazoo Promise was announced, the percentage of low-income students in KPS overall was 62 percent, with the low-income population at individual elementary schools ranging from 94 percent to 25 percent (the middle and high schools are already relatively integrated because there are fewer of them). With a relatively modest enrollment gain of middle-class students, KPS could become a mixed-income school district in only a few years.

What are the benefits of attending a school that includes students from diverse economic backgrounds? "While money matters a great deal in education, people matter more," writes Richard Kahlenberg (2007) of the Century Foundation, one of the leading experts on socioeconomic school integration. Myron Orfield, an expert in the decline of metropolitan regions, concurs: "Schools are not just instruction and textbooks but a complex web of social networks that reinforce student success or failure . . . Socioeconomically mixed schools improve poor children's academic achievement, high school graduation rates, and (most significantly) their access to further technical training, higher education, good jobs, and many other middle-class benefits" (Orfield 1997, p. 39). Parents, students, and teachers all play a role in this dynamic.

Parents. "It is an advantage to attend a school where parents are actively involved, volunteer in the classroom, and hold school officials accountable" (Kahlenberg 2007, p. 7). The reality of poverty means that low-income parents are less likely to be involved in their children's schools than are middle-income parents. Research shows that parents in middle-class schools are four times more likely than those in high-poverty schools to be members of the Parent-Teacher Association. Middle-income parents are also more likely to volunteer in the classroom, particularly during the elementary years, and are in a better position to provide financial support, whether through fundraising drives or the donation of supplies and services. High levels of parental involvement are good for schools as a whole, not just for the particular child whose parents are involved, meaning that the benefits extend across the learning environment.

Students. The sociological literature on peer effects shows that students learn from each other as well as from their teachers. Children from middle-income families arrive at school with larger vocabularies than children from low-income families, and the vocabularies of students at all income levels benefit from such a mixed-income environment. Students also learn behavior from their peers. Most parents would like to send their child to a school where his or her peers are academically engaged, don't skip class, and expect to graduate and go on to higher education. For a variety of reasons, these behaviors are found more often in middle-income than in low-income schools. If these behaviors dominate the learning environment, there is pressure on students from all socioeconomic backgrounds to conform to them.

Teachers. As a matter of public policy, it might make sense for the best teachers to be assigned to teach at the lowest-income schools, but in practice the opposite is true. Teachers in middle-class schools are more likely to be licensed, to be teaching in their fields of expertise, to have more teaching experience, and to have more formal education. They are also likely to have higher expectations of their students. For the most part, teachers consider it a promotion to move from a high-poverty to a middle-class school, simply because it is easier and often more satisfying to do one's job in an environment where there are fewer behavior problems.

Integrating a few middle-class children into a high-poverty environment can be detrimental to their academic achievement, but as long as there is a critical mass of middle-class students in a school, their achievement does not decline with the presence of low-income students. In other words, integration is not a zero-sum game in which gains for low-income children are offset by a reduction in the achievement of middle-class students.

Historically, school integration efforts have focused on achieving racial diversity in the interest of raising achievement levels among minority children and creating greater tolerance and understanding among children of all races. The U.S. Supreme Court ruling in 2007 that struck down school integration plans relying on race as a factor in student assignment was yet another blow to school districts hoping to integrate by race. But there is broad agreement that race-neutral alternatives, including family income, are perfectly legal bases for school assignment. And the overlap between race and economic status in the United States thus makes socioeconomic integration an effective, if indirect, path toward racial integration.

These multiple advantages have led approximately 40 school districts nationwide, educating 2.5 million students, to begin using socioeconomic status as a basis for school assignment, and many more are likely to do so in the wake of the Supreme Court decision. While the Kalamazoo Promise will almost certainly create greater income diversity within KPS, one of the big questions is whether socioeconomic integration will extend to individual elementary schools. One scenario is that the district integrates but the middle-income population clusters in certain schools, as is currently the case. If the middle-income population can ultimately be drawn into schools in poorer neighborhoods through the use of magnet schools and parental choice, Kahlenberg is hopeful about the impact of socioeconomic integration on student achievement in KPS: "*If* the college scholarship draws middle-class families into the district and, *if*, also, there is some effort at promoting equity within the school system—that is to say you don't have one part of the district that is overwhelmingly middle class and another part that is poor (in other words, *if* you get economic school integration)—that will be far more important than any of the traditional approaches of spending money on high-poverty schools."[20]

What can an urban community do if its boundaries are not elastic? According to Rusk, the municipalities within the region can move toward regional land use planning to help control sprawl, ensure that all suburbs have their fair share of low- and moderate-income housing to help dissolve concentrations of poverty, and implement regional revenue sharing to help reduce fiscal disparities (Rusk 1999, p. 11). (In the 1990s, Rusk was hired to develop such a plan in Kalamazoo only to have it shot down by surrounding municipalities intent on retaining their autonomy and ill-disposed toward joining forces with the city of Kalamazoo, home to most of the region's poor and minority residents.)[21] Another strategy for inelastic communities is to increase population density and the socioeconomic diversity of the urban core by enticing middle-class families to move into rather than out of the central city. This is one of the goals implicit in the Kalamazoo Promise and also a cornerstone of other efforts to revitalize cities.

The Creative Class and a Vibrant Downtown

The concept of the "creative class" developed by Richard Florida links the two strategies discussed above: worker productivity as a source of growth and the benefits of strengthening the urban core. Research by Nobel Prize–winning economist Robert Lucas has shown that denser urban areas enjoy an advantage in productivity because they combine people's creative energies in one locale. Building on this insight, Florida claims that the value of cities lies in their ability to centralize and thereby augment human capital: "Since places with more human capital grow more rapidly than those with less, urbanization (and the density that accompanies it) is a key element of innovation and productivity growth" (Florida 2005, p. 38).

Florida's arguments rest on the premise that place matters. Unlike those who believe that people make location decisions based on opportunities in the labor force, Florida maintains that many individuals, especially young people, choose a location first and then look for a job there. (A 2006 poll commissioned by CEOs for Cities offered some support for this claim, finding that two-thirds of college-educated 25- to 34-year-olds polled said that they will make the decision of where they live first then look for a job within that area [The Segmentation Company 2006].) University of Chicago sociologist Terry Clark has found that it is not the natural amenities of sunshine and temperatures that draw high human-capital individuals to cities, but "constructed amenities" from arts and culture to high-quality restaurants (Clark 2003). For Florida, it is the Three T's of technology, talent, and tolerance that "unleash the creative energy of lots of different groups trying lots of different things, some of which will make little difference and some of which will be successful" (Florida 2005, p. 54). In this he draws on James Surowiecki's powerful insight about the "wisdom of crowds" in coming up with aggregate solutions to complex problems: "They don't do so by all toeing the same moderate line, but rather by making independent and diversified guesses that can then be in some sense compiled. The natural variation that different human beings with different needs and desires bring to the table may, in this respect, be the most powerful tool we have for improving communities, regions, and nations" (Florida 2005, p. 54).

While investments in urban amenities targeted toward the creative class may help draw an increasing number of educated, skilled, and talented people to city centers, scholars such as Thomas Sugrue are skeptical about the ability of these trends to improve living conditions for most residents of urban areas. Writing about the cities of the rustbelt, Sugrue maintains that "there has been very little 'trickle down' from downtown revitalization and neighborhood gentrification to the long-term poor, the urban working class, and minorities. An influx of coffee shops, bistros, art galleries, and upscale boutiques have made parts of many cities increasingly appealing for the privileged, but they have not, in any significant way, altered the everyday misery and impoverishment that characterize many urban neighborhoods" (Sugrue 1996, p. xxv).

Regardless of where one comes down on this debate, cities may have little choice, according to Bruce Katz, vice president and director of the Metropolitan Policy Program of the Brookings Institution. Katz argues that drawing a critical mass of residents downtown is the key to urban revival and, ultimately, global competitiveness. "At a time of profound economic restructuring and demographic change, bringing residents downtown would have seismic implications. The critical massing of people would attract amenities that lure businesses and jobs for downtown and metro-area residents, shoppers and tourists and help stem the exodus of young workers" (Katz 2006a). Policies that support greater density in the urban core, rather than continued urban sprawl, are also favored by the environmental and land use movements, and they have gained new traction with oil prices that make public transportation increasingly desirable and cost-effective.

Like Florida, Katz is an optimist about the future of cities, arguing that the demographic, economic, and cultural shifts under way in the U.S. economy have given cities their best chance in decades to compete for new residents, their jobs, and their spending power (Katz 2006b). In the 1990s, the nation's largest cities have actually seen population growth that outpaces the previous decade, and growth has continued since 2000 (Katz 2006c). Katz and his colleagues have proposed a set of new federal urban policy initiatives to support this uneven but potentially important urban resurgence. One of these strategies is to invest in the growth of the middle class through investments in education. "The key to growing an urban middle class is simple: education," writes Katz (2006c, p. 15). "With residential choice dependent on school quality, cities need to ensure that their schools can attract and retain families with broader options."

Paths to Success—the Interrelationship of Education and the Economy

This chapter has addressed sequentially the policy areas of educational access and economic development, but the two issues are interrelated. On the Kalamazoo Promise Web site, the reasons given for offering college scholarships to KPS students are phrased simply but touch on both elements:

1) Education is an important key to financial well being.

2) It allows KPS to differentiate itself from other public and private school systems.

3) It provides a real meaningful and tangible opportunity for *all* students.

4) The Kalamazoo Promise will create opportunities for individuals who attend KPS and their current and future families. It follows—and studies have shown—that there is a strong correlation between overall academic achievement and a community's economic vitality and quality of life.

The program is designed to provide maximum benefit to long-term attendees of the district—reinforcement of the "stickiness" described above: "A desired outcome of the program will be to encourage families to make early decisions to enroll their students in Kalamazoo Public Schools, and to maintain that enrollment through graduation."[22]

This emphasis on long-term enrollment and the strictly enforced residency requirement lend credence to the idea that there is more to the Kalamazoo Promise than simply increasing educational opportunities for local students. As recounted in Chapter 2, Kalamazoo is in many ways a microcosm of the nation's older urban areas, a smaller and less acute case of the urban crisis described by Sugrue: a core city characterized by declining population, an increased percentage of low-income and minority residents, the deterioration of infrastructure, housing that is segregated by race and income, school attendance that corresponds largely to these segregated housing patterns, and higher crime rates than in surrounding suburbs. A climate such as this requires a powerful intervention to reverse negative trends long under way.

The Kalamazoo Promise is clearly meant as such a transformative investment—one that changes the incentives for diverse actors with attendant benefits for both educational attainment and the local economy. The W.E. Upjohn Institute developed Figure 3.1 to show the linkages between the educational and economic systems, as well as the critical decision points students and the community face on the path to success.

Pre-K through 12th grade education

The Kalamazoo Promise and programs modeled on it begin with the individual student enrolled in the public school district (some programs outside Kalamazoo also cover parochial schools situated in the urban core). The availability of full college scholarships to long-term residents creates an incentive for families with school-age (or younger) children to remain in or move into the district. Likely outcomes include increased public school enrollment, higher graduation rates, and a greater likelihood of high school graduates going on to some kind of postsecondary institution. Strong incentives are also created for the school district and community support organizations to provide the resources necessary for all students to take advantage of the available scholarships. This includes not just efforts to ensure that lower-achieving

Figure 3.1 Paths to Success

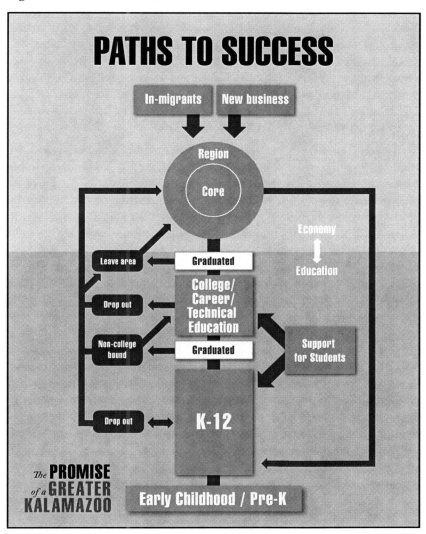

SOURCE: W.E. Upjohn Institute for Employment Research.

students are able to pursue and succeed in a postsecondary program, but also initiatives to keep higher-achieving students challenged and engaged. A related component is the need for effective, high-quality preschool and early childhood programs to ensure that all children start school prepared for success. Critical to all of these efforts are school- and community-based strategies to support parents and families, and to create a culture of college-going for youth of all backgrounds.

College, career, and technical education

Depending on the availability of local higher education options, students may choose to pursue their postsecondary studies or training within or outside the region. (In the case of the Kalamazoo Promise, students who decide not to continue their education immediately after graduation have the option of doing so at a later date because their scholarships can be used anytime within 10 years of graduation.) High rates of local college attendance have been seen with the first two classes of Kalamazoo Promise students—a pattern that strengthens the enrollment of local colleges and universities and keeps scholarship dollars within the region. Students who go away for college may choose to return to the community; conversely, students who attend a local postsecondary institution may move away after they graduate. In the aggregate, however, increased rates of high school graduation and postsecondary attainment for local youth should over time create a better-educated local workforce. Here, too, there is a strong incentive for postsecondary institutions to provide the support necessary for students—many of them first-generation college-goers—to succeed in their college or career/technical programs. The new opportunities provided by the scholarships also can serve as a catalyst for closer integration of postsecondary institutions and K-12 schools, as well as deeper engagement of area businesses in helping students define their career paths.

Workforce and economic development

The scholarship program offers short- and long-term advantages to businesses in both the urban core and the broader region. Companies in either locale can use the program as an incentive to recruit or retain employees, since workers can opt to live within the school district's boundaries where their children will qualify for the scholarships. The scholarship is also an enticement for entrepreneurs, freeing up college savings for business investment purposes. For businesses outside the region, the scholarship program provides the same tangible incentives, as well as an intangible but powerful signal that the community is one that values and invests in education. (The quality of the public schools is a critical factor in business location and expansion decisions.) As businesses relocate to or expand within the region, jobs and economic activity (such as home purchases and discretionary spending) will be created that benefit both existing and new residents. College graduates who left the area to attend school or work in a larger city may choose to return, especially when they are ready to buy a home or start a family. Increased regional economic vitality, together with the scholarship program, will support population growth, which will in turn contribute to increased enrollment in the public schools.

By targeting its scholarships toward students in the region's urban core, the Kalamazoo Promise overnight increased the attractiveness of the city to existing residents and created a magnet to draw in new residents and businesses. Many individuals without children also consider it a plus to live in a community that embraces education as the centerpiece of its economic development strategy. While these incentives are important, the extent to which the scholarship program can serve as a catalyst for broader economic and social transformation depends on several factors. Some of these, such as the condition of the state or regional economy, are largely beyond local control. Other incentives, however, are up to the community. Chief among the community's challenges are to ensure that the connection between education and economic vitality is broadly understood and that the potential regional benefits of the scholarship program are recognized.

Notes

1. For more information about the Clemens Foundation and Philomath, see Sabo (2002a) and Associated Press (2005). Filmmaker Peter Richardson, a graduate of Philomath High School, documented the dispute in a full-length documentary, "Clear Cut: The Story of Philomath, Oregon," which was shown at the Sundance Film Festival in 2006.
2. For the story of one such town, see Miller-Adams (2002, Chapter 3).
3. The IRS and state authorities approved the changes made to the scholarship

program based on the fact that the Clemens Foundation was incorporated as a charitable foundation with general grant-making powers, rather than specifically a scholarship-granting organization (Sabo 2002a,b).

4. The W.E. Upjohn Institute for Employment Research, the local think tank that is supporting the research and publication of this book, is also carrying out a multiyear net impact evaluation of the Kalamazoo Promise. Updates will be posted regularly on the Promise Web site: http://www.upjohninstitute.org/promise/index .htm.

5. E-mail message from Timothy Bartik, senior economist at the W.E. Upjohn Institute, to Julie Mack, November 8, 2006.

6. In 2008–2009, the average annual cost of tuition and fees at public, four-year institutions in the United States was $6,585; the average cost of public two-year institutions was $2,402, and the cost of private four-year colleges averaged $25,143. (College Board 2008).

7. Of Pell recipients who received their bachelor's degrees in 2004, 88.5 percent had student loans, compared to 51.7 percent of non-Pell recipients (Project on Student Debt 2007, p. 1).

8. For more on merit aid, see Heller and Marin (2004) and Heller (2006b).

9. Students with a household income of up to $50,000 at the time of application qualify; new rules introduced in 2007 impose an income limit of $100,000 at the time the student begins college for recipients beginning in 2009–2010. See the Oklahoma Higher Education Web site: http://www.okhighered.org/okpromise/ legislative-changes2007.shtml.

10. In November 2006, Michigan voters approved Proposal 2, which amends the Michigan constitution to ban public institutions from discriminating against or giving preferential treatment to groups of individuals based on their race, gender, color, ethnicity, or national origin, thereby making illegal the admissions practices of some of the state's leading educational institutions. Socioeconomic status is still allowable as a criterion for admission.

11. For more information, see the "I Have a Dream" Foundation Web site: http:// www.ihad.org.

12. See, for example, Committee for Economic Development (2006), Bartik (2006), and Dickens, Sawhill, and Tebbs (2006).

13. In the first year of the program, participating colleges and universities were limited to those surrounding Greene County, but the list of college options was expanded to the entire state in 2006.

14. According to College for Everyone director Pamela Hampton-Garland, class of 2007 students received more than $1 million in outside scholarships, so the original $300,000 scholarship fund was sufficient to cover their needs.

15. Information on the College for Everyone program was provided by Pamela Hampton-Garland in communication with the author, as well as McConkey (2005), Abernethy (2006), and Wayne (2007).

16. Promise Zones were initially called for in Governor Granholm's State of the State address in February 2007. Legislation introduced later in the year was passed by

the State House of Representatives in fall 2007 and as of spring 2008 was awaiting action in the Senate.

17. Thanks to Timothy Bartik of the W.E. Upjohn Institute for directing me toward this quotation and contributing his thoughts to this section of the chapter.

18. Alternatively, an industry cluster can be defined as "a group of firms and related economic actors and institutions, that are located near one another and that draw productive advantage from their mutual proximity and connections" (Cortright 2006).

19. See http://www.southwestmichiganfirst.com/wmlifesciencecompanies.cfm.

20. Author's interview with Richard D. Kahlenberg, The Century Foundation, January 24, 2006.

21. See Rusk (1998). In a report commissioned by the City of Portage in response to Rusk's proposal, two other consultants opposed such a compact, stating, "There is a strong argument to be made that the Kalamazoo region's existing form of government—one which features many, relatively small political jurisdictions—may actually contribute to the relative prosperity which the region currently enjoys" (Husock and Cox 1999).

22. The Kalamazoo Promise: Questions and Answers (Web site: https://www.kalamazoopromise.com).

Part 2

Impact

Many of the people who are watching around the country—and they are watching us—they don't realize that we are an urban core city. We have a poverty rate of 25 percent. We are one of the cities in this country that urban experts have debated about for the last decade—whether we have a future, whether our kind of city has a future in the new economy.

—Mayor Hannah McKinney, November 15, 2005

Along whatever lines we have been divided before, whether it was lines of income, lines of class, lines of color, lines of achievement, today we proclaim to all the world that we are one community with one vision and one common future . . . So, my brothers and sisters, whether we were expecting it or not, whether we want it or not, we are now ambassadors of the new Kalamazoo, and we must say to the world that we are the best, that we are an example for the rest of the world to follow.

—Pastor J. Louis Felton, November 15, 2005

4
The Challenge of
Community Alignment

When the Kalamazoo Promise was announced, the community's initial response of "Wow!" soon gave way to a collective "What now?" As it became clear that the anonymous donors were genuinely intent on remaining anonymous, this question took on added urgency. It was widely understood that the scholarship program was only a part of what it would take to achieve the full economic development potential of the Kalamazoo Promise, but there was quite literally no one at the helm to guide the communal effort that would be needed to advance the program's broader goals.

In this respect, the announcement came at an especially challenging time for Kalamazoo. Until the mid-1990s, most major community initiatives had depended heavily for both leadership and financial resources on the area's largest employer, the Upjohn Company. However, with the 1995 merger, downsizing of the local workforce, and the relocation of its corporate headquarters away from Kalamazoo, the company could no longer be relied upon to fulfill this role. Unlike in neighboring Battle Creek, where there are few contenders to assume the mantle of leadership from the Kellogg Company should it leave town, Kalamazoo is home to other large employers, such as Western Michigan University and two large hospitals. But no single entity is in the position to exercise the kind of influence the Upjohn Company once had. And even though this change had been under way for some time, the community had not yet fully adapted to it.

The anonymity of the Kalamazoo Promise donors is particularly important in light of this shift in the leadership paradigm. The donors' motivations for remaining anonymous have never been stated, but there are several plausible reasons. One is simply to avoid having to respond to any criticism of the program or concerns about conflicts of interest. (Negative publicity along these lines has indeed been an issue in several communities, including Denver and Pittsburgh.)[1] Another is to keep from being drawn into the day-to-day administrative or decision-making tasks surrounding the program. Also relevant is a long tradition of anonymous philanthropy in Kalamazoo suggestive of a genuine desire to avoid the spotlight. (The Kalamazoo Promise is only one, albeit the largest, of a number of sizeable gifts to community institutions given anonymously.) The donors' decision may also have been a strategic one made to maximize the catalytic impact of their gift—in other words, to prompt others in the community to step up and assume responsibility for implementing the Kalamazoo Promise and ensuring its success.

Whether or not this was their intention, the donors' anonymity indeed strengthened the program's catalytic impact by effectively creating a power vacuum at the center of the Kalamazoo Promise. And into this vacuum the community rushed with a myriad of initiatives and ideas (see the profiles highlighted in this chapter). Those prompted to act by the donors' investment responded in many productive ways. Parents volunteered in the schools, some for the first time. Churches introduced mentoring programs. New opportunities were created for students to recover credits and graduate on time. The local community college and university strengthened their services for first-generation college attendees. Businesses developed programs to support the economic goals of the Kalamazoo Promise. Yet even three years later, these efforts remained diffuse and uncoordinated.

It is easy to get excited about the Kalamazoo Promise. The scholarship program is inclusive (within the KPS district); generous; politically neutral, as it involves no use of public funds; and intended to last in perpetuity. But the Kalamazoo Promise was still a shock to the system, and the most pressing question to emerge since its announcement is how the community can best deploy its assets to make the most of such an unprecedented gift.

The response to the announcement of the Kalamazoo Promise is as complex as the issues raised by the program. The Promise has spurred some organizations to take on new tasks or conduct their business in different ways. It has brought some new entities into existence. And it has certainly increased civic pride and raised the spirits of longtime advocates for the urban core and the school district that serves it. But for many residents, the Kalamazoo Promise has had little impact and does not seem relevant to their work or lives.

There are several reasons why a strong and cohesive community response has not materialized. The first is that the potential of the donors' investment to transform the larger region is not well understood. In particular, the multiple linkages discussed in the previous chapter among an improved educational system, a healthy core city, and a stronger regional economy are not easy to grasp. It is much simpler to treat the Kalamazoo Promise as a scholarship program for KPS residents with school-age children. (Not surprisingly, the most vigorous responses to the Kalamazoo Promise have come from those segments of the community that are most directly affected by it, including not only the schools but also community organizations that support students, parents who have become more involved in their children's education, and real estate agents who expect the program to help them sell houses.)

A second explanation centers on the coordination problems posed by the Kalamazoo Promise. Even if the potential transformative effects of the program were well understood, the challenge of organizing and aligning a complex system, even in a community the size of Kalamazoo, is formidable. The transition to a new leadership paradigm and the lack of a clear coordinating structure compounds this challenge. It may just be a matter of allowing enough time for everyone to absorb the implications of the program. After all, according to Janice Brown, it took several years of conversation for the idea of the Kalamazoo Promise to take shape, and any expectation that the community would rapidly recognize and adapt to the new reality is probably unrealistic. It is more likely, however, that the very complexity of the program's impact is the reason for the lack of a unified response. The potential for widespread change in the educational, economic, and social spheres, coupled with the presence of multiple, overlapping organizations and leaders with longstanding vested interests, means that the Promise actually could exacerbate fragmentation and competition rather than generate greater unity.

The second half of this book examines the impact of the Kalamazoo Promise thus far.[2] This chapter traces the process through which the local community has organized itself since the announcement of the scholarship program; lessons for other communities are summarized at the end of the chapter. Chapter 5 looks at the impact of the program on students and the schools, and Chapter 6 examines its potential economic impact. Taken together, these chapters provide an account of the changes in social, human, and economic assets that have occurred thus far as a result of the Kalamazoo Promise.

Adams Outdoor Advertising: "It's What We Can Do"

When Mike Cannon, then the manager of Adams Outdoor's Kalamazoo office, first heard about the Kalamazoo Promise, he asked him-

self how the company could help. With 500 "faces," or billboards, in the Kalamazoo region, the answer was easy. Mike talked about his idea with the staff and they agreed that a positive gesture was called for. "The reason we picked the Promise is that more people were tearing it down than were building it up, and that bothered us," says Cannon.[3] Adams Outdoor worked with KPS to develop the message, then designed and produced a billboard and donated the labor, materials, and space to display it in three rotating locales on major thoroughfares in town. The message was simple and powerful: the phrase "Who Benefits From the Promise?" coupled with the raised hands of 15 diverse individuals.

"Based on the business we're in, we want a thriving community," says Cannon. "We need commerce, we need transactions happening. If the Kalamazoo Promise brings in more people, more jobs, if the school system improves, then if people had a little bit of money saved for college but they don't need it anymore, maybe they'll spend it in town—maybe they'll eat at that restaurant over there, maybe someone buys a new car over there. I'm not the smartest guy in the world, but what you're telling me is someone's going to pay for my kids' college—that could be $20,000–$30,000 apiece. So many people work their tails off saving that money just to give their kids that opportunity. And all of a sudden, someone's going to give that to my kids—and then to hear 'Oh, it's all just media hype.' We said, 'It's going to benefit everybody—potentially.' All we want is for people to think about that. That's why we have all different kinds of hands, all ages, all colors, working people."

Adams Outdoors' design was also featured on the cover of the AT&T White & Yellow Pages, published in August 2006 and distributed to 360,000 customers regionwide. AT&T donated the space in support of the Kalamazoo Promise, and Adams Outdoor followed up with a second set of billboards in the fall of 2006 with the message, "I Promise to Get Involved" and the address for the Promise of Greater Kalamazoo Web site.

"We have a vehicle that most companies don't have," explains Cannon. "I can pretty much reach the entire population of Kalamazoo over a certain period of time. That's a very powerful medium. We can put up any type of message and people are going to drive by and think 'What does that mean?' Then two days later they may see it again and think, 'Hmmm,' then business people will drive by and say, 'Maybe that affects me.' And suddenly they're thinking 'Maybe I should look into this.' There aren't a lot of other companies that can do this—it's what we can do."

Any account of the impact of the Kalamazoo Promise will require continual updating as the program unfolds, but a realistic ongoing appraisal is essential not only for Kalamazoo but for other communities developing similar programs. As city after city announces plans for a Promise-type plan, it has become clear that there are two equally important components to a successful program: the financial resources to pay for it, and effective community support or alignment. For Kalamazoo, the money was the easy part, arriving as a sudden and unexpected gift, while an aligned and organized community response has proven more elusive. And as time goes by it becomes increasingly clear that the provision of scholarship funds alone, no matter how generous, will fall short of yielding the kind of transformation the donors almost certainly envisioned for their community.

THE TRIUMPHS AND TRAVAILS OF THE SATURDAY
MORNING GROUP

The announcement of the Kalamazoo Promise on November 10, 2005, came just three days after local elections in the city of Kalamazoo. Hannah McKinney, an economics professor at Kalamazoo College and a member of the City Commission, would serve as mayor for the next two years by virtue of having won the most votes in the election.[4] On November 15, the same day that the community gathered in celebration of the Promise, Mayor McKinney announced plans to create a task force to study the institutional changes Kalamazoo should consider if it hoped to leverage the full benefits of the Kalamazoo Promise. "We face a much brighter future with greater options than we faced on election day," she told the *Kalamazoo Gazette* (Jessup 2005). Pointing out that the Promise has the potential to affect everything from economic development and housing to city budgeting, she stressed that city officials would need to move quickly to get ahead of the issues. "We're going to have more budget cuts next year, but now we have to cut in a way that still plans for future growth . . . now the budgeting process has to look at parks and recreation, different kinds of policing, and things like sidewalks. We want to be the right city for all of these new people." In a nod to the fact that the borders of the KPS district extend well beyond city limits, McKinney said the task force would include members of the broader community: "I'm not thinking the work stops with our city."

The first meeting of what came to be known as the Saturday Morning Group took place a month later, on December 17, 2005. The meeting was convened by three longtime community leaders: Randall W. Eberts, executive director of the W.E. Upjohn Institute for Employment Research; Jack Hopkins, the then president of the Kalamazoo Community Foundation; and Mayor McKinney. Fourteen other individuals representing the community's educational, governmental, business, nonprofit, and faith-based organizations were invited to the opening session. The original intention of those guiding the process was that a relatively small group would meet to plan a convening process for the broader community. The emphasis would be on leveraging the economic development potential of the Kalamazoo Promise, with the conveners asking the group "to consider a process to engage the broader

Huntington National Bank: Helping Prospective Homeowners

As a lifelong Kalamazoo resident and community president for Huntington National Bank's regional operations, Jerry Blaisdell thought he would enjoy attending the November 15, 2005, celebration of the Kalamazoo Promise. At the meeting, Janice Brown "conveyed the message that all of us in the community had a responsibility to make the Kalamazoo Promise come true, and that started my thinking about how Huntington could get involved," says Blaisdell (Mack 2006h).

Having secured corporate approval for his idea, Blaisdell announced in March 2006 that Huntington National Bank had created a $5 million loan fund for home buyers purchasing a residence within the KPS district. The program, aimed at buyers with little or no money for a down payment and/or credit scores that fall below the usual cutoff, offers a lower interest rate than other zero-down mortgages and waives the costly private mortgage insurance requirement.

The mortgages, which are available to anyone buying a home within the district whether or not they have children, are kept in the bank's own portfolio, which means they do not have to conform to the rules of the secondary mortgage market (for example, if a buyer has a credit score below the minimum cutoff of 620, he or she would need to turn to a subprime lender; Huntington can offer this customer a mortgage at the rate that those with credit scores above the cutoff would receive). The mortgage fund supports mortgages for up to 50 home buyers. By March 2008, $3.5 million in mortgages had been funded, the majority of which could not have been done conventionally. The program has been authorized through 2008, and may continue beyond that date.

If a customer's credit problems are too severe to qualify for the Huntington program, its loan officials refer them to the credit repair and home ownership program offered by Kalamazoo Neighborhood Housing Services (KNHS). "Some people can graduate out of KNHS and come back here. Because of the Kalamazoo Promise, if people start thinking early enough, and their children are young enough, they can do the rehabilitation, they can do the financial literacy to get ready and get into a home. I would be absolutely thrilled as an individual and as part of the community if we somehow were able to approve a deal and get a family or an individual into a household that they may not have otherwise been able to do. And I feel like we've done that."[5]

community in an inclusive discussion of the long-term economic issues presented by this unprecedented initiative."[6] The organizers hoped that this would be a short-term task, with both the narrow and broader convening processes occurring within a three-month period.

With the help of a facilitator, this group, along with some additional members, met again in January and February 2006 for lengthy discussions that focused on the potential of the Kalamazoo Promise as a transformative investment for the region. Among the positive economic development contributions identified were the possibility of reduced expenses for the criminal justice system, freeing up funds that could be more productively spent on economic development; the possibility of intergovernmental cooperation around issues like zoning and public services; and the likely enhancement of the image of Kalamazoo through efforts to position itself as the "Education City"—a community that has come together around the mission of education for all.

Some of the thorniest issues related to the Kalamazoo Promise also surfaced in these early discussions. Participants stressed that if children in the public schools aren't prepared to make use of the Promise, the community won't realize the long-term economic development opportunities the program presents. Cultural change in homes, schools, and neighborhoods would be required, with a higher value placed on academic achievement. Leaders would need to look honestly at issues of racism and economic disparity in Kalamazoo, as well as the lack of trust in the schools and city government harbored by some members of the community.

As the agenda grew beyond the initial question of leveraging the scholarship program for economic development purposes, it became clear that understanding the implications of the Promise, let alone aligning the community around it, would be a far more complex endeavor than first anticipated. (For example, at one of its early meetings the group generated a list of possible investments the community could make to leverage the Promise; there were 19 in all, ranging from helping students complete college and strengthening the area's infrastructure, to marketing the region and providing early childhood education.) To accommodate the expanding agenda, the group identified four strategic priorities, each to be explored by a subset of the larger committee and all embedded in the mission of making education the catalyst for regional vitality. The priorities were

1) to provide outstanding education to all students,

2) to engage the community to ensure every student succeeds,

3) to continue to revitalize the urban core, and

4) to create a "region of choice" for economic development.

On April 20, 2006, the full committee reconvened to hear reports on each subgroup's activities. Craig Misner, then head of the Kalamazoo Regional Educational Service Agency (KRESA), the region's intermediate school district, and Marilyn Schlack, the president of KVCC, had assumed responsibility for the "outstanding education" subgroup (Priority 1). They told the gathering about a meeting that had taken place among the area's three college presidents and 10 school superintendents. The conveners had made the case to their colleagues that the Kalamazoo Promise could serve to promote excellence in school systems across the region, rather than increasing competition among them. Embracing the idea of education as a catalyst for community transformation, the 10 superintendents had agreed to work together to use the Kalamazoo Promise as a positive tool for regional excellence in education, rather than allowing a competition for resources to erupt among them.

Pam Kingery, the head of Kalamazoo Communities In Schools (KCIS), David Gardiner, vice president for community investment at the Kalamazoo Community Foundation, and Pastor J. Louis Felton, president of the Northside Ministerial Alliance, were the conveners of the subgroup on student success (Priority 2). They reported on a March 22 meeting of 27 community organizations committed to thinking and acting cohesively to support students in light of the Kalamazoo Promise. This group became one of the most important drivers of community change in the months ahead.

Mayor McKinney and Mayor Peter Strazdas of the city of Portage had taken charge of the urban revitalization subgroup (Priority 3). Their initial endeavor was a town hall meeting to elicit public comment and allow residents to air their hopes and concerns about the impact of the Kalamazoo Promise. The message delivered by the mayors was that the urban core is not just the city of Kalamazoo, but includes much of Portage and neighboring townships and villages. Mayor McKinney was well acquainted with the economic development challenges posed by Michigan's little-box jurisdictional system, having firsthand experience of the tensions that surface from time to time between Kalamazoo and its neighbors over business subsidies, tax incentives, and the cost of services. One of her concerns was that the primary development impact of the Kalamazoo Promise might occur outside city boundaries (in the townships that are part of KPS) and contribute to greater competition among municipalities. The mayor encouraged government officials throughout the region to "buy in" to the Kalamazoo Promise and use it as a catalyst for collaboration among public sector entities. While not all the municipalities in the region are direct beneficiaries of the scholarship program, they all stand to benefit from any population growth, income growth, or business investment that might materialize in the wake of the Promise.

The regional economic development subgroup (Priority 4) was convened by the W.E. Upjohn Institute's Randall Eberts and David Sanford, acting president of the Chamber of Commerce. They reported on their conversations with business leaders and what they saw as their number one job: to make sure that businesses throughout the county understand the importance of education and its link to economic development and growth. The need for an effective communication strategy, including media outreach, the development of an integrated Web site, and the use of the Kalamazoo Promise as a "branding" tool for the community, would form an important focus of the work of this subgroup going forward.

At the conclusion of the Saturday Morning Group's April meeting, members expressed their intention to "move beyond process" and reconvene two months later with action plans in hand. Momentum at this point shifted to the four subgroups, some of which moved more decisively than others to advance their work. In August 2006, the conveners of the subgroups met for a planning session, although the larger group did not reconvene until September 2007.

How successful was this early steering process, and what did participants have to show for their effort? Much of the energy of the Saturday Morning Group was spent articulating a vision, identifying priorities, and exploring the connections among them. In retrospect, this conceptual work was tremendously valuable and continues to provide

The Kalamazoo Symphony Orchestra
"Harmony in Community"

The Kalamazoo Symphony Orchestra (KSO) was the first of the community's arts organizations to recognize the potential of the Kalamazoo Promise to provide a conceptual framework for its work. In 2007, the orchestra's marketing director, Thom Andrews, proposed to the staff and board a new way of thinking about KSO—as an organization whose goals and activities align with and support the educational and economic goals of the Kalamazoo Promise.

To remain vital, arts organizations continually seek to remain relevant to their communities. "In Kalamazoo, we are extremely fortunate to have a clearly articulated priority and confidence in the unwavering commitment of the community to this priority," says Andrews. "It is *The Promise of a Greater Kalamazoo*—an initiative built on the belief that education is the key to community building . . . The Promise is a long-term effort to convert Kalamazoo's economy from a manufacturing-based economy to a knowledge-based economy and to attract people to move to or return to Kalamazoo."[7]

To support this effort, Andrews proposed that the orchestra think about its activities in terms of the four subgoals of the Promise introduced during Promise Week in December 2006:

1) **Educational excellence**, encompassing the organization's arts-integrated curriculum, musical study opportunities, and youth concerts.

2) **Student success**, encompassing programs that award or honor exceptional musical achievement, provide performance experiences, and encourage musical exploration.

3) **Community vitality**, encompassing performances in Kalamazoo and surrounding communities, including free summer park concerts and collaboration with other arts organizations.

4) **Economic development**, encompassing KSO's economic impact on the region through the employment of staff and musicians, national recruiting efforts, and attraction of people from surrounding counties to the core city for KSO concerts.

Andrews recognized that this four-part framework reflects priorities that will be central to the community for the next generation. "There's really little risk in aligning yourself with this and probably greater risk in not . . . It means that we can dream with confidence."

Among the specific activities undertaken by KSO are using the symphony's opening night concert to promote and facilitate the recruitment of volunteers for community organizations, such as Big Brothers Big Sisters and Kalamazoo Communities In Schools; providing information about the scholarship program at KSO events; devoting the orchestra's January concerts (which often coincide with Martin Luther King Jr. Day) to an annual celebration of the Promise; and honoring school music programs during the symphony's observance of Music in Our Schools Month in March.

"Organizations wishing to be relevant in this community must be engaged in these efforts," says Andrews. "Those who engage strongly now will make the greatest impact in the long term and be in the best position to gain from the growth yet to come."

a robust framework for understanding the multiple challenges involved in a program such as the Kalamazoo Promise. The group's ongoing discussions helped clarify two distinct arenas for change—education (encompassing the first pair of strategic priorities, educational excellence and student support) and economic development (covering the second pair, the urban core and the broader region)—and identify the actors involved in each area. The loose coordinating structure also succeeded in setting in motion more intensive work by two of the four subgroups that had important implications for the community.

Yet as a central organizing structure for community efforts around the Kalamazoo Promise, the Saturday Morning Group had some serious shortcomings. First, and perhaps ironically, was the senior status of the people involved. While many of the community's most respected leaders participated in the process and gave generously of their time and knowledge, the group was made up of individuals who have demanding, full-time jobs, such as running school districts or heading colleges and foundations. The coconvener structure, with eight individuals guiding the process, suffered from the same problem, and without tangible and agreed upon milestones or other mechanisms for holding each other accountable, collective leadership was extremely difficult to sustain. In an effort to circumvent this problem, the coconveners at their August

2006 meeting discussed the idea of appointing a single person to serve as convener and spokesperson for the ongoing organizing process. The group's top pick for the role turned down the invitation because of other commitments, but the idea of finding an individual to act as a guiding hand—a sort of "Promise Czar"—has surfaced periodically since then.

A second shortcoming is that the group was never intended to be either responsive to or representative of the broader community, and this led some to question its legitimacy. In the absence of a designated leadership structure for the Kalamazoo Promise, it was up to the community to organize itself, and the group that assembled on that Saturday morning in December 2005 was largely self-appointed. Initially convened to discuss the regional economic potential of the Kalamazoo Promise, a number of key players were not present, and as the group's mission broadened to address virtually all aspects of economic and community development, their absence became increasingly problematic. Because the group brought together the usual roster of community elites, and because its conversations were carried out in closed sessions, unsure of what, if anything, they might yield, the process also intensified feelings of exclusion and disenfranchisement on the part of some of the community's grassroots leaders.

Perhaps most important, the effectiveness of the Saturday Morning Group was constrained simply by the fact that the real work of organizational alignment and system change cannot be done by a handful of senior leaders meeting every few months. It takes place through a deeper and more intensive process, when organizations and individuals recognize the need for change and implement it from within. Similarly, the idea of appointing a single leader or small steering committee to guide the course of community alignment does not sit well with many who believe that it would be a poor substitute for top-to-bottom (or bottom-to-top) community transformation.

THE COMMUNITY STEPS UP

At the same time that the Saturday Morning Group was working to create an overall framework for achieving the broader goals of the Kalamazoo Promise, grassroots organizations were developing local programs to transform their communities from within. Many of these were centered on Kalamazoo's Northside, a low-income, African American neighborhood adjacent to downtown. Within a few days of the announcement of the Promise, a group of retired educators and other concerned citizens began meeting at one of the area's large Baptist churches to discuss how children from their community could benefit from the Promise. Mentoring programs for area youth were initiated at several neighborhood churches. The Northside Ministerial Alliance's weekly meetings of religious and community leaders became a venue for information sharing about the Promise. Rallies and information sessions were held to mobilize families, assist with college loan applications, and provide information about the requirements for the program.

Because of the timing of the announcement, there was an intense focus on helping the current cohort of high school seniors, already halfway through their final year: "Since the announcement, we've been rushing, literally scrambling, to get them ready for college—get them to fill out college applications and so forth," said the Rev. J. Louis Felton, pastor of Galilee Baptist Church. "Some of these students never considered going to college until now" (Mack 2006f). Dr. Charles Warfield, a professor of education at WMU and one of the community's most respected African American leaders, pointed out some of the challenges these graduates and their parents would face: "Many will be first generation students at schools, which says many of them do not have a clue about what goes on in higher education, how it operates, and how to make its systems work for you." The high cost of textbooks and the meaning of standardized test scores are just two items of concern: "If I'm your professor and I tell you to get these books, and one book costs $100, you walk away saying 'I've got to have $500 here just for books.' Where's that money coming from? And again, just because educators know what the MEAP [Michigan's former standardized test] is does not mean the general public knows what it is. They know their kids take a test every year, but when you say, 'Well you got this MEAP score,' people just look at each other and say 'What's that?'"[8] By bringing together potential first-generation college students and church members with experience in higher education, Northside leaders hoped to arm students in advance with the knowledge they would need to manage the transition to college.

Another dimension of the grassroots response was an outpouring of support from KPS parents, many of whom called their child's school principal directly to ask how they could help. (One parent described the immediate emotional impact of the Kalamazoo Promise as "unimaginable," recounting the "looks of sympathy, pity, and shock" she had received in the past when telling friends or colleagues that her children attended a KPS school.)[9] It was clear immediately that individual schools would not have the capacity to channel the work of volunteers effectively, so KCIS was asked by the school district to coordinate volunteer efforts. (A link on the Kalamazoo Promise Web site under "Get Involved" takes users directly to the KCIS volunteer information form.) "It's extremely critical that volunteers experience success, and that's the specialty of Kalamazoo Communities In Schools," said Superintendent Brown. Timothy Bartik, the then president of the KPS board, concurred: "It's one thing to sign up volunteers. It's another to give them an experience that makes them want to continue to sign up, and still another to give them a project that will do students some good" (Mack 2006g).

To capitalize on the surge in volunteers and begin the process of coordinating the work of multiple community organizations, KCIS announced that a Community Partners Meeting would be held on February 8, 2006. For many, this would be their first opportunity to discuss student needs in the context of the Kalamazoo Promise, and the response was overwhelming. Organizers, who had initially expected 50 people to attend, changed the meeting's location three times to find a space large enough to accommodate all those who were interested. Ultimately, over 150 people were present for a morning-long session devoted to identifying priority needs and developing strategies for getting resources into the schools.

The Community Partners meeting set the agenda for much of the work on student support that would take place over the following year and provided a venue for a diverse set of speakers who crystallized both the opportunities and challenges inherent in the Promise, as the following sampling of comments reveals:[10]

- Superintendent Janice Brown spoke of how the Promise had changed the rules by making every KPS student "college material." The question is no longer "*Are* you going to college? It's

Where are you going to college?" Given the potential of this opportunity to alter students' life prospects, failure is not an option.

- Pastor Louis Felton stressed the need to address not just the ideal vision of Kalamazoo, but also the reality, including the fact that "we live in one of the most segregated communities in Michigan." Another painful reality is that the current educational system has tacitly acknowledged that not every student will succeed. He called on community members to find something in every child that can be awakened and transformed: "Every Kalamazooan should be a donor to the Promise, a partner with, an investor in, a stakeholder in the Promise."

- Von Washington, Jr., at the time principal of the alternative high school, called school a "daily drudgery" for many students. "The kids don't know what this means," he said. "They don't believe it is something for them. Their dreams are very few and very minimal at this point."

- Lauren Daniels-Davies, a junior at Kalamazoo Central High School, shared a list of needs that had been identified in a survey of 120 high school students. Among the priorities mentioned were undisturbed sleep, mentors, a library card, YMCA memberships, alarm clocks, health care, college visits, bus tokens to attend after-school programs, tickets to plays, and help getting an e-mail address—basic needs that many of those in attendance had not thought of.

- Kevin Campbell, the principal of Milwood Middle School, decried the unofficial "tracking" of children as early as kindergarten. "By second or third grade," he told the audience, "some kids are identifying themselves as nonachieving, and they've essentially abandoned literacy by the time they're in middle school. We're trying to convince kids to get on a path that they don't believe they're on." A change in the mindset of both students and teachers is needed if the potential of the Promise is to be realized. "WMU could be in Canada for many kids," said Campbell, speaking of the lack of familiarity many residents have with the higher education resources in their midst. "Their world is their neighborhood."

As attendees discussed student needs in the areas of academic and life skills, mental health and substance abuse, college admission and retention, physical health and basic needs, and parental and family support, the breadth of the issues facing the community began to take shape. Participants recognized that the school district cannot and should not be responsible for meeting all of these needs and that the support of churches and community organizations was essential. Parents, especially, would need to change their mindsets, and if they can't support their children's aspirations, another positive adult relationship must be forged. At the meeting's conclusion, everyone present was asked to submit a Promise Commitment Card asking what resources or services their organization could contribute to the daunting task ahead.

The issues that surfaced at the Community Partners meeting were taken up by the community engagement task force that coalesced a month later as a result of the Saturday Morning Group process. Charged by its conveners with "helping us think and act as one community to help all of our children succeed," this group of two dozen individuals from educational, nonprofit, and social service organizations met regularly from March through August 2006. In its work, the task force relied on consultants funded by the Kalamazoo Community Foundation and the Greater Kalamazoo United Way, who identified high-impact strategies to improve outcomes for students at all developmental levels and undertook a landscape assessment of local organizations in the community already using these strategies. Ultimately, four high-impact areas—parental involvement, in-school health care (including mental health), out-of-school time programming, and mentoring—were identified as key strategies for focusing KCIS resources most effectively.

A second community engagement process was launched in November 2006 under the leadership of Joseph Kretovics, head of the GEAR UP program based at Western Michigan University's College of Education.[11] Those close to the process saw this initiative as a reflection of dissatisfaction with the engagement efforts already under way, particularly the degree of minority representation. Indeed, the group's first meeting drew 40 attendees, many of whom had not taken part in other efforts, and the discussion centered on leadership and whether the current engagement process, including the Saturday Morning Group and the community engagement task force, was sufficiently inclusive. There was general agreement on the need to avoid duplication and build on

Pathways to the Promise: Supporting Children and Families

With professional backgrounds as school psychologists and counselors, Ruby Sledge and Cassandra Bridges can recognize a struggling child when they see one, and their church, Mt. Zion Baptist in Kalamazoo's Northside neighborhood, is a place where the families of many such children worship. In 2001, with financial support from the church, they founded the After School Homework Center to provide local elementary school children with homework assistance, tutoring, and leadership training. The program, which operates four afternoons a week during the school year, draws an average of 40 elementary school children daily. A year later, the church added a Summer Youth Program that offers six weeks of full-day programming that combines a focus on academic skills with the kind of camp experience many of these children have never had, such as tennis instruction, swimming, photography, and arts activities. When the Kalamazoo Promise was announced, the staff and volunteers involved in Mt. Zion's youth ministry activities found a new focus, structure, and energy for their work: they added a teen homework program, as well as a component for parents. The entire set of family support efforts was given a new name: Pathways to the Promise.

Sledge and Bridges drew on their own life experiences in creating Pathways to the Promise. Both women have lived through times of racial, geographic, and socioeconomic tensions. While their parents were not highly educated, they understood that education was critical to the success of their children. The message they passed along is that "success is not based only on whether you have the financial means to further yourself. Children can be successful based on what their parents believe, what they believe, what they do and what they say."[12] The Parent Program seeks to instill this conviction in church families regardless of their income or educational standing. At meetings, parents are asked to create mission and vision statements for their families to help them internalize the message that they are also responsible for their children's outcomes. These statements are used to identify short- and long-term goals and define the respective roles of the parent and child. Discussion of the importance of family structure and rules, as well as the idea that learning is something that goes on in the home every day, has helped parents find ways to be-

come more supportive, consistent, and positive in their interactions with
their children.

Retired and current educators who are members of the church support Pathways to the Promise on a volunteer basis as teachers, mentors,
aides, program evaluators, and counselors. Several small local grants
have also enabled the program to hire local teens as teacher aides and
tutors and provide gift certificates for school supplies and clothing to
families that have participated successfully in the parent program.

Long before the Kalamazoo Promise was created, Ruby Sledge and
Cassandra Bridges acted on their belief that "all children have the opportunity to graduate and go to college. You are smart enough, you have
everything you need. You are going to succeed. There are no excuses."
By using the resources of their church and fellow congregants to connect
families with the support they need, they are making this belief real.

existing infrastructure but a lower degree of consensus over the role
of KCIS. (Some observers point out that WMU faculty and staff were
overrepresented in this group, perhaps indicating the university's desire to become more involved with the Promise, as well as the need
for closer integration between WMU and the broader community.) The
debate shifted when Janice Brown joined the conversation, which was
taking place in a meeting room at the KPS administration building, and
forcefully enjoined the group to embrace KCIS's leadership: "KCIS has
been identified as the lead group for organizing community resources
around students." In her characteristically direct style, Dr. Brown asked
those present, "Are you willing to be led?" And while perhaps not the
most tactful language in a roomful of leaders who had invested years
in building their own organizations, those present seemed willing to
consider the idea. Pastor Milton Wells, leader of the Eastside neighborhood's Open Door Ministries, spoke on behalf of many when he
replied, "We already have a structure; now we have to decide if we're
going to work together."[13]

There were two impediments to KCIS successfully fulfilling this
lead role. First, the organization is funded through private contributions
and grants, and lacks sufficient resources to respond to the new demands being placed on it. The presence of a site coordinator in fewer

than half of the district's school buildings has created a two-tiered system through which services are accessed, as well as varying degrees of resentment by other area school districts whose students are not served by KCIS. Second, some community members distrust KCIS, a few because of negative personal experiences, others because they view the organization as allied with a school district and its leadership that, in their view, had failed to address the needs of low-income, minority children. If stronger leadership were to be placed in the hands of KCIS, it was widely recognized within and outside the organization that these concerns would need to be addressed.

With parallel community-wide engagement processes under way, a coordinated response seemed further out of reach than ever. But subsequent meetings of the GEAR-UP-initiated group led to a general acceptance of the premise that the most effective route to providing young people with support is to have a single organization coordinate services. Two suggestions for addressing community concerns included a broadening of the KCIS board to involve parents and leaders of youth-serving organizations (the organization's board consists mainly of well-connected representatives of business and government agencies), and to ensure that KCIS is able to link children with services delivered through churches and neighborhood organizations, not just the schools.

Ultimately, a document expressing these views was presented to and endorsed by the boards of KPS, KCIS, and the Kalamazoo Regional Chamber of Commerce, and KCIS launched a process of organizing its activities around the four high-impact strategies identified by the community engagement task force. Recommendations were developed for implementing each of the strategies, and advisory groups were formed to guide the implementation process. Kalamazoo Communities In Schools staff members charged with facilitating the groups cast their nets widely, inviting grassroots leaders and practitioners to participate. Each of the advisory group's membership includes a cross-section of human service representatives who meet regularly to coordinate service delivery. The KCIS board also announced an ambitious capital campaign to raise $2.7 million in operating funds for the organization for 2008–2010 in order to support an expansion of its capacity.

While these community engagement processes were unfolding, another effort got under way—this one aimed at a constituency outside of Kalamazoo. In spring 2006, a self-appointed group that included school, government, and community leaders began meeting to explore whether the funding from a major national foundation might be secured to create a systemwide approach to investing in children. Operating on the assumption that Kalamazoo is an ideal laboratory for observing the effects of system change, the group explored the idea of integrating schools and the community into a seamless web of support for children from birth to adulthood. The group did this through

- a customized learning approach that actively engages parents during the first years of school, identifies children who need a designated educational coach to provide continuity for school success, and assists parents in advocating for their children;

- a comprehensive menu of options (e.g., early childhood education, mentoring, health and mental health services, summer study opportunities, tutoring) for parents/guardians to select based on an individual child's educational needs;

- an information system to facilitate the creation and monitoring of a personalized success plan for every KPS child; and

- extended learning opportunities beyond the traditional school day and year for all students who need them.[14]

Working with Jack Hopkins of the Kalamazoo Community Foundation, the group crafted a letter that would be used to contact national foundations interested in youth development and community change in order to assess their interest in the concept. One of the notable features of this exploratory process is that the letter to foundations was signed by leaders of virtually every major educational, governmental, and business organization in the community, suggesting that at least when it came to presenting itself to the outside world, Kalamazoo was able to speak with one voice.[15]

EVOLUTION OF THE KALAMAZOO PROMISE SCHOLARSHIP

While the community was engaging with the implications of the Kalamazoo Promise, the scholarship program itself was evolving. Early on, there was considerable speculation about how the Kalamazoo Promise would be organized: if it was set up as an endowment or made up of annual contributions from the donors, what guarantees were in place that funds would be provided indefinitely, and where the program would be housed? In the first months after the November announcement, the Kalamazoo Promise was run temporarily from the superintendent's office with no dedicated staff. Kalamazoo Public Schools executive director for communications Alex Lee handled press inquiries, and information about program requirements was accessed through the KPS Web site. It is no surprise that there was some confusion about the fact that the Kalamazoo Promise is organizationally distinct from KPS. (The slogan, "The Kalamazoo Promise, kept exclusively at Kalamazoo Public Schools," probably didn't help.)

It was not until March 2006 that the program hired its first dedicated employee, Kalamazoo Promise administrator Robert Jorth. (As of June 2008, Jorth remained the only employee of the organization.) Jorth's official role is to determine eligibility, maintain a database of students eligible for and receiving the scholarship, and paying scholarship funds to colleges and universities. (Like most scholarship programs, funds are paid directly to the schools.) With no precedents available, Jorth had to create his own procedures for carrying out this work. Moreover, the system would need to be flexible enough to accommodate the terms of the scholarship program, especially students' ability to access funds any time within 10 years of high school graduation.

Jorth's background, including 20 years of corporate experience in quality assurance and database programming, as well as a master's degree in public administration, had prepared him well for such a task. The administrative systems he devised have successfully accommodated the complex data needs of the program while keeping the administrative processes streamlined enough to be carried out by one individual. (The Kalamazoo Promise scholarship application form, for example, fits on a single page.) Jorth also took on responsibilities that go well beyond program administration. "I got my bachelor's degree in English and religion, with the intent of going to seminary," says Jorth, "so I've always had this social ministry thing. All this came together with this job—it just seemed to fit my skill set."[16] Along with Janice Brown, Jorth has served as the public face of the Promise, visiting schools, churches, businesses, and community organizations to talk about the program and answer questions. He has called students at home to ask why they haven't filled out their application forms or when they plan to register for classes. He has initiated a mentoring program in which current Kalamazoo Promise recipients support incoming freshmen at their colleges and universities. And he spent part of the summer of 2007 meeting with students who had lost their scholarships due to poor academic performance in order to learn what had gone wrong and how it might be addressed.

Jorth does not know who the donors are, and he interacts with them primarily through Janice Brown. But he is clearly inspired by their gift and fulfilled by his role in implementing it. "I have been just stunned by their generosity," says Jorth, "because every time we've gone back to ask them, it is that they want to give this money out, they want people to take advantage of this. This isn't about trying to narrow it down, which I think was the natural inclination of everyone. You'd go to meetings and people would say, 'Do you have to do community service to qualify? Do you have to do this? Do you have to do that?' No, no, and no. I think [the donors] understand that if this is really going to be an economic development initiative, and they really want to address the core city, then they have to be fairly liberal in their interpretation in order to make it possible for people to qualify and take advantage of it."[17]

In fall 2006, Jorth moved out of the school district building and into an office at KCIS's new downtown facility (a space donated by one of the city's real estate developers). A new Web site was established with its own domain name—https://www.kalamazoopromise.com—and the Kalamazoo Promise was incorporated as a 501(c)(3) organization. With these changes, the Kalamazoo Promise is more clearly positioned as an entity independent of KPS. The program Jorth runs remains a model of efficiency, with a single person tracking the eligibility of more than 11,000 students and disbursing $3 million in scholarships to 20 schools. Administrative costs in the first three years of the program were under 5 percent of annual scholarship dollars. Jorth remained the sole employee of the Kalamazoo Promise organization until September 2008, when Janice Brown joined as executive director. Her role is to help align the community and leverage the broader potential of the scholarship program.

The First Day Shoe Fund:
Meeting Children's Most Basic Needs

While the Kalamazoo Promise generated a wave of new volunteers in the public schools, for some it simply added new urgency to ongoing work. One example is The First Day Shoe Fund, an initiative to provide low-income KPS children in grades K-2 with a pair of new shoes at the beginning of each school year.[18]

The organization was founded by Valerie Denghel, a longtime community resident who initially became involved with KPS as a tutor. "I've always loved to read," says Denghel, "and I figured that I could impart my love of that particular subject to those children who were just starting out. What I found out is that many children were coming to school in shoes that were too big, too small, torn, or worn. Some of them didn't even have shoes, and were kept home because of that fact. So I started to bring a few pairs in at the beginning of the school year and each semester that number grew until I realized I needed help."[19]

With a grant from Bread for the Journey and working through Kalamazoo Communities In Schools (KCIS), Denghel bought and distributed 160 pairs of shoes for low-income students attending summer school in 2005. With shoes left over, she donated the extras to two elementary schools where they would be distributed to kids in need. "I realized we were just scratching the surface," says Denghel.

Inspired by a Community Partners meeting in February 2006 where "a young woman got up and said how wonderful the Promise is, but in order for students to take advantage of it they needed to be ensured basic needs like transportation, food, and clothing," Denghel assembled a board and incorporated The First Day Shoe Fund as a 501(c)(3) organization. In 2006, her organization distributed 307 pairs of shoes; in 2007, the number grew to 691, and in 2008, Denghel expected to give away 950 pairs to children attending summer school. "This allows kids to start the semester on an equal footing with their peers, to participate in gym and play outdoors. We want to expand to the whole county, but we have to start somewhere. We decided to start with KPS not just because of the Promise but also because of the need."

Denghel tells the story of an elementary school student who asked the KCIS site coordinator at her school in January 2007 for a single shoe for her younger brother—over the winter break he had lost one and was being kept home because it was his only pair. The site coordinator had some of

Denghel's shoes left over from the summer and sent a pair home with his sister. After missing almost a week of school the boy was back in class the next day.

"I had this idea and it's no big deal," says Denghel, "but what's important is everyone else who's picked up on it—KPS, KCIS, board members of the First Day Shoe Fund, and all the generous people in the community who have helped us. Not everyone needs to start their own 501(c)(3), and not everyone needs to have a million dollars. You can have a few dollars, you can have time. Time is sometimes more valuable than money. Anyone who's interested in children can become a part of the Promise."

RESEARCH AND EVALUATION ACTIVITIES

Just as KCIS came to play the central role in coordinating student support services, another institution with deep local roots assumed responsibility for coordinating data collection, research, and evaluation efforts around the Kalamazoo Promise. The W.E. Upjohn Institute for Employment Research, founded in 1945 with an endowment from the founder of the Upjohn Company, is an internationally known think tank that focuses on employment issues. As a nonprofit organization with a respected record of nonpartisan research, the Upjohn Institute was the logical place for the school district to turn for assistance with its data needs. A $303,000 grant from the W.K. Kellogg Foundation in nearby Battle Creek, one of the nation's largest philanthropies, played an important role early on, enabling the Upjohn Institute to assist KPS in purchasing a data warehousing system that would allow the district's multiple databases to be accessed through a single interface. (The grant has also supported a variety of research and convening activities around the linkages between education and economic development.) An agreement with the Greater Kalamazoo Association of Realtors that gave the institute access to housing market data, along with its ongoing economic analysis and forecasting role, positioned the Upjohn Institute as the chief conduit for research and data related to the Kalamazoo Promise. But, as with many entities involved in the Kalamazoo Promise, the Institute's role has expanded to meet new needs and opportunities.

One of the Upjohn Institute's first Kalamazoo Promise–related activities was to convene researchers with a shared interest in the program.[20] At three meetings in the spring of 2006, employees of the institute, WMU's Evaluation Center, WMU's School of Education, and other local and visiting academics met to exchange information and discuss data needs and evaluation efforts. (Representatives of KPS were also present at these meetings.) Among the projects to emerge from this ad hoc collaboration was a survey of KPS high school students carried out at the end of the 2005–2006 academic year to assess the initial impact of the Kalamazoo Promise on their plans, and a successful application to the U.S. Department of Education for a grant to evaluate the Kalamazoo Promise. The grant, which provides $348,000 over three years for research carried out by the WMU Evaluation Center, the Upjohn Institute, and the Midwest Educational Reform Consortium based at WMU's School of Education, was made in a category where only 1 in 70 applications was funded, suggesting strong federal policy interest in this local experiment.

The Upjohn Institute also worked closely with an Ann Arbor–based think tank, the Center for Michigan, and local partners to organize a town hall meeting on education and Michigan's economic future held in Kalamazoo in January 2007. The event, which attracted more than 200 local and state business leaders, educators, legislators, and individuals, was convened to explore the importance of education to the state's ongoing economic transformation and consider whether a statewide program modeled on the Kalamazoo Promise should be pursued. In a survey completed at the end of the day-long meeting, conference participants overwhelmingly supported a scaling up of the Kalamazoo Promise (70 percent said it should be offered statewide), although opinions varied on how such a program should be funded and who should pay, with some participants arguing that a statewide initiative would undermine the local economic development impact of a Promise-type program.[21]

A major and unanticipated responsibility of institute staff has been to provide information to other communities that are developing initiatives modeled on the Kalamazoo Promise. The intense national interest generated by the program was one of its least-expected consequences, and no one was quite prepared for the barrage of queries about the scholarship's structure and impact. Along with Janice Brown and Alex

Lee from KPS and Bob Jorth from the Kalamazoo Promise, it was Institute staff that handled most of these inquiries, serving as an ongoing resource for representatives of other communities and local and national press. In line with this effort, the Upjohn Institute created a section of its Web site for Kalamazoo Promise–related information in order to support researchers and other communities seeking a central source of data. In its first year, the Web site had well over 13,000 downloads; by mid-2008, the rate of downloads reached 2,000–3,000 per month.[22]

As the second anniversary of the Kalamazoo Promise approached, the impact of the program had spread far beyond Michigan. With the launch of Promise-type scholarship programs in Denver, El Dorado, Arkansas, and Pittsburgh, and new initiatives being announced almost weekly, the Upjohn Institute initiated discussions about the value of linking these communities into some kind of learning network. A planning meeting in December 2007 brought together community leaders from Kalamazoo with representatives of Promise-type programs in other locales, and in June 2008, more than 200 individuals from more than 80 communities converged in Kalamazoo for PromiseNet 2008—a networking conference designed to bring together and share knowledge among communities that are putting education at the heart of their economic development efforts. The Kalamazoo Promise has continued to attract national, even international, interest. Kalamazoo no longer has a monopoly as a model (PromiseNet 2009 will be held in Denver), but observers still look to the Kalamazoo area as the place where any positive effects of such a program will be the first to materialize.

PROMISE WEEK

To return to the local scene, in the summer of 2006 the members of the Saturday Morning Group working on regional economic development began planning a community-wide event to mark the first anniversary of the Promise. The goals of what became known as "Promise Week" were to celebrate the creation of the scholarship program, to inform community members about the broader vision of education as a catalyst for regional vitality and achievements to date, and to engage the community in future work around this vision. With a short planning window, responsibility for organizing the week's activities was delegated to Blaine Lam of Lam and Associates, a local public relations firm specializing in community development. Lam created several working groups to move the process forward, including teams devoted to community outreach and creative work in support of upcoming events. A special effort was made to reach the city's low-income and minority population through churches and community organizations.

The first annual celebration of Promise Week took place December 6–10, 2006. Events included a town hall meeting attended by approximately 300 people and preceded by an information fair that drew close to 50 nonprofit exhibitors. Smaller sessions included a forum of area economists and a panel of educators. A Web site was created to provide a unified point of entry to the community—http://www.greaterkalamazoo.com—and a community report card, an annual tracking mechanism designed to increase accountability, was distributed. The *Kalamazoo Gazette* published a special supplement about the Kalamazoo Promise's first-year achievements, and area media gave extensive coverage to the events of the week.

One of the few disappointments of the first Promise Week was the small number of minority and low-income parents who attended the town hall meeting and information fair. To explore whether a different model of community convening might be more effective in reaching these groups, the Upjohn Institute contracted with Lam & Associates to organize two neighborhood forums in low-income neighborhoods. Two events focusing on the needs of children were held in the first half of 2007, and both were attended by large contingents of parents and residents. Organizers attribute the showing to the fact that these events took place at public schools within neighborhoods and at a convenient time for parents and families, as well as to the involvement of neighborhood associations and trusted community organizations as sponsors.

The second annual celebration of Promise Week took place from November 10–16, 2007. The planning process began earlier this time, with several groups meeting regularly to move things forward again under the leadership of Blaine Lam. One of the concerns voiced by organizers is that the first Promise Week had been heavier on celebration than on information and engagement. A second concern is that events had highlighted issues related to the core city and school district rather than the broader region. Thus, there was a strong effort from the beginning of the planning process to engage diverse elements of the community in conversation about the benefits of alignment, and to focus on the broader vision of education as a catalyst for regional vitality rather than the scholarship per se. Those involved in the planning also worked to ensure that the community's racial and economic diversity was reflected as fully as possible in the speakers invited to participate and that events were conveniently located, scheduled at appropriate times, and included incentives, such as child care, prizes, and food, to ensure maximum participation.

In retrospect, organizers, who this time included two energetic KPS trustees, along with Blaine Lam and Upjohn Institute staff members, felt that these goals were largely met. The week was billed as an opportunity to "join the conversation," with community events focusing on arts and education, the connection between business and education, and the ways in which the community markets itself to the outside world. In addition, Promise Week included a parent appreciation night sponsored by the Northside Ministerial Alliance, as well as a Promise School and Community Celebration at one of the district's high schools, where books created by students from each KPS school were presented to Dr. Brown on the occasion of her retirement. This event also featured performances by student ensembles and informational tables set up by about 40 youth-serving organizations.

Among the main achievements of the second Promise Week were its regional focus, the substantive nature of most of the discussions, and the involvement of a broad range of community organizations. The Arts Council of Greater Kalamazoo hosted the arts and education conversation, which included panelists from a dozen arts organizations. The business event was sponsored by the Chamber of Commerce, Southwest Michigan First, and KRESA, and featured a productive exchange between educators and representatives of both small and large firms. The external marketing event was hosted by the Greater Kalamazoo Association of Realtors and included presentations by the Convention and Visitor's Bureau, Southwest Michigan First, WMU, and Downtown Kalamazoo Inc. For the third annual Promise Week, scheduled for November 10–14, 2008, planning responsibility was decentralized even further, and events around the theme of "leading by example," highlighting organizations that have already focused on the vision of Kalamazoo as the education community.

While Promise Week has served as a welcome opportunity to reflect on the work that goes on day in and day out by organizations and individuals throughout the region, its substantive contribution to community alignment should not be overstated. Thus far, Promise Week's utility has been mainly to allow the community to pause and take stock of where it stands in relation to the broader vision of the Kalamazoo Promise. As more community organizations become involved, it is likely that Promise Week will continue to serve this purpose.

As the second anniversary of the announcement of the Kalamazoo Promise approached, the Saturday Morning Group reconvened for two meetings. One motiviation was for participants to hear from each other about any progress related to the strategic priorities set forth the previous year. Another was to bring new players into the process in recognition of the leadership changes under way during the previous year, including new school superintendents in Kalamazoo and Portage, a new president at Western Michigan University, and new leadership on the horizon at KRESA and the Kalamazoo Community Foundation.

The meetings, held in September and October of 2007, underscored once again the challenge of community alignment in a decentralized leadership environment. The agenda summarized several principles centering on the idea of education as the cornerstone of quality of life and economic development in the region. The group was asked to consider ways to

- expand the community's focus from the Kalamazoo Promise scholarship program to the principle of educational excellence for everyone,
- find a common purpose for and benefits from collaboration,
- align and leverage community resources, and
- create partnerships organization by organization.

These principles, which had grown out of earlier discussions, could be summed up with the slogan "think regionally but act locally": while unified action on the part of such a diverse community may be unrealistic, the community response to the Kalamazoo Promise will be amplified if organizations do their work with a common goal and direction in mind. Although no one objected to these ideas, the absence of a clear task for the group and a lack of professional facilitation meant that the discussion once again got bogged down in process. Several members expressed frustration at having what they felt was the same conversation that had taken place two years earlier, and some said that they were no longer interested in attending such meetings.

Even so, the meetings gave rise to some honest, even heated, conversation reflecting the reality of the Kalamazoo Promise. Much of this related to what had been revealed by the program's first year of operation, especially a lack of preparedness of many high school graduates for success in college. This problem is most pressing for the local community college, which bears the burden of remediation not just for Kalamazoo Promise recipients but for other underprepared students from throughout the region.

Another point of contention was whether the resources for student support, coordinated through KCIS, should remain focused on KPS or be extended to other districts in the county. On the one hand, KPS is where the largest number of minority, low-income, and underachieving students are found. The district's success is also essential to the vitality of the urban core. On the other hand, if education is to be the cornerstone of the region, the focus cannot be only on KPS; indeed, some of the county's rural districts are in worse shape than Kalamazoo when it comes to graduation rates and test scores. Without tangible incentives for improvement, other districts will be marginalized and the spotlight will remain focused on KPS and the Kalamazoo Promise. In response to this predicament, Craig Misner, the outgoing head of KRESA, presented his idea of assembling a pool of foundation funds that could be used to reward innovative pilot projects in all the county's districts. Yet this proposal was met with skepticism by some who wondered whether philanthropic resources would be spread too thinly and whether such an initiative was duplicative of earlier community efforts.

There was also little consensus over the ongoing role of the group itself. Some members proposed that there be no more meetings, while others suggested the group meet only once or twice a year as a way of "checking in" on the state of community alignment. Still others drew an analogy with previous community organizing efforts, such as assembling the funding needed to build the downtown festival site, and suggested that a small task force be charged with a specific responsibility and meet weekly until it is accomplished. Perennial concerns about representation resurfaced, with an overwhelmingly white, middle-class body once again attempting to steer the response of a community fragmented by race and class. But the question of whether the organizing process should be more inclusive fell victim to the question of what that process should look like and what its overarching purpose should be. Overall, the powerful sense among many that "something" needed to happen was trumped by a lack of consensus over what that should be.

The meetings did yield some important achievements. First, they served as an opportunity to address the reality that many students entering the local community college are woefully unprepared to succeed there—something that has long been the case but that the Kalamazoo Promise has brought to greater light. Every high school graduate or holder of a GED is indeed entitled to *enroll* at the community college, but they are not entitled to stay if they cannot pass their classes. Some students with Kalamazoo Promise scholarships have argued that their scholarships entitle them to remain at KVCC, with the responsibility for remediation falling on the college. KVCC president, Marilyn Schlack, spoke about being caught in a double bind, with the failings of the K-12 system being laid at the doorstep of KVCC, and community-based efforts to support students focusing on the K-12 years rather than a successful transition to higher education. One outcome of this discussion was agreement that the strategic priorities of educational excellence and student support need not only to be coordinated closely with each other, but must extend across the span of students' pre-K–16 education.

The group's members also expressed a belief that if educational excellence is given top priority, the vitality of the urban core and regional economic development will follow. Although this point is debatable, it was striking to hear the region's leading economic development official Ron Kitchens say at the meeting, "We don't have an economic development problem; we have an education problem."[23] (Others might contend that we have a jobs problem that will not be resolved simply through investments in education and student support.)

A third area of consensus was the need to set realistic, measurable, and attainable goals and hold each other accountable for meeting them. Kalamazoo College President Eileen Wilson-Oyelaran asked her fellow members to think about what they would like the community to look like in five years. Should the minority and income achievement gap be cut in half? Should businesses be giving employees time off to attend parent-teacher conferences? What would an "acceptable" college retention rate look like? Should the community expect to see a drop in the school-to-prison pipeline? Rather than promoting lofty and unattainable goals or circling around the same issues over and over, agreement on a limited number of specific goals would be the best avenue for achieving tangible results. While several members agreed to meet to consider some of these indicators and then report back, as of this writing more than one year later, this effort had not yet gotten off the ground.

By the end of the second meeting in the fall of 2007, there was a sense among members that the larger group had played itself out and that a new approach was needed. In retrospect, and not to diminish the value of its work in framing the challenges ahead and facilitating discussion across sectors, the Saturday Morning Group was both too large and too small for effective action—too large to undertake or complete any concrete tasks, and too small to represent or speak for the broader community. As one participant put it,

> Their organizational bias is to find a way to simplify things: 'If only we had one voice. If only we had one vision. If only we had one leader. If only we had one goal. If only we could find one model.' Our community leaders use this approach in their organizations, and it is successful. But education is the most fractured, most political, most difficult to measure and most complex of community issues, so this approach only intensifies the frustrations of unappointed leaders attempting to exert more and more control in a setting in which they have precious little. I'm reminded of the ant on the log floating down the river, proclaiming he's driving it. It's just not possible.[24]

Aligning a community, even a relatively small one, around education as a cornerstone for regional vitality is a vastly more complex undertaking than building a festival site, as hard as that may be. The very complexity of the undertaking is reflected in the four strategic priorities identified by the group early on, which remain a powerful organizing device. Alignment does not require that community members decide whether to focus on KPS to the exclusion of other school districts, or whether helping high school students is a more or less pressing goal than providing college students with support. It does not even mean that education should take precedence over economic development. Rather, if every organization can begin to think regionally and act locally—that is, determine where its interests and priorities lie and, if appropriate, orient its activities with the broader vision in mind—the community will be transformed naturally from within. The challenge of alignment will then shift from resolving turf battles and allocating resources to one of identifying where various actors in the community compete or overlap, and where collaboration is necessary.

As of the summer of 2008, a new process was in place that bodes well for precisely this kind of organic and productive change. With guidance from the W.K. Kellogg Foundation and initial funding from the Kalamazoo Community Foundation, Boston-based consultant Steve Greeley began working to engage individuals and organizations in the Greater Kalamazoo area around the cause of education-based economic development. Greeley's firm, DCA, was founded in 1991 and helps communities build support for large-scale social change.

The process pursued by DCA in Kalamazoo began with conversations with a wide range of leaders (both formal and informal) asking what they would like to see as major areas of collaboration if Kalamazoo is to become a premier educational community. Discussions were held with close to 60 individuals representing parents, students, teachers, workforce development professionals, and community members from the private, public, and philanthropic sectors. From these conversations DCA drew out common themes and aspirations. Chief among these were

- agreement across all sectors with the fundamental premise of the Kalamazoo Promise—that education should be at the center of the region's economic development strategy;
- consensus around the need to do much more to provide educational support to community youth;
- awareness that the community has an abundance of services, but they are largely supported independently and have not been required to collaborate; and
- a hunger to move from process to action.

In a presentation to community leaders in July 2008, the consultants reported that the Promise had accelerated change in Kalamazoo and raised educational advancement to the top of the civic agenda, while drawing increased attention to barriers to progress and work to be done. The engagement process had revealed a shared vision of the community as one in which all students have a love of learning, a solid foundation of school readiness, literacy and learning skills, opportunity to explore their interests and develop their talents, a sense of purpose about their futures and pathways to their goals, positive peer relationships and consistent adult support, and abundant choices for future learning and careers.

They proposed that community members and organizations align their work by "doing what they do best" so that students

- develop the skills that form the foundation for academic achievement and lifelong learning;
- have ready access to high-quality academic reinforcement, opportunities to explore interests and develop talents, and social/emotional support;
- connect learning to earning, develop career objectives, and understand the pathways to realize them; and
- receive help when faced with serious challenges that undermine their ability to learn.

Going forward, DCA recommended the formation of a set of working groups around critical issues related to these goals, such as early childhood development or the education-workforce connection, as well as a defined leadership and advocacy group responsible for promotiong the overall agenda, encouraging resources to flow where they are needed, and influencing policy.

Going forward, Greeley anticipates activity on two levels: The first is a set of working groups to be formed around the issues of early childhood development, including an emphasis on parenting skills; the physical and mental health of school-age youth; out-of-school support, including social, cultural, and academic enrichment; and tightening the connection between educational institutions and the workplace. These groups may build on existing networks, such as the Great Start Collaborative, which already connects organizations interested in early childhood, or they may represent new partnerships established by participating organizations. The second level will consist of a defined leadership and advocacy group made up of community leaders responsible for promoting the overall agenda, encouraging resources to flow where they are needed, and influencing policy. Unlike the Saturday Morning

Group, this coordinating body will have some kind of staff to serve as a liaison between the working groups and the leadership body.

Despite the reluctance of some leaders to commit to yet another consultant-led process (a common structure for Kalamazoo's repeated forays into community change), the lack of concerted action to mobilize collective assets on behalf of the Promise during its first two and a half years generated considerable enthusiasm for DCA's efforts. Especially encouraging was the close alignment of the themes emerging from DCA's work with the priorities of KPS under Dr. Rice's leadership (see Chapter 5). Moreover, Greeley and Rice both recognize that they are engaged in a process with ramifications that extend beyond Kalamazoo. The biggest social challenges facing much of the nation—economic dislocation, rising wealth disparity, continued racial segregation—are all present in Kalamazoo, along with a rich array of institutional assets. With the scholarship program as a catalyst, the greater Kalamazoo region has the potential to deploy those assets decisively and together, and in doing so to serve as a laboratory for other communities. "If we can figure it out here, it can be a model elsewhere," says Greeley, adding that, "The country is watching. If you want to convey that you're happy with the status quo, that's one answer, but if you aspire to something better there are some questions that need to be answered." Change may be complex, but the questions are simple: What do we as a community want every child to have? How can we ensure that every child has the resources needed from birth on to ensure that he or she is a successful learner? How can we ensure that all children are educated in their choices? The responsibility for answering these questions, then implementing the solutions, belongs not just to educational institutions but to churches, community centers, social service organizations, businesses, arts groups, and others, making the challenge of alignment all the more complex but critically important.

Notes

1. In the case of the Denver Scholarship Program, early negative publicity focused on how the program's chief donor became so wealthy; see Raabe (2007). In Pittsburgh, the University of Pittsburgh Medical Center—the main donor to the Pittsburgh Promise—was charged with holding its gift hostage to tax breaks requested from the Pittsburgh City Council; see Boren (2007).

2. This account is current as of September 2008. For updates, see the W.E. Upjohn Institute Web site at http://www.upjohninstitute.org/promise/index.htm.

3. This and other quotes in this section are from the author's interview with Jerry Blaisdell, Huntington National Bank, May 10, 2006.

4. In the November 2007 election, Bobby Hopewell, an African American businessman and longtime commission member, was elected mayor, and Hannah McKinney returned to her previous position on the commission as vice-mayor.

5. Author's interview with Jerry Blaisdell, Huntington National Bank, May 10, 2006.

6. Kalamazoo Promise Planning Session, December 17, 2005, Meeting Review (author's files).

7. This and other quotes in this section from the author's interview with Thom Andrews, March 1, 2007.

8. Author's interview with Dr. Charles Warfield, January 25, 2006.

9. Author's conversation with a KPS parent.

10. This section draws on the author's notes from the Community Partners meeting on February 8, 2006, as well as KCIS's subsequent summary of that meeting.

11. Gaining Early Awareness and Readiness for Undergraduate Programs (GEAR UP) is a federally funded, competitive grant program designed to significantly increase the number of low-income students who are prepared to enter and succeed in postsecondary education. The Midwest Educational Reform Consortium, housed within WMU's College of Education, operates a GEAR UP program in several school districts in southwest Michigan, including Kalamazoo Public Schools.

12. This and other quotes in this section from author's interview with Ruby Sledge and Cassandra Bridges, Mt. Zion Baptist Church, August 9, 2007. Thanks to Bridget Timmeney for her assistance with this section.

13. Reverend Milton Wells of Open Door Ministries, comment at a meeting of community organizations, November 8, 2006.

14. From final national foundation letter template, March 29, 2007.

15. The letter's signatories represented the city of Kalamazoo, KPS administration and trustees, Kalamazoo College, Kalamazoo Community Foundation, Kalamazoo Communities In Schools, Kalamazoo Regional Chamber of Commerce, KVCC, Northside Ministerial Alliance, Southwest Michigan First, W.E. Upjohn Institute for Employment Research, and Western Michigan University.

16. Author's interview with Robert Jorth, July 18, 2006.

17. Ibid.

18. See http://www.firstdayshoefund.org.

19. This and other quotes in this section from the author's interview with Valerie Denghel, founder of The First Day Shoe Fund, June 6, 2007.

20. The Upjohn Institute also made a grant to the author of this book in January 2006 to follow the community's progress in responding to the Kalamazoo Promise.

21. For more information, see material posted on the Web site of the Center for Michigan: http://www.thecenterformichigan.net/blog/education-michigans-economic-future.

22. As of December 31, 2007 (first 11 months), 21,192 page views and 13,011 downloads were recorded.

23. Ron Kitchens, chief executive officer of Southwest Michigan First, comment at Saturday Morning Group meeting, September 29, 2007.

24. Private e-mail to author.

5
Impact on Students and Schools

In the months following the unveiling of the Kalamazoo Promise, a growing number of communities, large and small, announced plans to develop their own programs inspired by what was happening in Kalamazoo. The first cities to signal their intentions did so only a few months after the introduction of the scholarship program. These included Newton, Iowa, a company town adjusting to the imminent departure of the Maytag Corporation; Hammond, Indiana, a shrinking industrial city on the south shore of Lake Michigan; and Flint, Michigan, the distressed former home to General Motors' main production facilities and the setting for Michael Moore's movie *Roger and Me*. Leaders in these communities saw in Kalamazoo something akin to their own challenges and recognized the potential of the scholarship program to transform both a struggling school system and a troubled economy.

By the first anniversary of the Kalamazoo Promise in November 2006 the floodgates had opened, with city after city announcing its own version of the program. From large, industrial cities in the Northeast to small, resource-dependent towns in the South, this movement was reinforced by two local indicators released in the summer and early fall of 2006: an enrollment jump of close to 10 percent over the previous year for KPS, and an apparent increase in housing prices within the district. Newspapers across the nation printed leads like this one, which appeared in the Warren, Ohio, *Tribune-Chronicle* (2007): "Since the 'Kalamazoo Promise' began in November 2005, the school district has had the biggest enrollment growth in the state, and home prices rose 6.8 percent, even though the rest of Michigan has seen home prices decline."

These two developments—the reversal of an urban school district's long-term enrollment decline, and the potential economic benefits of a scholarship program as reflected in the real estate market—offer an ideal rubric for assessing the initial impact of the Kalamazoo Promise. This chapter surveys what has happened to Kalamazoo's students and schools as an immediate result of the Promise, while Chapter 6 turns to the question of economic impact.

ENROLLMENT GROWTH IN THE KALAMAZOO
PUBLIC SCHOOLS

Much of the national and local media coverage of the Kalamazoo Promise has emphasized its impact on individual students and their families, but the most immediate beneficiary of the scholarship program was the school district itself. Within a few days of the announcement of the Kalamazoo Promise, KPS officials had received more than 100 e-mails and phone calls from families interested in transferring into the district. While the assumption of an enrollment increase was widely shared, it was anyone's guess what its size and distribution might be.

One of the annual challenges for public school administrators is to forecast how many students will show up for the first day of school. Advance registration is not required, and public schools are legally bound to accommodate any student residing in a district even if he or she arrives in the middle of the semester. So, planning for a new school year—including decisions about class size, teachers, and bus routes—is a complex endeavor. With an unprecedented intervention such as the Kalamazoo Promise, the exercise was all the more difficult.

During the summer months of 2006, KPS officials publicly projected a net increase of 450 students over the previous year. Instead, 1,040 more students were enrolled in class for the September 27, 2006, head count that largely determines state funding, bringing the district's total enrollment to 11,212, up 10 percent over the previous year. The "blended count" (based on a combination of enrollment from September and the previous February) was 10,993, an increase of 899 students, or 8.4 percent. As Figure 5.1 shows, this increase marked the reversal of a long-term downward trend in KPS enrollment that, at its high point in the late 1960s, had reached 18,956 before falling to 10,187 in 2004–2005, the year before the Promise was announced.[1] In reality, the enrollment figures represented an even larger shift, since two years earlier the district had lost 500 students and in a typical year district officials would have projected an annual loss of 350 (Associated Press 2006a). In fact, as the Warren *Tribune-Chronicle* had reported, the numerical increase in KPS students was the largest increase in enrollment in 2006 among Michigan's 552 school districts. (In percentage

Figure 5.1 Long-Term KPS Enrollment Trend

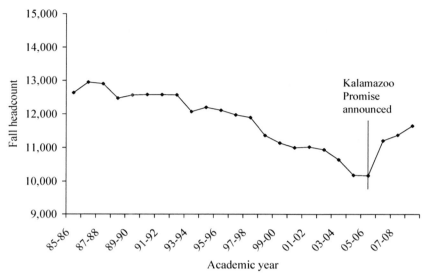

SOURCE: Data provided by KPS.

terms, the district ranked fourth among systems with at least 50 students [Mack 2007a]).

The rise in enrollment, although twice as high as projected, was accommodated relatively smoothly. Much of the increase came in elementary school buildings where there was room to expand, and the district had purchased extra materials, outfitted additional classrooms, and lined up substitute teachers in case its estimates had been too cautious. In addition to the 71 teachers hired before the beginning of the school year (a number that includes replacements for retiring teachers), another 29 teachers were hired after classes had started. The addition of several new bus routes completed the transition picture. While the first few weeks of the term were reportedly a bit chaotic in the more crowded buildings, the adjustment period was short lived.

Gains in enrollment were spread throughout the district, with most at the elementary level where the number of students increased by 12.8 percent over 2005. Middle school enrollment rose by 5.2 percent and high school enrollment by 6.8 percent. Double-digit percentage increases occurred in 9 of the district's 16 elementary schools, with especially large gains at schools in mixed-income neighborhoods and at two magnet schools.[2] Maple Street Magnet School for the Arts was the only middle school to register a substantial enrollment jump (15.6 percent), while Kalamazoo Central High School grew by 11.4 percent and Loy Norrix High School by 2.1 percent. The district's alternative schools also grew in size, including the Reach and Teach program for students who have been expelled, where enrollment rose 21.3 percent, from 61 to 74 students.[3]

The monetary value of the new students in terms of the state's per-pupil foundation grant of $7,556 was $6.8 million.[4] The costs associated with the larger student body in terms of staffing, supplies, and transportation amounted to $4.1 million, which meant that KPS did not have to cut its budget for the first time in many years. Deputy Superintendent Gary Start has been preparing the district's budgets since 1983, when enrollment stood at about 12,500. "I've done a lot of budget cuts," says Start, explaining the vicious circle that until 2006 had affected Kalamazoo along with almost every other urban school system in Michigan. "Urban districts throughout the state are declining enrollment districts. All urban districts are subject to constant budget cutting, and what that creates is a downward spiral. You lose students so you cut the budget because you don't have the money, and the act of cutting the budget—be it adversarial negotiations or budget cuts (like closing buildings)—that creates a loss of more students, which means you cut again."[5] Over the seven years prior to the Kalamazoo Promise, KPS had to trim about $20 million from its budget (the 2006–2007 annual budget was $103 million), with finances made even tighter by increases in the cost of health care premiums, teachers' pensions, and energy prices. These nondiscretionary increases required the district to reduce program services simply to pay for ongoing fixed costs. As Dr. Brown commented about a promised increase in state funding of $250 per student that had been budgeted for 2006–2007, "I'm getting supposedly $250 more per kid per year. That $250 is going right into my adults."[6]

The Kalamazoo Promise eased this financial bind, but only slightly. As Start points out, in school budgeting there is often a misperception about the connection between available resources and what they actually buy; for example, 10 new teachers spread across 25 school buildings will make only a dent in class sizes. For 2006–2007, approximately 1 percent of the total budget, or $1.7 million, was available for new programs and additional teachers. "It's way better than a $5 million cut," said Start before the budgeting process began, "but the other side of the coin is that I'll be seriously lobbied with all kinds of great ideas to spend money. The belief that there is lots and lots of money and we can do anything we want could even make budget negotiations more difficult than in the past."[7] In fact, the school board faced a major challenge in deciding how to allocate the available funds, with the administration proposing four new programs, only two of which could be funded (see below).

Assessing the enrollment impact of the Kalamazoo Promise is made more complex by the need to account not only for new students but also for those who have opted not to leave. "One of the biggest factors [in rising enrollment] is that people are choosing to stay," explains Start. "Where we had a lot of students exiting before, now they're staying."[8] The number of KPS residents who sought waivers to enroll in other public school systems in the region, which historically had averaged 350 a year, declined to 248 the year after the Promise was announced. And the fall-to-winter head count for 2006–2007 showed a net loss of 131 students, well below historical levels of 250–350 per year. The conclusion of the 2006–2007 academic year brought more positive news, when KPS granted diplomas to 567 graduating seniors, up 10 percent over the previous year. Especially notable was a 31 percent rise in the number of African American students graduating.

ENROLLMENT IMPACT ON NON-KPS SCHOOLS

When the Kalamazoo Promise was announced, one of the first concerns voiced by observers was the potential negative impact on neighboring school districts, as well as private and charter schools. Kalamazoo County, with a population of 240,000, encompasses nine separate school districts, and their proximity to each other means that families living in one district can switch to another by moving only a few miles in any direction. This easy mobility is one of the factors that facilitated flight out of Kalamazoo and contributed to KPS's past enrollment decline. With the Kalamazoo Promise providing a substantial incentive for families with school-age children to move into KPS, neighboring school districts feared that the scholarship program might reverse this pattern of outward migration. Kalamazoo is also home to many families that have opted out of public school altogether, choosing private or parochial schools or homeschooling, and there was uncertainty about whether the new incentives provided by the Kalamazoo Promise would draw some of these students into the public school district.[9]

Early evidence suggests that KPS's enrollment increase did not come solely, or even primarily, at the expense of neighboring districts. An examination of the data for students entering KPS in fall 2006 showed that they came from 88 different Michigan communities and 32 different states.[10] Almost half of the newly entering students had moved to the district from outside Kalamazoo County, suggesting that the Promise had brought a substantial number of new families to the county. But with about 500 students transferring into KPS from neighboring public, private, or charter schools, much of the first-year enrollment impact resulted from a shift in the distribution of students and families throughout the region rather than growth in their number. (The economic impact of population shifts is discussed in the next chapter.)

The increase in enrollment was especially pronounced within the broader regional context. Twenty of the 33 school districts in southwest Michigan reported enrollment declines from the previous year, and 8 of those reported a drop of at least 3 percent. Some of this decline was simply a continuation of ongoing trends related to the weak economy and population loss. But some of it was also due to the impact of the Kalamazoo Promise. One of the steepest drops came in the Comstock public school district that borders Kalamazoo; it lost 274 students, or 9.4 percent of its enrollment. Of these, 85 transferred into KPS. Parchment, a second school district that lost students, is also contiguous with KPS. In these communities, a new school district can be accessed by moving across the street or down the block—an especially easy choice for renters who don't need to worry about selling their homes in a depressed real estate market. In the past, such shifts have resulted in net losses for KPS and increased enrollment for Comstock and Parchment, whereas in 2006 the direction was reversed.

The only school district in the region of comparable size to KPS is Portage Public Schools, which for years had been the district of choice for many middle-class families with young children. While Portage experienced a decline of 212 students to 8,649, this amounted to only

2.3 percent of its enrollment. In the fall of 2008, net enrollment in the Portage Public Schools was down by only 12 students.[11] Portage Public Schools officials say that job losses at Pfizer were as important a factor as the Kalamazoo Promise and, indeed, KPS records showed only 70 students from the city of Portage entering KPS in 2006.

It was expected that the Kalamazoo Promise would hit private and charter schools especially hard, and the numbers bore this out. Most of the private and parochial schools in the area suffered enrollment declines, although these too had been under way for some time and reflected economic conditions as well as competition from KPS. Enrollment at the area's Christian and Catholic school systems, each of which serves over 1,000 students, fell about 6 percent in 2006–2007 over the previous year. Two of the four small, secular private schools were down in size, while the third held steady and the fourth expanded slightly with the addition of a new facility. The steepest enrollment decline in the area—21.9 percent, or a loss of 84 students—was experienced by Kalamazoo Advantage Academy, a public charter school that had become one of the schools favored by low-income African American families because of its small class sizes, an emphasis on discipline (including the wearing of uniforms), and parental dissatisfaction with levels of minority student attainment in the public schools. The Kalamazoo Promise, as well as the perception of improvement in the public schools, changed the calculus for many low-income families who were now willing to give the public schools another try.[12]

In August 2007, Kalamazoo Advantage Academy responded to the drop in enrollment by announcing that it would provide its students with college scholarships equivalent to that percentage of the Kalamazoo Promise they would forfeit by attending the charter school for grades K-8. The Gift for Tomorrow program, offered by Mosaica Education Inc., the company that operated the school, would cover 35 percent of college tuition for students who attended for all nine years instruction is offered, thereby eliminating the financial incentive that would motivate Advantage Academy parents to move their children to KPS before high school. Few people understood this as a business decision that made excellent financial sense for Mosaica. Charter schools receive the state foundation grant per student enrolled each year (for 2007–2008 the amount was $7,638). The total financial loss in operating funds to Kalamazoo Advantage Academy for the 2006–2007 school year was thus in the neighborhood of $650,000. If the charter school were able to retain a single student for his or her first nine years of school, that would be worth almost $70,000 (at current state funding levels). If that child did attend KPS for grades 9-12, then decided to go to college, the 35 percent portion of the scholarship for which Mosaica would be responsible would have been calculated after all other sources of financial aid were applied for and would amount to a trivial sum compared to what the company had received to educate that child. (As it turns out, the Gift for Tomorrow program is now useful mainly by way of illustration, since Kalamazoo Advantage Academy lost its charter due to poor test scores and declining enrollment, and closed its doors before the 2008–2009 academic year began.)

It is hard to disentangle the multiple reasons for the enrollment declines experienced by non-KPS schools. While the Kalamazoo Promise was clearly a factor, it was probably no more significant than the restructuring of local firms and a struggling state economy that has forced many families to leave Michigan to find jobs. Of course, these economic factors are also a drag on any potential enrollment increase for KPS. In September 2007, KPS experienced its second consecutive enrollment gain, but of a much smaller magnitude than the previous year, with net new enrollment of 166 students or 1.5 percent over the previous year. Enrollment grew by 276 students, or 2.4 percent in 2008—a number that included many former students from the charter school that had closed. Observers agree that, despite the attraction of the Kalamazoo Promise, enrollment will not increase substantially until the local economy improves. "I think there's a real desire for folks to come here, but no jobs to fund that desire," KPS spokesman Alex Lee has said (Mack 2007b). But even the more modest increases of 2007 and 2008 and their distribution across the grade levels have meant that an elementary school building taken out of use in 2003 returned to its former status and is now home to four kindergarten classes from a nearby school. This recommissioning of one of the many school buildings that had fallen out of use as enrollment in KPS declined is a small but potent sign of a public school system that appears to have turned the corner in terms of enrollment.

WHO IS USING THE KALAMAZOO PROMISE?

In its simplest incarnation, the Kalamazoo Promise is about creating incentives for KPS graduates to extend their education beyond
high school. The nature of this incentive, however, varies according to
a student's educational aspirations and family income. In other words,
while the Kalamazoo Promise can be said to offer something for everyone, that "something" is not the same for everyone. Pam Kingery, executive director of Kalamazoo Communities In Schools, which serves
students at many different levels of need, is an astute observer of this
tiered effect. While she believes that all of the following groups will
benefit from the Kalamazoo Promise, she points out that the nature of
those benefits will vary.[13]

- For middle- and upper-middle-class students who already plan to
  go to college, the availability of the Kalamazoo Promise allevi-
  ates much of the debt burden they and their families will face and
  frees up college savings for other purposes, including graduate
  school.

- For middle-class students who may not be sure about college, the
  Kalamazoo Promise creates a tangible incentive for them at least
  to consider postsecondary education, while encouraging full-
  time attendance and alleviating the need many college students
  have to work full time.

- For the children of working-class families who aspire to go to
  college but for whom the financial barriers are too high, the Kalamazoo Promise creates a new set of opportunities. ("If we do
  this well and create some other supports to help them navigate
  the system, I think we will mobilize another group of this working-class, first-generation population," says Kingery.)

- For low-income students, the Kalamazoo Promise opens up a
  new sense of possibility and hope, especially for younger children who may lack college-going role models in their own families but who will now spend their K-12 years in a school system that expects them to continue their education beyond high
  school.

Kingery is most concerned about those students who are so far behind in terms of their academic skills that they can't attempt college without serious intervention. "If we don't figure out how to remediate that, we won't have really fulfilled the true potential of the Promise," says Kingery.

Not only does KPS's diverse student body complicate the task of providing support to students, it also complicates the analytical task of assessing the Kalamazoo Promise. It is not enough to ask how many students receive a scholarship or what schools they choose to attend. Instead, any evaluation of the program's impact must address what these students would be doing in the absence of the scholarship. Would they be attending less expensive schools, or perhaps be living at home instead of on campus? Would they be working full or part time while in school? How much debt would they or their parents be assuming if the scholarships were not available, and how might this affect their subsequent career and educational choices? Has the scholarship limited the choices of students who now feel compelled to attend in-state or public universities? In investigating these questions, it is also critical to keep in mind the long-term nature of the program, which is set up to continue in perpetuity. The impact on student options and decision making may be quite different a decade or two after the program's introduction than it is in its early years.

With these caveats in mind, the analytical task begins with an examination of who used the Kalamazoo Promise in the first three years it was offered. As Table 5.1 shows, of 517 graduates in the class of 2006, 409 were eligible to receive scholarships based on their KPS residency and attendance. Some of those eligible did not apply for the scholarship either because they did not plan to attend college, had already decided to attend a private or out-of-state school, or had received scholarships from other sources. Forty students had their applications approved on appeal.[14] Among those eligible, 73 percent (or 303 students) used their scholarship to enter college in fall 2006. Data for the class of 2007 and class of 2008 show gradually improving results, with increasing rates of eligibility and scholarship usage in the first semester following graduation. A different set of numbers suggests the value of the scholarship program's flexible terms of use. By the fall of 2008, 342 students or 83.6 percent of eligible students from the class of 2006 had used some portion of their scholarship, as had 405 students or 80.8 percent from

Table 5.1 Kalamazoo Promise Summary Data

	2006	2007	2008	Total
Number of KPS graduates	517	579	548	1,644
Eligible for the Promise	409	501	474	1,384
% of graduates eligible for the Promise	79.1	86.5	86.5	84.2
Number of graduates using the Promise the first semester after graduation	303	359	370	—
% of eligible students using the Promise the first semester after graduation	72.7	74.6	78.1	—
Number of graduates who have used the Promise[a]	342	405	370	1,117
% of eligible students who have used the Promise[a]	83.6	80.8	78.1	80.7

[a] Students who have used at least some portion of their scholarships as of fall 2008.
SOURCE: Data provided by Kalamazoo Promise administrator.

the class of 2007. This suggests that while most Kalamazoo Promise users begin college immediately after graduation, others are entering postsecondary institutions a year or two after graduation.

In a July 2006 editorial, the *Kalamazoo Gazette* noted the high proportion of students planning to attend college, calling it "amazing," especially since the Kalamazoo Promise had been announced only nine months earlier. "Many at-risk students—those who come from low-income families with low levels of educational achievement—certainly were not even thinking about college when they woke up on November 10, 2005, the day the Promise was announced . . . It is astonishing how a rare opportunity like this can make young people with few prospects suddenly begin to envision a life of greater possibilities and shift gears quickly" (*Kalamazoo Gazette* 2006a).

With only three years of data, it is early to detect patterns in usage, but several interesting findings have already emerged. First, while the demographic profile of students eligible for Kalamazoo Promise scholarships closely matches the demographic profile of the graduating class, eligible students have used the scholarship at different rates depending on their race and gender. As Table 5.2 shows, female graduates have used the Promise at a slightly higher rate than male graduates and with one exception (African American females from the class of 2006), African American students, both male and female, have used

Table 5.2 Demographic Data for Kalamazoo Promise Users

Class	Number of graduates	Eligible for the Promise	% of graduates eligible for the Promise	Number of graduates who have used the Promise[a]	% of eligible students who have used the Promise[a]
2006	517	409	79.1	342	83.6
Female	247	196	79.4	170	86.7
African American	94	72	76.6	64	88.9
Hispanic	21	17	81.0	12	70.6
Caucasian	128	106	82.8	93	87.7
Male	270	213	78.9	172	80.8
African American	101	71	70.3	52	73.2
Hispanic	14	11	78.6	9	81.8
Caucasian	147	124	84.4	107	86.3
2007	579	501	86.5	405	80.8
Female	303	265	87.5	215	81.1
African American	130	113	86.9	84	74.3
Hispanic	15	13	86.7	13	100.0
Caucasian	148	133	89.9	114	85.7
Male	276	236	85.5	190	80.5
African American	129	104	80.6	82	78.8
Hispanic	9	8	88.9	6	75.0
Caucasian	126	115	91.3	96	83.5
2008	548	474	86.5	370	78.1
Female	263	230	87.5	183	79.6
African American	128	108	84.4	85	78.7
Hispanic	8	7	87.5	3	42.9
Caucasian	119	108	90.8	89	82.4
Male	285	244	85.6	187	76.6
African American	117	97	82.9	65	67.0
Hispanic	16	15	93.8	11	73.3
Caucasian	144	125	86.8	105	84.0
Total	1,646	1,384	84.1	1,117	80.7

[a] Students who have used at least some portion of their scholarships as of October 2008.
SOURCE: Data provided by Kalamazoo Promise administrator.

the scholarship at a lower rate than white students. When it comes to socioeconomic level, the pattern of scholarship usage matches closely the demographics of the graduating class. For example, 33.5 percent of Promise users from the class of 2006 came from low-income families (as measured by eligibility for the federally subsidized lunch program), relative to 34.9 percent of low-income graduates in the class of 2006 overall. For the class of 2007, 31.3 percent of Promise users were classified as low-income, relative to 36.9 percent of the graduating class.[15]

A second finding is that the overwhelming majority of Promise users have opted to enroll at local institutions. A full 70 percent of scholarship recipients from the class of 2006 attended either WMU or KVCC (see Table 5.3). While this number seemed high to many observers, it was less surprising in light of WMU's free room and board offer, which drew students who might otherwise have gone elsewhere, including to more selective schools, such as Michigan State University or Kalamazoo College. KVCC, which is open to all high school graduates, was the school of choice for many of those students who did not have college plans at the time the Promise was announced. Yet the pattern recurred in subsequent years, even though WMU's free room-and-board offer was not renewed, and by fall 2008, over 60 percent of Kalamazoo Promise recipients were enrolled at a local institution (see Figure 5.2). The pattern of strong local scholarship use suggests that many students are opting to remain close to home, whether for financial reasons or because of their familiarity with local institutions. It also provides a direct economic benefit to the local economy and means that the costs of the program have been lower than anticipated (KVCC tuition is substantially lower than tuition at the state's four-year universities). The other two largest recipients of Promise students have been the state's two leading universities, the University of Michigan and Michigan State University. A dramatic rise in the number of KPS graduates attending the University of Michigan—from just 12 in 2005 to 49 in 2008 (Mack 2008a)—suggests that many of the district's most academically talented graduates are opting to use their scholarships to attend the state's premier educational institution rather than go out of state or opt for a private college.

Of course, the value of the Kalamazoo Promise lies not just in being admitted to college but in succeeding once there. The third early finding is that during the first two years of the program, college persistence rates for Kalamazoo Promise students were in line with national

Table 5.3 College and University Attendance by Kalamazoo Promise Users, Fall Semester 2008

School	Total	Percentage
Four-year universities		
Central Michigan University	17	2.0
Eastern Michigan University	9	1.1
Ferris State University	21	2.5
Grand Valley State University	20	2.4
Michigan State University	105	12.6
Michigan Technological University	8	1.0
Northern Michigan University	9	1.1
Oakland University	2	0.2
Saginaw Valley State University	2	0.2
University of Michigan	95	11.4
Western Michigan University	242	29.0
Wayne State University	14	1.7
Total four-year universities	544	65.2
Community colleges		
Glen Oaks Community College	2	0.2
Grand Rapids Community College	4	0.5
Kellogg Community College	3	0.4
Kalamazoo Valley Community College	272	32.6
Lansing Community College	4	0.5
Lake Michigan College	1	0.1
Washtenaw Community College	4	0.5
Total community colleges	290	34.8
Combined total	834	

SOURCE: Kalamazoo Promise administrator.

norms, with 59 percent of scholarship recipients from the class of 2006 still enrolled in school in fall 2008.[16] However, retention rates varied widely across the schools attended by Promise recipients.[17] Academic performance by the first group of Kalamazoo Promise recipients attending a four-year university during their freshman year (2006–2007) was within the norm for all first-year students at these institutions. None of the 18 students attending the University of Michigan lost his or her scholarship. At Michigan State University, 3 of 31 Promise users (or 8 percent) had their scholarships suspended in the fall of 2007 and 3 more

Figure 5.2 Number of Kalamazoo Promise Users Attending Local Institutions, Fall 2008

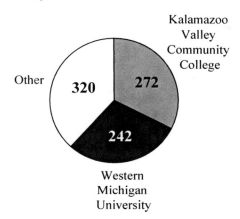

SOURCE: Kalamazoo Promise administrator.

received warnings. At WMU, 13 of 104 Promise users (or 12.5 percent) had their scholarships suspended while another 15 received warnings. At the local community college, however, the percentages were much higher, with two-thirds of Promise users unable to maintain a 2.0 GPA.

In fall 2008, 51 percent of class of 2007 users who started at a community college were in good academic standing, compared to 87 percent of class of 2007 users who started at a university.[18] This gap suggests the widely varying degrees of college readiness of KPS graduates and poses a major challenge for the school district. But freshman retention rates reflect more than simply a student's academic preparedness. Bob Jorth's conversations with Kalamazoo Promise recipients on probation and those who lost their scholarships suggest that many of these students were overextended, taking too many classes and working too many hours at one or more jobs. In 2008, rules requiring full-time college attendance by Kalamazoo Promise users were changed to permit students at KVCC to attend part-time. (Part-time attendance at other institutions is allowed on a case-by-case basis.) For other students, their grades had foundered on a lack of appreciation of the demands of college-level work or poor time management skills. Still others responded to the freedom of a college setting by choosing not to study or go to class, suggesting a low level of social and emotional preparedness. Thus, strategies to improve college success for KPS graduates must include not only stronger academic preparedness but also the acquisition of skills that many children of college graduates take for granted.

At KVCC, where the need for remediation is highest, a number of such strategies have been put in place. The school has a transitional studies program for students who need support in basic skills, including a course called College Success Strategies, which focuses on reading comprehension, note taking, outlining, time management, research skills, and test awareness. Students in the district's high schools can dual-enroll in these courses before graduation to help them prepare for a smoother transition to college. Once at KVCC, they have access to the Student Success Center, inaugurated in 2007, which offers traditional services such as tutoring and career counseling, while also helping students with practical needs like financial planning, transportation, and child care. Other colleges provide varying levels of support to incoming freshmen. Some schools have summer preparatory programs for students who are the first in their families to attend college. At Michigan State University, incoming students may be required to take remedial courses as part of the condition of admission, and students on probation are required to meet with an academic adviser who connects them with support services. At other schools, support systems are available but not mandatory. Western Michigan University, for example, offers tutoring, mentoring, counseling, career and graduate school planning, and other resources designed to enhance a student's education and success, but there is no automatic referral system for struggling students.

Students in the class of 2006 were privileged to be the first to receive the scholarship, but they were also disadvantaged in having so little time to accommodate to the new reality. The sudden introduction of the Kalamazoo Promise six months before graduation affected students in varying ways. Some chose to attend more expensive schools or live away from home because tuition costs would now be covered. Others opted for a public in-state university over a private college or out-of-state school. Still others gave up their places at more selective institutions to accept WMU's room-and-board offer. The most difficult decisions were those faced by students who had never intended to go to college. Presented with the potential for a full scholarship as their K-12 education neared its end, some scrambled to get into schools with competitive admissions policies while others opted for community college with open enrollment policies. Others abandoned their plans for military service now that their college education would be free.

The announcement of the program also stimulated some changes in attitude about high school and college. A survey of KPS high school students given six months after the Promise was introduced found that almost half the students reported that teachers were expecting more from them and that the availability of information about higher education opportunities had increased. One-third of the students surveyed said they were working harder in school because of the Promise, and more than 20 percent indicated in written responses that the Promise had changed their life by making college a possibility (Miron, Spybrook, and Evergreen 2008). For many students, the Kalamazoo Promise did not mark the critical dividing line between college and no college, but it did ease their concerns about the financial strain of higher education. "It gave me more confidence and reassurance that I really could go to college and be a nurse without having to worry about so much debt," wrote one student (p. 7), while another commented, "Now I can afford to go to college and still afford to take care of my daughter" (p. 18).

Much remains to be done to ensure that students fully understand the implications of the Kalamazoo Promise. Stories shared by students both publicly and privately suggest a lingering misconception of the terms of the scholarship. Despite plentiful information to the contrary, some students still believe they have a guaranteed right to go to the college of their choice, not understanding that they need not only to graduate from high school but also earn the grades needed for admission and remain in good academic standing once enrolled. "Students now think they can slide through and get mediocre grades," said Jaquay Ollie, a 17-year-old senior at Kalamazoo Central. "Work ethic in the schools is starting to diminish. Students see this as a gift you don't really need to earn." Other students have adopted the attitude that they won't need to work hard once they get to college because "it's not their money" (Tibor 2007). Some of the attitudinal changes have been more positive. Sherry Ransford, a high school English teacher at Kalamazoo Central who retired in 2008, commented that her more advanced students were palpably more relaxed and less competitive during the college-admission and financial aid season since the Promise had been announced. In past years, students would apply to colleges but until financial aid packages were announced would have no idea whether or not they would be able to afford to attend. With the financial pressure removed, the focus shifted to getting into the best school possible and the extent of competition with one's peers was eased. On the other hand, Ransford noted that even as soon as the second year, students seemed to have shifted from seeing the Kalamazoo Promise as a gift to more of an entitlement.[19]

ENSURING STUDENT SUCCESS

In August 2007, Michael Rice, former superintendent of the Clifton, New Jersey, public school district became superintendent of KPS. Superintendent Janice Brown had announced her retirement in December 2006 after serving in the position since 2000.[20] Dr. Rice moved quickly to establish his priorities for the district and enlist community support for them. Within weeks of the beginning of his term, KPS contracted with Phi Delta Kappa, a national education organization, to conduct a curriculum audit that would assess the district's strengths and weaknesses in comparison to national standards. In his first months on the job Dr. Rice created advisory councils of staff members, union leaders, parents, and students with whom he meets monthly. He launched a strategic planning process to develop year-by-year expectations for students and parents covering academic, cognitive, and social skills. The hours devoted to testing were reviewed with the goal of freeing up additional instructional time. New procedures were introduced for reinstating students who had been suspended or expelled, and hiring and evaluation practices for teachers were strengthened.

Much of Dr. Rice's message focused on the need to treat the Kalamazoo Promise as a process rather than a "carnival prize" awarded at graduation. At a reception in Kalamazoo's Northside neighborhood early in the school year, Dr. Rice put aside pleasantries in favor of candid dialogue with African American leaders. "We're not doing kids any favors when we tell them, 'Stay in school and you'll get the Promise.' The fact is, you have to read well, you have to write well, you have to do math well to succeed in college. That's the dirty little secret" (Mack 2007d). In all of Dr. Rice's extensive interactions with community groups, he asked for the continued involvement of parents and residents. "Everybody involved in crafting the expectations [for students and the adults that support them] would be responsible for helping to fulfill those expectations. If you want to put your oar in the water, God bless you, but then you need to keep your oar in the water" (Mack 2007e). At the same time, Dr. Rice has voiced concern about the multiple efforts under way to support student achievement: "There's enormous goodwill in this community—people starting programs, people wanting to help. There are all these wonderful things, but the issue is to what extent we're working together and what times we're working against each other. The cohesion needs to improve very, very substantially" (Mack 2007f).

Dr. Rice has also stressed the value of making decisions about programs based on clear evidence of their effectiveness. The Kalamazoo Promise has brought to the fore a number of challenges for the district, the most pressing of which is a seemingly intractable gap between the academic achievement of middle- and lower-income students. (The close correlation between income and race in KPS—and indeed throughout the nation—makes the achievement gap by income a rough proxy for the black-white achievement gap.[21]) While a variety of strategies have been implemented to address the achievement gap, in Dr. Rice's view insufficient resources have gone into measuring and reporting on their results. He is adamant about the need for assessment and seems willing to ruffle some feathers along the way: "If we're doing something and it's not having the results we want, we have the right and responsibility to be flexible and make changes," Rice has said. "We don't want to be stuck on stupid" (Mack 2007f).

The district's priorities, all of which to some degree predate the Kalamazoo Promise, include increasing academic rigor, reducing the dropout rate, deepening the college-going culture, and addressing behavior problems that interfere with student learning. These interlocking goals are congruent with a broader state and national context that emphasizes testing as a gateway to promotion and tighter curriculum requirements.

Increasing Academic Rigor

"The literature is clear that high expectations drive student achievement," says Dr. Rice (Mack 2008b). Several initiatives to raise expectations are under way, ranging from new practices governing promotion from one grade to the next to the crafting of a community commitment to increase student success. Kalamazoo Public Schools for many years had a policy of social promotion for students in kindergarten through 8th grade based on research claiming that providing support services to failing students is preferable to holding them back. The counterargument is that social promotion reduces the incentives for students to maintain their academic progress and contributes to large numbers of high school freshmen being held back or dropping out. (In recent years, approximately one-third of KPS freshmen have ended the school year without earning enough credits to move on to the 10th grade.) In March 2007, KPS announced a plan that broke with the tradition of social promotion. Struggling students in the 1st and 8th grades are now offered support services during the school year. If they fail to gain ground they are required to attend summer school. Those students who do not comply must repeat the grade, while those who do are evaluated to determine whether or not they should advance. In 2007, 150 or 15 percent of 1st graders and 175 or 21 percent of 8th graders were required to attend summer school. Overall, the district enrolled about 1,500 students in summer 2007, compared to 900 the previous year, at a cost of $800,000, almost double that of summer 2006 (Mack 2007i).

Testing requirements, too, have been tightened. In part to assess whether schools are making adequate yearly progress under the federal No Child Left Behind law, the state of Michigan now requires all juniors to take the Michigan Merit Exam, which includes the American College Test (ACT), in order to graduate. This means that the ACT has become one of the de facto requirements for receiving a Promise scholarship. The test, which had been administered on a Saturday at a cost of $70 per student, is now given during the school day and costs nothing. In a district seeking to prepare every graduate for some form of higher education, having an ACT score is an important step in helping students decide where to apply to college. In addition, those who score high enough are eligible to receive a $4,000 Michigan Promise merit scholarship. (Promise recipients can use these funds for books and transportation, substantial costs not covered by the Kalamazoo Promise.)

In 2007, the state of Michigan also introduced more rigorous high school graduation requirements. The decision was controversial, with educators concerned that many high school students who are unable to meet the existing requirements would now be that much further from being able to graduate (Bartik and Hollenbeck 2006). While KPS's graduation requirements were already closely aligned with the 2007 law, the new requirements do pose a challenge to some of the district's alternative education programs that have fewer requirements and lack the resources to teach the science and language classes that are part of the new state rules. The new graduation requirements take effect for the class of 2011.

An emphasis on academic rigor cuts both ways for KPS. On the one hand, it increases the likelihood that students who graduate from high school will be better prepared to succeed in a postsecondary setting. On the other hand, it raises the bar for all students, meaning that those who are already struggling will need to meet even higher standards and may be more inclined to give up. This is why KPS's approach to academic rigor seeks not just to strengthen standards but also to enlist students, parents, and the broader community in ensuring that every student succeeds.

The recognition that schools cannot operate in a vacuum was reflected in the district's 2007–2008 strategic planning process, which focused on crafting a set of expectations for students and the adults who support them. Year-by-year academic goals were established to correlate with state benchmarks while social expectations were developed through a participatory process that involved 250 volunteers from the community. Presented in five subcommittee reports and summarized in a colorful wall chart posted in schools and community venues are expectations for every year of a child's development (KPS 2008). For example, a kindergartner is expected (among other things) to be able to count to 30, play cooperatively with others, and recognize letter sounds, while his or her parents are expected to attend all parent-teacher conferences and provide children with a quiet space to do their school work. Educators are expected to reinforce positive student behaviors and base their instructional decisions on data. The broader community is expected to support and provide positive, enriching after-school activities and ensure that every elementary school student has a relationship with at least one adult who supports their educational development. Dr. Rice has called the exercise "the beginning of our long-term effort to improve schools for children by creating clear and high expectations for both children and adults" (Mack 2008b). Galvanizing diverse audiences around a common set of expectations can also help increase account-ability and support for low-income and minority children who are more likely to struggle in school.

Reducing the Dropout Rate

The Kalamazoo Promise requires KPS to ensure that, in Dr. Rice's words, "every child is college ready" by the time he or she graduates from high school. This is a formidable challenge that begins with keeping students in school. Like urban districts throughout the nation, KPS has grappled with high dropout rates that are especially acute for minority students. For KPS in 2007, the dropout rate after four years in high school was 20.8 percent: 16 percent for white students versus 24 percent for African American students, a disparity of 8 percent. For the same period, the four-year graduation rate was 69 percent: 78 percent for white students compared to 63 percent for African American students, a disparity of 15 percent.[22] While the Kalamazoo Promise provides an incentive for students to stay in school, other, more direct interventions are needed to reduce the dropout rate. Among those initiated at the high school level, some prior to the Kalamazoo Promise, are the reopening of the district's alternative high school, the introduction of smaller learning communities within the large high schools, freshman academies to ease the transition from middle school, and the expansion of in-school and out-of-school credit recovery programs to enable students to regain missing credits and graduate. The district has also introduced targeted interventions, such as early literacy programs, that strengthen academic performance before dropping out becomes an option. Other initiatives, including the federally funded GEAR UP program, provide middle and high school students with a range of supports, including college visits and innovative summer experiences.

Deepening the College-Going Culture

The Kalamazoo Promise does much to increase the attractiveness of postsecondary education, but a deeper cultural shift is needed to support the higher-education aspirations of all KPS students. Heightened awareness of postsecondary education is reflected in the college pennants that line hallways and appear on teachers' doors, classroom visits by students and faculty from local colleges and universities, and many in-school programs that ask students to think about potential careers and the education required for them. Frequent invocation of the Kalamazoo Promise by teachers and administrators also plays a part: "There's a common language that the kids are beginning to use about going to college," says Tisha Pankop, an English teacher at Loy Norrix High School. "They ask each other 'Aren't you going to college? Where are you going to college?' And I find more students anticipating going to college as a result of the Promise." Yet the barriers facing students are formidable. "In one class, I have two homeless students," continues Pankop, "a student who's a mom and one who's about to be, and two who are the primary caregivers for siblings. Most of the kids who have supportive families, or families where someone has gone to college, are pretty realistic about what it takes to succeed. It's the kids who've never done it before who are not realistic. They'll say, 'I'm going to be a basketball star, a lawyer, a doctor,' but they don't have a clue what they are up against."[23]

Several programs designed to help build an understanding of what is required for college success were catalyzed by the announcement of the Kalamazoo Promise. Kalamazoo Communities In Schools began organizing an annual College Awareness Week that brings community volunteers into the elementary schools to read to second graders. The book selected for the program, a copy of which every child receives, is *I Know I Can*, by Wendy Rouillard, which introduces students to four furry creatures exploring the types of careers they want to pursue. Kalamazoo Communities In Schools also initiated a "Promise Fellows" program that pairs Americorps/VISTA volunteers with first graders attending summer school to boost their literacy skills (Mack 2007g). Students from Kalamazoo College and volunteers from the Junior League and other civic organizations participate regularly in literacy projects with elementary school children. Other programs run the gamut from GEAR UP–sponsored visits to WMU for middle school students to college fairs at KPS elementary schools, from a college-prep program specifically for Hispanic youth to mentoring through the African American woman's organization, the LINKS, Incorporated.

Changes in school policies that push in the direction of greater academic rigor include a new system of weighting grades for advanced placement classes (an extra point is awarded) to reward students for taking more advanced courses. A second change is the introduction of pluses and minuses to the grading scale to give students an incentive to work toward better grades and to give teachers more grading options.

There have also been new efforts in the community to provide one-on-one relationships for students who need extra support in school and in navigating successfully the high school to college transition. A number of area churches have created tutoring and mentoring programs or expanded existing programs. Kalamazoo Communities In Schools, which inherited an earlier Chamber of Commerce–sponsored mentoring program (the Kalamazoo Area Academic Achievement Program), introduced a program called "Promise coaching" that for two years piloted a life-coach model to help first-generation, college-bound high school students prepare for getting into college. Big Brothers Big Sisters has scaled up its mentoring programs, doubling the number of children served and developing new methods of recruiting mentors by partnering with schools, businesses, and religious institutions. The Promise has had an impact not only on the availability of mentors, but also on the focus of the organization's programs. "Mentors are coming forward at a much higher rate than anticipated," says Big Brothers Big Sisters executive director Peter Tripp. "We've been able to encourage [them] to take a more active role in kids' education, school performance, and career interests. That's always been a piece of these relationships, but because of the Promise it has become more meaningful."

Efforts such as these are especially important for students who are the first in their families to attend college and who may lack the basic knowledge about what is involved. Evidence suggests that it is not financial barriers that constitute the primary roadblock to attending college—after all, a multitude of scholarships are available for low-income students—but rather a lack of academic and social preparedness, an absence of college-going role models, a less than supportive peer group, and the need for hands-on support to access the college admissions and financial aid process. The barriers, of course, are not insurmountable, but children who face them are at a distinct disadvantage. Kalamazoo Public Schools teacher Tisha Pankop recounts her own experience.

> I was the first in my family to go to college. I knew I wanted to go, but I couldn't fathom how I was going to do it. I didn't have anyone helping guide me through it, and so when everyone else was applying for college when we were seniors I didn't even think

about it, but at the end of my senior year I got a little scholarship and I thought 'Well, I have this money and I don't want to waste it,' so I went to the community college. But when I'd go home to my family, there was no one to ask me about how things were going. They just didn't understand. I wound up going to three different colleges, and it took me seven or eight years until I graduated. A lot of that had to do with not having that support.[24]

Pankop and others believe that a supportive individual is the single most important intervention a student can be offered. "Kids need support, not just information. They need someone to follow up and ask, 'Are you getting enough sleep? Are you studying enough? What classes are you taking? What else are you up to?'" The support person does not need to be a parent or formal mentor. Teachers can play this role, as can a friend's parent. In the case of Joanne Sloan, it was her husband, himself a first-generation college graduate who went on to earn a graduate degree, who served as her inspiration and supporter. Ms. Sloan had drifted away from high school before graduation, but after meeting her husband went back for a GED and attended college—a big step for a woman whose father was a blue-collar worker with a 6th grade education. "Education did not have a high value in my home," says Sloan. "My parents never went to even one of my parent-teacher conferences." Her husband's experience was different: "His mom encouraged him to reach. She did value an education and she knew that he was smart, that he could go on."[25] From the first days of their marriage, the Sloans instilled in their two children the expectation that they, too, would go to college. The expectation was backed by the Sloans's commitment to prepaying their children's college tuition through the Michigan Education Trust even when finances were tight ("It was pretty much like an extra house payment," says Sloan about their monthly contributions). Their children, both products of KPS, now have access to both the Kalamazoo Promise and their MET savings. Their daughter attends Michigan State University and their son, now in middle school, has his eye on the University of Michigan. Both expect to complete college without taking on any debt.

Addressing Behavior Problems

Since the 1970s, KPS has suffered from negative stereotypes related to its status as an urban school district serving a student body with
a large poor and minority population. Kalamazoo Public Schools officials trace some of this back to the racial unrest of the desegregation era
and argue that most of the negative comments come from people who
haven't been inside a KPS building for years. Parents are sometimes
surprised when they visit their children's schools to find a high degree
of supervision and an orderly environment. Still, annual surveys by the
district show student behavior regularly among the top concerns for
both students and their parents, and teachers are the first to acknowledge that students with behavioral problems interfere with the learning
of others.[26]

The district has taken an aggressive approach to preventing and
managing behavioral problems for several years. The implementation
of a positive-behavior and literacy-support model within the district's
elementary and middle schools stresses consistent rules and focuses
on interventions, academic and otherwise, to address student behavior.
The district reopened its alternative high school and related programs
in 2005–2006 (the previous program had been closed, and students with
alternative education needs transferred to neighboring districts). A police liaison at each of the comprehensive high schools serves as a de-
terrent to illegal behavior, as well as a resource for conflict resolution.
Despite these efforts, the rate of suspensions remains extremely high
(in 2006–2007, 30 percent of all high school students were suspended
at least once, and the 857 students involved averaged three suspensions
each). The suspension and expulsion rates are especially high for African American males (Mack 2007f,h).

The Kalamazoo Promise has placed the school district's management of behavioral problems under greater scrutiny. In September 2006,
officials took action after fights broke out at a basketball game between
the two large high schools. The students involved were suspended, and
an upcoming football game between the schools was rescheduled for a
Saturday morning. One of the high schools canceled its homecoming
dance because of threatened disruptions, but the decision was reversed
when a group of seniors pledged to discourage any violence. At a subsequent board meeting, two mothers whose children had just transferred

into a KPS middle school complained about disruptive behavior and fighting. A series of incidents at Loy Norrix High School the following year, including fights in a park across the street that spilled onto campus, drew renewed attention to school security. Tensions were especially high in 2007, a year during which five teenagers were the victims of homicide in the city of Kalamazoo. In December 2007, the school board voted to approve the new superintendent's recommendation to add several hundred security cameras at the high schools, as part of a system to provide additional surveillance of corridors, stairways, lobbies, parking lots, student entrances, building perimeters, the cafeteria, and the gym. Dr. Rice and his staff are also considering improved video surveillance of school buses and the addition of buzzers, intercoms, and cameras at the main entrances to the district's elementary schools.[27]

"Some of the kids are so full of anger that they're self-destructing in middle school and high school," says Scott Hunsinger, who has taught middle school in the district since 1995. "The Promise does very little for those kids. If you really want to transform them, it will take parenting classes and other kinds of support. You would need a whole other Promise to do that." The paradox, of course, is that the families that need help the most are the hardest to reach. "The public schools are expected to be the silver bullet for a whole range of societal ills," continues Hunsinger.[28] This may be an unfair expectation, but schools are one of the few places where the hardest-to-serve children can be found, provided support programs start early enough. The middle school behavior program initiated by KPS in 2008, as discussed in the following section, is a sign that educators recognize high school may be too late for particular interventions.

Increasing academic rigor, reducing the dropout rate, deepening the college-going culture, and addressing behavior problems all share the common goal of increasing the likelihood that students enrolled in KPS will graduate from high school and be prepared to succeed in some kind of postsecondary program, whether it be a four-year college, a two-year college, or a career or technical training program. Much work remains to be done. In a pattern that roughly mirrors the national experience for urban school districts, close to one-third of KPS students drop out before graduation. Among those who do graduate, half attend a four-year college and the other half opt for a two-year program. Of those KPS graduates who enroll at KVCC, approximately one-third graduate, one-third end up on probation, and one-third drop out. In very broad terms, according to Dr. Rice, this means that fewer than half the students who enter high school navigate successfully the transition to postsecondary education, a situation that is deeply problematic for educators, young people, and the nation's economic health.[29]

DIFFICULT TRADE-OFFS

The impact of the Kalamazoo Promise, as well as broader changes in the nation's educational system, guarantees that KPS is a district in transition. But the question of its ultimate shape or even its current direction has been made more complex by the introduction of the Promise. Perhaps the most fundamental issue any school district faces is who it serves. The short answer is easy: all KPS students and their families. The longer answer must address the competing needs of different groups of students and their families. In the case of KPS, these groups include the roughly one-third of students who have significant problems in school, the most advanced students who need special challenges to remain engaged, and those in between. The task of serving these diverse groups is even more difficult in a climate of limited resources. The middle-income families that the region is trying to attract from an economic development standpoint will look at KPS to see if it offers the kinds of choices and opportunities that more affluent suburban school districts provide. The lower-income students who make up the majority of the district's enrollment will now pay a much steeper cost—the forfeiture of a free college education—if they do not succeed in school. The "revolution of rising expectations" brought about by the Kalamazoo Promise means that time is short for the school district to produce visible results that speak to the needs of both audiences.

The trade-offs and conflicts that can emerge from this dynamic are most evident in the context of budgetary decisions. In spring 2007, the school board faced the task of allocating funds for new programs for the coming academic year. Earlier that spring, Dr. Brown had proposed raising the cap on enrollment in kindergarten through 3rd grade classes from 24 to 29 (26 for kindergarten) at the district's five lowest-poverty elementary schools in order to maintain the cap at 17 at the six highest-poverty schools. (The other five elementary schools would have kept the 24-student cap.) In suggesting the plan, the superintendent cited rising enrollment as well as changes in federal grant rules mandating smaller class sizes for high-poverty schools. Arguing that "equity does not mean equality," the superintendent presented the case that high-poverty schools need smaller classes because so many students are at risk of academic failure.

The outcry was immediate and intense. Parents from the affected schools flooded a meeting of the school board threatening strategies ranging from recalls to petition drives to e-mail campaigns. "I have no problems pulling my kids out and going to Otsego" [a neighboring public school district], said one parent. "I would like the Promise, but I don't need it" (Mack 2007j). Another said, "It smacks of bait and switch—come to KPS and we'll raise class size . . . I told my husband, we can put our child back in Montessori so fast it can make their heads spin. But that's not what I want, and it's not what they want" (Mack 2007k). Having promoted small early elementary class sizes as essential for student learning, the district had boxed itself in on the question. The board, which had not yet signed off on the class-size plan when it was floated, overruled the superintendent within a matter of weeks. One result was that the coming budget debate was constrained by the need to add teachers to maintain existing class sizes, at a cost of roughly $600,000.

It is worth noting that KPS parents appear to accept the principle that class sizes may differ across the district based on the percentage of low-income children being served; in other words, that schools facing challenges related to a high-poverty population are entitled to additional resources. It was the scale of the imbalance—17 students per class versus as many as 29—that brought the parents of children at the mixed-income schools out in force.

Given the outcry, keeping class sizes constant in the mixed-income elementary schools became the top priority for the budget. As for the remaining available funds, the board was presented with four options, only two of which it could afford: a 1 percent across-the-board pay increase for teachers, a small reduction in the size of core high school classes through the hiring of six new teachers, the introduction of a behavior program for high school or middle school students, and changes in a Spanish/English dual-language program that enjoyed strong support from the parents of those who participated. Until fall 2007, students at one of the district's elementary magnet schools had the option to enroll in a dual-language program taught half in Spanish and half in English. The program was popular with many of the district's Hispanic families, as well as a vocal group of white parents; however, its location as a separate entity within an inner-city school had created a two-tiered system, with the lower-achieving students (many of them African American) not participating in the dual-language curriculum. When the district announced plans in 2006 to phase out the program to focus on improving the school's test scores, parents of the immersion students organized a campaign to retain the program or move it to a new site. The proposed behavior program had no parallel advocacy group—almost by definition, the parents of most of these children are not prone to show up at school board meetings or write letters to the editor—but administrators, teachers, and parents have long argued that behavior problems must be addressed before the critical transition to ninth grade. In the final budget, advocacy or not, the board opted to fund the first two priorities—a small teacher raise and a modest class-size reduction—a decision that spread the benefits of the additional funds as widely as possible. It also left behind an angry group of parents of dual-language students and a pressing need for services for those students whose behavior is responsible for much of the disruption in the middle and high schools.

A year later, when the 2008 budgeting process occurred, both the dual-language program and a middle school behavior program were funded. Of the projected new resources of $1.35 million available for 2008–2009 (relative to an operating budget of $120 million), $755,000 was allocated to the behavior initiative—a full-year program requiring new teachers and facilities—while $332,000 went to fund a dual-language curriculum that would serve K-4th grade students in its first year, then expand to all elementary grades. The dual-language program would be housed in a refurbished elementary school near the city's center that had been closed almost three years earlier, a decision that reflected both the need for new space in light of expected enrollment growth and the strong support of neighborhood leaders for reopening the shuttered school.

The largest budget initiative was the introduction of full-day kindergarten at 14 of the district's 17 elementary schools, a move that was paid for entirely through reallocation of the district's federal Title I budget at no cost to local taxpayers. At two schools, where fewer than 40 percent of students are low income, and at the new dual-language school, the state of Michigan prevented KPS from using the Title I funds that would pay for full-day kindergarten. Instead, parents of prospective kindergarten students at those three schools were given the opportunity to move their children to one of the other 14 schools or stay at their current school, which would provide half-day kindergarten accompanied by a half day of wraparound, a child care program led by paraprofessionals. In all, the 176 students in full-day kindergarten in 2007–2008 would become approximately 900 in 2008–2009—an increase of roughly 400 percent. Kalamazoo Public Schools kindergartners would receive an estimated 371,000 additional instructional hours under this plan.

The choices made in the first three post-Promise budgets offer some insight into the balancing act KPS performs as it strives to increase the achievement of low-income children while providing the enrichment opportunities that middle-income families demand. This balancing act brings to mind Albert O. Hirschman's theoretical insights into the process of organizational decline. According to Hirschman, when people are dissatisfied with a product, they have two options: "exit" by switching to a competing product (or school district) or "voice," the process of agitating and exerting influence for change from within (Hirschman 1970). In the past, exit was the preferred path for families disenchanted with KPS who voted with their feet by switching districts or sending their children to private or charter schools. With the new incentives provided by the Kalamazoo Promise, more families are choosing to stay and fight. As in other policy arenas, the poor tend to have less "voice" than those who are better off, which makes it a particular blessing that many of the middle-income parents who have chosen KPS precisely because it is a diverse school district are prepared to advocate not just for their own children but for their children's less well-off classmates.

Middle-class families may no longer be leaving the district, but they are becoming more vocal about its shortcomings. At the same time, advocates for at-risk children are demanding that they too be prepared to utilize the Kalamazoo Promise. Teachers are feeling the strain. Classes are packed, with some high school classes at the 37-student maximum.

The expectations engendered by the Kalamazoo Promise are stressful, in part because they seem out of reach to those in the classroom day in and day out. Yet the Kalamazoo Promise is a universal program, available to every graduate of KPS provided that the minimal attendance and residency requirements are met. For the most part, teachers are embracing that challenge and recognize that triage and tracking are no longer acceptable strategies. Since the announcement of the program, teachers' expectations of their students have risen as well. According to researchers at the WMU Evaluation Center, the Promise has created a renewed sense of urgency and excitement in the schools that has helped teachers define priorities, increase support for students, and push college as an option for more of the student body (Jones, Miron, and Kelaher Young 2008). As Theresa Williams-Johnson, a teacher with 20 years of experience at Hillside Middle School, reports, "Before the Promise, I did a lot of talking to students about college and about finishing high school. When I would ask, 'How many of you are going to college?' there was never a time when I got every kid to raise their hand. Every hand goes up now. I can promise you, every hand will go up this year."[30]

"As much as you say it doesn't matter, we're middle-class people teaching sometimes very low-income children," says Sue Larsen, a music teacher at a high-poverty elementary school and the mother of three KPS students. "You can't help but make a judgment that these kids are bound for college and these kids aren't. [The Kalamazoo Promise] really changed my mind set. The first thing you think is that we have to make all of these children college ready. That meant looking at all of my students like my children, truly not as anybody else's children."[31]

Sherry Ransford, another KPS teacher, agrees: "It used to be that teachers could say, 'You can be anything you want to be,' and not mean it at all," she says. "There is no way that they could legitimately believe what they were saying. Now they can. I think we all stepped up with the Promise. All of us now really believe that all kids should be college ready. It was pointless before. Why make a kid college ready when they wouldn't be going, when that was beyond our ability?"[32]

An apt metaphor is offered by middle school teacher Scott Hunsinger. "To me, the Kalamazoo Promise is nothing short of a miracle. It gives hope to kids who would not have been able to afford college. It removes one of the biggest hurdles stopping them from getting a college education. Bam! It took one of those hurdles away. But what's happening to teachers is that we're going through a psychological process of feeling so grateful that this big hurdle's gone, but then starting to realize how many other hurdles are there that were probably not as clear to us before. We usually never got beyond that first hurdle. Now we're realizing all the other hurdles that lie beyond it, and that can be deflating and depressing."[33]

What are those hurdles? A lack of academic preparation and insufficient literacy, low expectations that some adults have for students and that some students have for themselves (multiple generations of non-college-going means that many students still don't believe they can or should go to college, Kalamazoo Promise notwithstanding), inadequate attention to the non-academic skills needed to succeed in college, and, for some, mental health issues related to psychological and social trauma. Hunsinger calls it a stern reality check. "If your goal is to serve kids from struggling low-income families who never would have had a shot of going to college and are way behind academically, this is a huge challenge. It may take generations." But Hunsinger and his colleagues are also optimistic: "One of the reasons the Promise is a gift and a blessing is that the conversation we're having has changed. We would not be as ambitious about the number of struggling kids we're going to help get into college if not for the Promise."[34]

Notes

1. Enrollment data presented in Figure 5.1 begins in the mid-1980s, after the demographic surge related to the baby boom had aged out of the K-12 system.
2. The elementary schools with the largest increases in enrollment were Milwood Elementary, 25.9 percent; Parkwood-Upjohn Elementary, 23.9 percent; Woodward School for Technology and Research, 19.5 percent; Lincoln International Studies School, 18.3 percent; Indian Prairie, 17.5 percent; and King-Westwood Elementary, 14.2 percent (data provided by KPS).
3. Data provided by KPS.
4. Figure derived from 899 blended enrollment increase multiplied by $7,556 foundation grant for 2006–2007.
5. Author's interview with Deputy Superintendent for Business, Communications, and Operations Gary Start, KPS, March 22, 2006.
6. Author's interview with Dr. Janice Brown, Superintendent, KPS, June 30, 2006.
7. Author's interview with Gary Start, March 22, 2006.
8. Ibid.
9. Estimates put the number of children in grades K-8 who opt out of the public schools at 4,000, or more than one-third of total KPS enrollment (Mack 2006i).
10. This informal assessment was carried out by Bob Jorth, Kalamazoo Promise administrator, based on data provided by KPS.

11. Author's conversation with Tom Vance, Community Relations, Portage Public Schools, September 8, 2008.

12. One of the more unusual responses to the Kalamazoo Promise came from a banker at a Connecticut-based investment firm that underwrites bonds for charter schools, who asked whether the Kalamazoo Promise donors are philosophically opposed to the charter school movement; author's notes, 2006.

13. Author's interview with Pam Kingery, executive director, Kalamazoo Communities In Schools, January 27, 2006.

14. The appeals process involves submitting a letter with appropriate documentation to the appeals committee, a three-person committee appointed by the board. The appeals committee reviews the material and makes a decision on whether the student will receive a scholarship and for how much. Appeals are limited to seniors. The committee meets approximately quarterly. Students with a short lapse or lapses with significant enrollment in KPS are those most likely to receive some kind of scholarship, usually related to family hardship, emotional issues, learning needs, custody, abuse, or neglect. Reasons such as out-of-district residency or not graduating from KPS do not get approved. Approximately 75 percent of those submitted to the committee by Bob Jorth are approved.

15. These percentages are substantially lower than either the 65 percent low-income proportion of KPS enrollment overall or the 56 percent low-income designation of district high school students for two reasons. First, low-income students become less likely to apply for free and reduced-price lunch assistance as they reach middle and high school. Second, it is likely that low-income students are overrepresented among those who fail to complete high school, thereby lowering the proportion of free and reduced-price lunch recipients within a graduating class. Data provided by KPS. Overall free and reduced-price lunch numbers are from October 2007 data.

16. Retention data reported by Bob Jorth, Kalamazoo Promise administrator.

17. The rules governing continued eligibility for the scholarship generally mirror the "satisfactory academic progress" requirements of the state's public colleges and universities. Students must complete 75 percent of the credits for which they enroll and receive a GPA of at least 2.0, or a C average. If these criteria are not met students are put on academic probation for one semester. If the situation still does not improve their scholarship is suspended. The scholarship can be reinstated if a student returns to good standing with a 2.0 G.P.A. or higher. This provision holds true for 10 years following the student's graduation from KPS unless interrupted by military service (see https://www.kalamazoopromise.com).

18. See note 16.

19. Author's interview with Sherry Ransford, KPS teacher, January 8, 2008.

20. For the 2007–2008 year, Dr. Brown stayed on in a consulting role she had worked out with the board before her retirement. This was a controversial arrangement, but was accepted because the plan had been developed before the school board knew whether or not it would be hiring an experienced administrator and because of Dr. Brown's connection to the Kalamazoo Promise donors; see Mack (2007c).

In September 2008, Dr. Brown was appointed executive director of the Kalamazoo Promise organization.

21. According to KPS data from October 2007, 81 percent of African American students in KPS qualify for the federally subsidized free and reduced-price lunch program as compared to 40 percent of white students.

22. The 2007 graduation rate, which the state of Michigan calculated for the first time based on a four-year cohort graduation rate, includes only "on-time" graduates—those who complete high school within four years. The dropout rate includes those who left high school permanently at any time during the four-year period for their cohort or whose whereabouts are unknown. The difference between the two rates is attributable to those students who did not graduate on time but also did not drop out during the four-year period (Center for Educational Performance and Information 2008).

23. Author's interview with Tisha Pankop, KPS teacher, December 19, 2007.

24. Ibid.

25. Author's interview with Joanne Sloan, KPS teacher, July 26, 2006.

26. This finding is not unique to KPS. In national polls, respondents consistently identify a lack of discipline, fighting, and violence as among the biggest problems facing the public schools (Rose and Gallup 2007).

27. Kalamazoo Central High School will go from having 16 cameras to 129, Loy Norrix High School will go from 42 to 164, and the Kennedy Center, which houses alternative programs, will go from 15 cameras to 22. Norrix has the most because of its sprawling layout. A federal grant covered the $288,000 cost of the cameras, and the district spent another $131,000 from its 2006 bond issue to install the cabling infrastructure (Press News Service 2007).

28. Author's interview with Scott Hunsinger, KPS teacher.

29. Author's interview with Michael Rice, KPS Superintendent, April 1, 2008.

30. Author's interiew with Theresa Williams-Johnson, September 19, 2008.

31. Author's interview with Sue Larsen, KPS teacher, May 26, 2008.

32. Author's interview with Sherry Ransford, KPS teacher, January 8, 2008.

33. Author's interview with Scott Hunsinger, KPS teacher.

34. Ibid.

6
Prospects for Economic Change

While the Kalamazoo Promise has had an immediate effect on students and the schools, its influence on the local and regional economy is a longer-term proposition. The scholarship program was introduced at a time when economic trends in the state of Michigan were extremely negative, and this broader environment has thus far overshadowed any major economic gains that might materialize as a result of the Promise. In addition, business decisions that could have a sizable impact on the economy almost always unfold over a long time frame, and it is still too early to know if the Kalamazoo Promise will lead directly to new, job-creating investments in the region. Finally, the community alignment and engagement efforts necessary to leverage the Promise, especially on the part of the business community, have been slow to emerge. Even so, the announcement of the scholarship program has had some important initial effects that reinforce encouraging trends already under way and increase the community's attractiveness to outside investors, as well as its appeal to those businesses already based here.

This chapter provides an assessment of the economic implications of the Kalamazoo Promise, both achievements thus far and prospects for the future. Some of these are difficult to quantify, as they involve changes in Kalamazoo's culture and reputation, but it is important to attend to them nonetheless. It is precisely such intangible factors that can shift the attitudes of residents and outsiders away from the specter of urban decline and set in motion developments that lead to positive economic change.

ECONOMIC DEVELOPMENT CHALLENGES

If the Kalamazoo Promise is to serve as a catalyst for regional economic development, its impact must be strong enough to overcome some deeply negative economic trends. Michigan has struggled since

2000 to adapt to the decline of the state's auto industry and the associated manufacturing industries that shaped its economy for 100 years. The numbers paint a bleak picture.

- Economic growth for the state has lagged the national average since 2002. In 2004, Michigan was the only state whose economy contracted, and in 2007, the state ranked 49th out of 50 in terms of growth (Bureau of Economic Analysis 2007). In March 2008, Michigan's seasonally adjusted unemployment rate was the highest in the nation, at 7.6 percent, compared to 4.4 percent nationwide (W.E. Upjohn Institute for Unemployment Research 2008a).

- While median household income for state residents has historically been above the national average, by 2005 it had fallen to average or below-average levels (CRC 2007a).

- Michigan leads the nation in outward migration, especially by young people. The state ranks 49th out of 50 in retaining young adults (ages 18–24), and census data show that the population of 25–44-year-olds declined by 268,382 between 2000 and 2007. One of the nation's largest moving companies, United Van Lines, reported that in 2006 Michigan exceeded all other states in the proportion of residents departing, with 66 percent of the company's shipments outbound (CRC 2007a).

- Even after shedding 24.3 percent (or 217,900) of its manufacturing jobs between 2000 and 2005, Michigan remains heavily dependent on manufacturing. The state's employment location quotient for automobile, light truck, and parts manufacturing is 7.88, meaning that the state's share of employment in this industry segment is 7.88 times the national average (Fulton and Grimes 2006).

Kalamazoo County is less dependent on manufacturing than southeast Michigan, and the economic base of the region has retained its comparative diversity. But growth has been slower, household incomes lower, and unemployment higher than for the nation as a whole. A weak job market is perhaps the biggest constraint on the economic impact of the Kalamazoo Promise, limiting the potential increase in population and related economic growth.

A second challenge in assessing the economic impact of the Kalamazoo Promise is the time frame over which business decisions unfold. According to economic development officials, it routinely takes five to seven years for major investment deals to come to fruition. A number of encouraging economic developments that emerged in the three years after the scholarship was introduced actually originated prior to its announcement. Ongoing downtown revitalization, including the city's first multiplex cinema, and major construction projects, such as the $30 million Miller Canfield building across from Bronson Park that broke ground in September 2006, have contributed to a relatively positive economic outlook, but these projects all predate the Kalamazoo Promise. Even the Monroe-Brown Foundation internship program, designed to assist with the retention of local graduates, and the KPS bond issue approved in May 2006 had both been in the works well before the scholarship program was announced. Of course, it is quite likely that some of these developments were initiated by the same wealthy individuals responsible for the scholarship program, which was in a planning mode for several years prior to November 2005. It is also likely that the community's leading economic development organizations, including Southwest Michigan First, Downtown Kalamazoo Inc., and the Southwest Michigan Innovation Center, all of which have been extremely active in recent years, number among their board members at least some of the anonymous donors.

The positive economic news that seemed to cascade from the pages of the *Kalamazoo Gazette* in spring 2008, especially the announcement that local bioscience company MPI Research would create 3,300 jobs over the subsequent five years, was a post-Promise development, but it is not clear how directly the scholarship program played a role in corporate decision making. Still, the Kalamazoo Promise has indeed given a boost to the local economy. It is much too early to assess whether the Promise will be seen as the spark that ignited a regional economic recovery, but its initial impact has reinforced positive trends already under way and changed the collective view of the community's economic potential. The effects range in scope from the direct economic impact of the scholarship program on family resources to a substantial increase in national attention and recognition granted to the Kalamazoo region.

MODEST GAIN FROM SCHOLARSHIP FUNDS AND
SCHOOL SPENDING

A small but direct impact of the Kalamazoo Promise on the local economy resulted from the decisions of scholarship recipients about where to attend college. Seventy percent of Promise recipients from the class of 2006, the first to receive the scholarship, opted to attend either WMU or KVCC. These individual decisions meant that approximately 60 percent of scholarship funds, or close to $1 million, flowed directly from the Kalamazoo Promise 501(c)3 organization into local institutions of higher education.[1] The scholarships also affected families who had prepared to finance at least a part of their children's tuition expenses. While the magnitude of this effect is impossible to quantify because of variations in household resources and needs, some families undoubtedly experienced an unexpected windfall from the sudden availability of Kalamazoo Promise funds. Anecdotal evidence and interviews suggest that one result was a reduced need for students or parents to take out loans, as well as new resources for discretionary spending. Again, it is impossible to know where these discretionary funds went, but it is reasonable to assume that at least a portion was invested in the local economy.

Another direct economic impact of the Kalamazoo Promise has come from construction projects supported by the bond issue passed by KPS voters in May 2006. Plans for an infrastructure bond predated the announcement of the scholarship program, but it was the expectation of a Promise-driven enrollment boost that led KPS to increase the size of the request and designate the proceeds for the construction of new school buildings—the first for KPS in 35 years. (The newest building in the district at the time the Promise was announced was Kalamazoo Central High School, opened in 1972; six of the school buildings currently in use were constructed before 1930.) With the bond issue on the horizon, some KPS officials believed it would take at least a year to develop a comprehensive building plan, but others urged putting something on the ballot right away because of the positive momentum created by the Promise. In January 2006, a quickly organized telephone survey of likely voters gauged community support for such a plan. Officials were pleasantly surprised by the results: 92 percent of respondents supported a bond request for facilities upkeep, 74 percent supported a new elementary school building to replace an overcrowded school on the West Side, and 63 percent backed construction of a new middle school. Millie Lambert, president of the KPS teachers' union commented, "I was really surprised that, given what's going on in this town economically, people are still saying that education is a high priority, and if they have to pay, they'll pay" (Mack 2006j). The bond allocated $24 million for construction of the middle school, $11 million for the elementary school, and the remainder for technology and facilities maintenance and upgrades. It was financed at a lower interest rate than previous issues and yielded total savings to the district of $5.9 million over its 20-year life. Deputy Superintendent Gary Start attributed the favorable financing to "the strong national interest in Kalamazoo, mainly because of the Kalamazoo Promise" (Ricks 2006).

The location of the new middle school was more contentious than its financing. Multiple sites were considered, including a 27-acre downtown parcel once occupied by a paper mill and the site of a costly environmental cleanup, a 227-acre site on the east side that included an area where sludge had been dumped from the city's old wastewater-treatment plan until 1968, and 160 acres of undeveloped land owned by the WMU Foundation on the west side of town just inside the city's boundaries. In October 2006, the district's announcement that the school would be built on the west side site was met with an angry response from some residents and community leaders. In addition to concerns about the limited degree of public input, critics claimed that the decision represented an abandonment of the city's core, the area in greatest need of investment. From the perspective of the district, however, the decision was an easy one. A collaboration with the WMU Foundation, which sold KPS the land (appraised at $2 million) for the bargain price of $1 million, and the city of Kalamazoo, which committed to $2 million in infrastructure investments, as well as nearby housing and commercial development, the deal brought together three of the community's leading public institutions. The new middle school is at the geographic center of KPS, making it accessible to the fastest-growing area of the district, and its location should stabilize residential housing in the nearby Arcadia neighborhood, which is home to a growing number of student rental properties.

In fall 2007, local elections resulted in the approval of school mill-ages in four neighboring districts, including the Portage Public Schools, the region's second-largest school district. In promoting an earlier ver-sion of this request, the then Superintendent Peter McFarlane had asked voters to support the Portage school millage as an "extension" of the Kalamazoo Promise, not a reaction to it. "All of the education entities need to take a look at what is necessary to be competitive and to draw attention to the quality that's there . . . We think this is another compo-nent of developing this education region here" (Chourey 2007). Even in the throes of an economic downturn and a state budget crisis that is con-straining public investment in education, the school bond votes showed "a community that has been willing, over and over again, to dig into its pockets to fund education" (*Kalamazoo Gazette* 2008a).

Support from the region's voters for educational spending was re-affirmed in May 2008, when a countywide millage renewal passed by a 57 percent margin (Mack 2008c). The campaign was notable for the connection made between education and economic development. "For many communities," wrote the editors of the *Kalamazoo Gazette* in urging a "yes" vote on the tax, "the renewal . . . isn't just about gutting school programs and laying off teachers. It's an economic development issue . . . The Kalamazoo area, bolstered by the Kalamazoo Promise and reinforced by fine higher education institutions, has been transform-ing itself into the Education Community—a place where companies seeking highly skilled, well-educated employees can set up shop and thrive" (*Kalamazoo Gazette* 2008b). Ron Kitchens, the head of South-west Michigan First, supported this view in urging a vote in favor of the tax: "One of the top priorities for businesses, whether they are already here or considering locating here, is the condition of K-12 education. They never ask if we have average school systems. They want to know their families will have superior opportunities through the public school systems" (Kitchens 2008). The millage, which generates over $11 mil-lion a year for the county's nine school districts, or $335 per student, had been approved in 2005 by a 51 percent margin. At that time, the measure had squeaked through on the strength of "yes" votes in the urban core; outside Portage and Kalamazoo, ballots ran 2–1 against the tax. This time, the urban vote held steady, but in the rural townships the proportion of "yes" votes jumped from 32 percent to 43 percent. The gains were spread throughout the region, with the percentage of voters supporting the tax going up in 17 of the 19 municipalities involved in the election despite an energetic campaign by the local antitax group (Mack 2008d). Growing support for school funding even among voters traditionally opposed to public spending of all kinds suggests that voters in the region are coming to understand the critical importance of high-quality education to their economic future and are willing to contribute at a time when state education spending has remained flat or declined. It also lends credence to the idea that the Kalamazoo Promise is not a zero-sum proposition—if KPS gets more, everyone else will get less—but instead can serve as a tool to leverage educational improvement throughout the region. "People were able to get beyond taking a narrow view of self-interest—to me, that's the story of the millage campaign," said Tim Bartik, one of the proposal's chief advocates (Mack 2008d).

THE HOUSING MARKET PUZZLE

Housing market trends are one of the most perplexing issues for researchers engaged in assessing the impact of the Kalamazoo Promise. Unraveling their meaning is especially important, since publicity about the relative strength of the housing market in response to the announcement of the scholarship program has been one of the chief arguments used by advocates for similar initiatives in communities throughout the nation.[2]

Recognizing its potential to drive home sales in a slack market, area real estate agents were among the first to incorporate the Kalamazoo Promise into their marketing strategies. Within days of the program's announcement, "College Tuition Qualified" signs were posted in the yards of homes for sale in the district, houses pictured in real estate ads had the words "Kalamazoo Promise" superimposed on them, and typing the phrase "Kalamazoo Promise" into an Internet search engine took one directly to the Web sites of local real estate agents. In September 2006, the Greater Kalamazoo Association of Realtors (GKAR) released data showing that home sales within KPS had outperformed the region for the first time in five years. For the 12 months ending September 30, 2006, sales of homes within the school district were up 6.7

percent, compared to a countywide decline of 5.2 percent; in the two-thirds of the region not within KPS, the drop in sales was 10 percent. Similarly, the median price of homes within KPS rose 3.6 percent while it fell across the region by 1.4 percent.[3] Although the gains have since dissipated, these were the numbers that were seized upon by national media and made their way into the lexicon of immediate benefits generated by the Kalamazoo Promise.

Local real estate agents say that the Promise has already altered the dynamics of the local housing market, even if not quantifiably. As John Jackson of Prudential Preferred Realtors recounts, "When I started in 1971, and even until recently, when someone moves here from Ann Arbor or California or New York, I'll get a call from the relocation director. They'll say, 'Pick them up and show them around town.' So, I'll pick them up and I'll say, 'What is it you're looking for?' And they'll tell me, 'I want a wonderful old home, I'm looking for character, 3 bedrooms, 2½ baths, *not* in the Kalamazoo school system.'"[4] (Jackson speculates that the aversion to KPS had mainly to do with social issues rather than the quality of education, noting that when prospective residents could be convinced to visit a district school they would wonder why they had been warned away.) Jackson says that his job and that of other Kalamazoo real estate agents has been made easier by the Kalamazoo Promise, with prospective buyers often now asking to look only at homes within KPS district boundaries.

At the same time, several countervailing trends cast doubt on any positive housing market impact. In the year following the announcement of the Promise, instead of a projected tightening in supply, more homes actually came onto the market, perhaps because many homeowners in the district decided it was a good time to sell. (In September 2006, the GKAR reported that the number of homes listed for sale had risen 14 percent, from 1,848 to 2,133, during the previous year, while sales grew by less than 7 percent.) And the sluggish regional economy exercised a powerful constraint on housing prices. "Although some area experts said they think the local residential real estate market is on its way back up," wrote the *Kalamazoo Gazette*'s real estate reporter in 2007, "a thorny mix of factors is still depressing the market and financially undermining many would-be home sellers" (Miron 2007a).

Southwest Michigan was largely immune to the housing bubble that drove prices up elsewhere in the nation, and the collapse of the market, too, has been much less dramatic than in many other regions. Even so, there has been a slowdown in both housing sales and prices. From 2000 to 2005, annual home sales in the Kalamazoo market had fluctuated between 4,243 and 4,954 units, with sales in 2006 of 4,614. In 2007, sales dipped below the 4,000-unit level for the first time in years, to 3,990 (a drop of 13.9 percent relative to 2006). The median sales price of homes in the area also fell, from $133,000 to $128,700, while the ratio of the listed price to the sales price declined slightly, from 96.75 percent to 95.98 percent. In all, the value of residential property sales fell 18.2 percent in 2007 over the previous year. Sales of all other categories of property, including land, multifamily buildings, and commercial/industrial sites were also down in 2007.[5] Another troubling indicator was a surge in the number of homeowners in some stage of foreclosure. In January 2008, Kalamazoo County officials reported that a record number of residents—969, up from 762 the previous year and more than double the total of three years earlier—had lost their homes in 2007 because they were unable to pay their mortgages. Even more hardship was on the horizon, with about 2,400 properties in the county in some stage of foreclosure (Nixon 2008a,b).

At this point any findings about the impact of the Kalamazoo Promise on the real estate market remain inconclusive. A definitive analysis is complicated by several factors: first, it is possible that the extent of the weaknesses in the housing market simply outweighs any potential benefits of the scholarship program. Second, without data from an appropriate comparison group it is difficult to assess how much worse the market might have been in the absence of the Promise. At the same time, city officials and real estate agents claim that downtown office vacancy rates are falling, rental demand is strong, and the small downtown residential market is booming, with only 2 percent vacancy in 2007 and more construction under way.[6] How much this has to do with the Kalamazoo Promise, how much with ongoing downtown revitalization efforts, and how much with the community's changing demographics (with more young and retired people interested in living downtown) is unclear. In the meantime, outside the downtown district it is a buyer's market, with properties for sale at every price point and housing costs well below the national average.

The mixed picture extends to home construction, where rosy forecasts had followed in the immediate aftermath of the Kalamazoo Promise. Early excitement by developers was reinforced when a housing development that sat idle for three years sold out in nine months following the November 2005 announcement (Beeke 2006). The area's largest home builder, Allen Edwin Homes, which built the development, made plans to purchase $7 million of property within KPS boundaries and build 500 new homes by 2009. And Hometown Building Co., a builder from the east side of the state that had recently opened a Kalamazoo division, said it planned to build 75–100 homes in each of the next few years, primarily on property it already owned on the west side of town (Miron 2006). However, these projections were cut back in light of the weakness of the local job market and negative trends in the housing market nationally (Miron 2007b).

The Kalamazoo Promise may have been a factor in where new housing starts occurred in 2006, with the largest number (133) in Oshtemo Township, two-thirds of which lie within the KPS district. The older and denser areas of the district saw fewer housing starts, with only 18 in the city of Kalamazoo and 40 in Kalamazoo Township (Miron 2007c). Building permit data for 2007 mirrored the housing start data, with a growing proportion of new residential permits issued for sites within KPS even as the volume of total permits fell.[7] Here, too, most permits are for the townships surrounding the urban core, with 338 in Oshtemo and Kalamazoo Townships and 52 in the city of Kalamazoo. A third housing-market indicator may also be related to the Kalamazoo Promise. The taxable value of homes in Kalamazoo County rose to $8.3 billion in 2008, a 3.96 percent increase over 2007. County officials had anticipated a smaller increase and identified the Kalamazoo Promise as a factor in the stronger-than-expected growth: "What kept the taxable values from going down was all the new residential construction in the Kalamazoo Promise areas," said Bonnie Payton, director of the county's equalization department. The strongest rise in values came in the townships—Oshtemo with 4.98 percent and Kalamazoo Township with 4.03 percent—while a more modest rise of 3.45 percent occurred in the city of Kalamazoo. Communities outside the district (with the exception of Texas Township, a small portion of which lies within KPS) had slower growth in home values (Killian 2008).

Builders remain optimistic. As Greg DeHaan, co-owner of Allen Edwin Homes, told the *Wall Street Journal* in July 2008, his company hadn't build a single home in the KPS district for 12 years before the

Promise was announced. Now, home sales in KPS account for 20 percent of the company's overall business, with the number of Promise-eligible properties built by Allen Edwin rising from 47 in 2006 to 87 in 2007. "The Promise has just given us this renewed sense of optimism," DeHaan says (Bennett 2008).

RAISING THE COMMUNITY'S PROFILE

One of the most important effects of the Kalamazoo Promise, albeit one that is difficult to quantify, has been a dramatic increase in the national profile of the Kalamazoo region. While the ultimate impact on the economy cannot yet be ascertained, local officials say this development is of great importance to future economic growth. Ron Kitchens cites surveys that consistently identify the top two reasons for business location decisions as, first, learning about the community from someone who lives or works there, and, second, reading or hearing about the community in the media. The Kalamazoo Promise contributed to both, creating excitement among residents who were eager to share the news with friends and associates outside the region and generating intense media coverage as well as a string of awards and honors. "There are 36,000 economic development groups globally all selling the same product: 'Invest here,'" says Kitchens. "Anything that makes a community stand apart is incredibly valuable." In short, the Kalamazoo Promise put Kalamazoo on the radar of the nation's major companies and leading media outlets—something that would have been tremendously hard to achieve in its absence.

A report on ABC World News that aired in September 2006 stands out among the national and international media coverage of the Kalamazoo Promise, which also included feature articles in the *Chicago Tribune*, the *Economist*, the *International Herald Tribune*, the *Los Angeles Times*, the *New York Times*, *USA Today*, the *Wall Street Journal*, and the *Washington Post*, as well as repeated coverage by National Public Radio. The three-minute ABC segment featured families from Arizona and Hawaii who moved to Kalamazoo to take advantage of the program, as well as a visit by anchorwoman Katie Couric and Dr. Brown to Kalamazoo Central High School. One of the program's results was a surge in phone calls and e-mails to Southwest Michigan First—60 in three days—from business people who had seen the segment. "It's amazing how many companies are now calling," Kitchens told the *Kalamazoo Gazette* (Chourey 2006a).

The awards began piling up at the same time that press coverage increased. While not all of these honors cited the Kalamazoo Promise, many were related at least in part to greater national awareness of the community. Several accolades were publicized in the first 18 months following the announcement of the scholarship program.

- *Expansion Management Magazine*, which serves company executives interested in expanding or relocating their facilities, included the Kalamazoo-Portage metropolitan statistical area among 73 communities across the nation on its 5-Star Quality of Life Metros list. The region was the only one in Michigan to be included. The magazine's quality-of-life indicators are intended to quantify what its editor describes as "employees being able to tap into the American dream . . . being able to afford to own a home, to be able to send your children to good schools, to feel safe from crime, to live in a place with a reasonable cost of living" (Chourey 2006b).

- Partners for Livable Communities, an organization that promotes progressive urban development, chose Kalamazoo as one of three cities to receive its Entrepreneurial American Leadership Award. "We give this award to communities where there are specific programs that we feel are really exemplary and something that needs to be modeled elsewhere," said Irene Garnett, chief operating officer of the Washington, D.C.–based nonprofit. "[The Kalamazoo Promise] is an economic-development strategy that really hasn't been used before. We think it's an example of something that can work in Michigan and other towns in that part of the country" (Mack 2006k).

- America's Promise, an alliance for youth, rated Kalamazoo as one of the nation's "100 Best Communities for Young People" based in part on the Kalamazoo Promise. The ratings were announced on ABC's *Good Morning America*. The 750 communities that applied for the honor were asked to demonstrate their support for youth, the availability of crucial resources for children, and positive results from community efforts on behalf of youth development (Jessup 2007).

- Kalamazoo was included in "The 6th Annual Fast 50," 50 portraits of "people and businesses writing the history of the next 10 years" compiled by *Fast Company* magazine. Kalamazoo was the only geographic region to be recognized with this honor, which was based on the Kalamazoo Promise, Southwest Michigan First's venture capital fund for financing life science startups, and community efforts to keep WMU's engineering school local (*Fast Company* 2007).

- Southwest Michigan First was one of four U.S. organizations honored by CoreNet Global, an Atlanta-based trade association for real-estate executives, for excellence in economic development. Southwest Michigan First received one of two Economic Development Leadership Awards in the Leadership and Innovation category, based on its presentation of the organization's model of "community capitalism," which includes the Kalamazoo Promise (Miron 2007d).

- Kalamazoo was named one of the top 10 turnaround cities in the country by the Urban Land Institute. The announcement noted improvements Kalamazoo had made to its downtown with new business, arts, and locally owned restaurants (Nyren 2007).

- The Metropolitan Policy Program of the Brookings Institution commissioned a study of the Kalamazoo Promise as part of its "Blueprint for Prosperity" series. The Brookings researchers proposed a role for the federal government in supporting an expansion to other communities of the education-centered economic development strategy pioneered by the Kalamazoo Promise (Brown, Affolter-Caine, and Dimond forthcoming).

While such honors may go unnoticed by the general public, they have drawn attention to Kalamazoo within business and policy circles and increased the community's bragging rights. They have also been avidly embraced by Southwest Michigan First and the city of Kalamazoo as marketing tools to recruit new businesses seeking a high quality of life for their employees.

The *Wall Street Journal* returned to the topic of the Kalamazoo Promise in July 2008 with an article reporting on the economic impact of the scholarship program. Citing the positive job news of the past six months, the reporter quoted an official of the California-based Kaiser Aluminum Corp., a firm that recently announced the creation of 150 jobs at an $80 million office and research center to be built in Kalamazoo. "We are building a sophisticated facility with new technology, and we want well-educated people who will work with us and want to live in Kalamazoo," said Martin Carter, vice president and general manager of common alloy products at Kaiser Aluminum, noting that the company considered cities in three states as the site for its new facility. "Some of the other sites gave a lot of talk about future education plans, but in the case of Kalamazoo, they already had a commitment to developing a well-educated community" (Bennett 2008). On the other side of the equation—new workers—the reporter included in his account the story of Efeosa Idemudia, a personal banker at J.P. Morgan Chase & Co. in New York who was preparing to buy an $800,000 home in Brooklyn when he saw an evening newscast about the Kalamazoo Promise. Mr. Idemudia was in Kalamazoo looking for homes a few weeks later. "When I went to college I had to work a full-time job and go to school," said the father of three. "I want my kids to focus on their education so they can do a whole lot better than I did" (Bennett 2008).

For communities emulating the Kalamazoo Promise, the national media "bang" from their programs is likely to be much quieter than it was for Kalamazoo. However, a community's commitment to education and its role as a powerful attractor of businesses like Kaiser Aluminum and families like the Idemudias will be a reality even if other communities are pursuing similar goals.

BUILDING AN EDUCATED WORKFORCE

For the Kalamazoo Promise to achieve its economic development potential, the region will need to move into that virtuous circle of economic growth underpinned by a highly educated workforce, as described in Chapter 3. Both sides of the equation are essential: skilled and educated workers who opt to live in the region and employers who value their labor. In this regard, the Kalamazoo Promise is not only a powerful recruitment tool, but also something that enhances the "stickiness" of the community, defined by Kitchens as "anything that makes Kalamazoo a place where people who have a choice choose to live."

An exodus of young, educated workers is a critical concern both for the region and the state as a whole. Between 2000 and 2005, Michigan lost 22,000, or 2.2 percent, of its population of young adults ages 18–24. The *Kalamazoo Gazette* (2006b) spoke for many when it commented in an editorial, "It makes us wonder what will become of all the promising young people graduating from Kalamazoo Public Schools with the Kalamazoo Promise college guarantee in their hands. If [these] grads are unable to find jobs here when they finish college, then the ultimate benefit of the Promise will go to the economies of other states." In its annual economic outlook for 2006, area economists agreed that retaining young people was a critical priority for the region, and that doing so will require a deepening of the manufacturing-to-services transition under way. The W.E. Upjohn Institute's George Erickcek characterized this change as going from "producing for a living to thinking for a living" (Miron 2005).

One strategy is to provide more support for recent graduates of local colleges and universities who often leave town for larger cities upon graduation. The Monroe-Brown Internship Program is a step in this direction. The announcement of the Kalamazoo Promise led the Monroe-Brown Foundation and Southwest Michigan First to scale up the program, which serves as a vehicle for retaining the community's intellectual capital. In 2007 and 2008, the program provided paid summer internships to approximately 50 local college students. Interns received a salary, bonus, scholarship funding, and a network of business connections at local firms.[8] Eighteen companies have participated in the program. "We wanted to create an internship program that would reward students for staying and growing in Kalamazoo . . . These are talented individuals that may have otherwise spent their summers working in other cities, but they have chosen to stay here. We hope they make that decision again after graduation," said Monroe-Brown Foundation President Bob Brown (Southwest Michigan First 2007). The assumption is that students may end up with job offers from the firms where they were interns, as often happens with similar programs in larger cities.

Plans call for marketing the program to additional firms and seeking an expanded funding base for it.

Another strategy is to promote the community as one that is especially hospitable to entrepreneurs. Much of the effort in this area has focused on positioning southwest Michigan as a home to the life science industry and retaining researchers who were laid off from Pfizer in subsequent waves of downsizing. The Southwest Michigan Innovation Center (SMIC), a business incubator funded by Southwest Michigan First and the city of Kalamazoo and housed within Western Michigan University's Business Technology and Research Park, has played a critical role in fostering entrepreneurship in the life science field. Between its establishment in 2003 and 2008, the center housed a total of 23 start-up companies, not one of which has failed. (Similar incubators generally aim for an 80 percent success rate.) Three of these firms have moved into their own facilities, including drug-development firm Kalexsyn Inc., which built a 20,000-square-foot headquarters and laboratory in the Business Technology and Research Park in 2007 (Mackinder 2008). The *Kalamazoo Gazette* has called life sciences "the still-young, and somewhat unsteady, horse to which economic developers have hitched their growth-industry wagon" (Jones 2007). Many observers would like to see the connection with entrepreneurs in other sectors strengthened. Some envision a support network for young entrepreneurs—even those still in college—that would include a business incubator and venture capital, services now reserved mainly for more experienced business owners or researchers.

A third strategy is to market the community to young people who were raised in or attended college in the region then departed for the enticements of bigger cities. (Chicago seems to be the prime destination for area graduates.) Many of these individuals have since started families and, confronted with high housing prices and troubled public schools in most of the nation's major metropolitan areas, might consider a return to their home community. Lam & Associates has developed a Web site aimed at this population, with the message that the community has changed since they lived here. "Our goal is to attract and retain our 20- and 30-somethings in a community dedicated to improvement and quality of life. We expect to create momentum, and help create new jobs, as we build on our community's most appropriate focus on education as the key to our future," wrote Blaine Lam in introducing his

Web-based campaign, "Share Kalamazoo."[9] The school improvement efforts discussed in Chapter 5 are critical to such a campaign; while cities have shown that they are able to attract young people regardless of the problems that plague many urban school districts, good public schools are a must if they are to retain these residents once they have school-age children.

And what of Kalamazoo's less-educated workers? Trapped in minimum-wage jobs, unemployed or underemployed, does the Kalamazoo Promise offer them something, or does its value lie mainly in expanding the educational opportunities available to their children? Mattie Jordan-Woods, the head of the Northside Association for Community Development and a powerful advocate for economic growth in Kalamazoo's low-income neighborhoods, stresses that there is nothing automatic about the scholarship program's impact on either parents or children: "The Kalamazoo Promise does one thing and one thing only: It provides scholarship dollars for any kid who is academically able to graduate [from high school] and go on to college. This creates new opportunities for low- and moderate-income people whose kids are doing well in school, but it does nothing by itself to bring up the academic competitiveness of kids who are struggling."[10]

Like others, Jordan-Woods believes that one-on-one tutoring programs, as well as strategies to address the social problems found in many households, are essential for this group of students, but she also stresses the importance of the physical environment in which low-income children grow up. "You need to have an environment that celebrates education and says that things are happening here. If you change the physical environment of a neighborhood through better housing, nicer buildings, and more playgrounds, businesses will invest because they want to be there," says Jordan-Woods. And with businesses come jobs for the parents who live in that neighborhood. "When a majority of people [in the neighborhood] are working, it creates an expectation of what the neighborhood should look like." She says it also raises children's expectations about their own futures. "When children see their parents and neighbors go to work every day, it increases their appetite for education."

In this sense, the most commonly understood logic of the Kalamazoo Promise—improve educational opportunities in order to bring about a healthier economy—is reversed. It is economic opportunity that reinforces the demand for higher education, not the other way around. "Watching your mama get up and go to work, even if she earns only $9.00 an hour, and not wait on the check every two weeks, is going to make them want to go to college," says Jordan-Woods. "They'll want $13.00 an hour; they'll want something better." In her own work, Jordan-Woods remains focused on the economic and physical development of the Northside, chiefly the improvement of the neighborhood's infrastructure and appearance, and the creation of jobs for its low-income residents. This neighborhood focus is an essential complement to the work of economic development officials to attract high value-added jobs to the region.

The heightened national profile of Kalamazoo and the alignment of local officials around the goal of education-based economic development, both related to the Kalamazoo Promise, began to yield results on the job front in the spring of 2008. The MPI Research expansion, which will include the creation of 400 jobs downtown, where the company will occupy two buildings formerly owned by Pfizer Inc., grabbed most of the headlines. (In a testament to the ongoing role of a few prominent families in Kalamazoo's history, MPI Research's chairman and CEO, William U. Parfet, himself a former Upjohn Company president, noted that his grandfather, W.E. Upjohn, had built the buildings and his father had worked in them.) MPI Research will receive property tax abatements on the downtown buildings and will have the opportunity to buy them for the sum of $1 in 2013 if its job creation obligations have been met. While not referencing the Kalamazoo Promise directly, Parfet said the reasons he chose to expand in the region are the quality of the local workforce and access to higher education institutions that help recruit scientists and other skilled workers to the area and create a pool of local talent. "Seventy percent of the people who work at MPI have at least a bachelor's degree," he said. "Low taxes are important, but quality of education is critical" (Mack 2008e). MPI Research and Kaiser Aluminum were not the only companies to announce the creation of new jobs in the Kalamazoo region in the first half of 2008. Four local firms, including Fabri-Kal Corp. and AT&T, plan expansions that together will create hundreds of new jobs (Jessup 2008).

In March 2008, while the unemployment rate for the state hovered at close to 8 percent, the Kalamazoo-Portage area had a significantly lower level of 5.6 percent. The gap, a fairly steady one, is evidence of the relative diversity of the Kalamazoo region. "The country's future is not in automobiles," said Ron Kitchens, commenting on the job growth announcements. "It's in companies that offer brainpower, knowledge and entrepreneurship . . . When most communities lose their national or global relevance, they never come back. But Kalamazoo has done it over and over again, from sleds to stoves to celery, to paper to pharmaceuticals to medical devices . . . People who have made money stayed here and they become mentors who pull others along" (Jessup 2008). It is reasonable to conclude that such multigenerational wealth and a commitment to the community are also at the heart of the Kalamazoo Promise, whether the precise identity of the donors is known or not. And while the connection between the scholarship program and job creation is not a direct one, the alignment of community leaders around a strategy of education-based economic development is critical to the region's economic future.

FORECASTING THE FUTURE

The impact of the Kalamazoo Promise on regional economic growth is a long-term proposition, but it is possible to envision how it might come about. To illustrate how the Kalamazoo Promise could contribute to employment and income growth in the region, the Upjohn Institute's George Erickcek has developed a model based on his 20 years of experience in forecasting regional economic trends for southwest Michigan.[11] The model embodies a set of conservative assumptions about likely increases in student enrollment, population growth, employment opportunities, and earnings. While the gains it predicts are modest in the context of the overall regional economy, the forecasting process illustrates how a growing population and increased disposable income resulting from the Promise could brighten prospects for both employment and income growth.

An obvious and immediate effect of the Kalamazoo Promise is to increase disposable income for households whose children qualify for the scholarship. This increase will generate economic activity through increased consumer spending, which in turn will support the creation of a small number of new jobs. Based on assumptions about the annual outlay for each scholarship round, the college retention rate, and the proportion of new students entering college as a result of the Promise, Table 6.1 shows the projected annual increases in disposable income for the families of Kalamazoo Promise recipients. In 2006, this reached just over $1 million; by 2017, it is expected to rise to $6.4 million (in 2006 dollars).[12]

A second, more subtle effect is an increase in economic activity due to the new students expected to enter KPS annually. As shown in Table 6.2, in 2006, KPS attracted approximately 368 new students from outside the county, a number that declined in 2008 but remained positive. The assumption used in the model is that 125 new students will come from outside the county in each year of the forecast period (2007–2017). The impact on the labor force is calculated based on the assumption of an average of 1.8 parents per new student, with 70 percent of these adults entering the local labor market. These assumptions yield a growth in the labor force due to the Kalamazoo Promise of approximately 158 workers per year (see Table 6.2).

The forecast scenario is based on the assumption that the annual increase of 158 new labor force entrants will find jobs either by joining an existing firm at present wage levels or by starting their own businesses. For purposes of the model, and based on the composition of employment in the region, these jobs are evenly divided among the following

Table 6.1 Projected Increase in Annual Disposable Income for KPS Families (in thousands of $)

2006	1,081
2007	2,157
2008	3,249
2009	4,354
2010	4,647
2011	4,949
2012	5,225
2013	5,481
2014	5,718
2015	5,947
2016	6,184
2017	6,432

SOURCE: Forecast data from the W.E. Upjohn Institute.

Table 6.2 Population and Labor Force Assumptions, 2006–2008

	2006	2007	2008
Net new students in KPS	368	125	125
Net new parents (1.8/child)	662	225	225
Cumulative population increase	1,030	1,380	1,730
Net new labor force participants (70% of parents)	464	621	779
Net population increase by year	1,030	350	350
Net labor force increase by year	464	158	158

SOURCE: Forecast data from the W.E. Upjohn Institute.

industries: banks and other financial institutions, insurance companies, real estate, professional and technical services, educational services, and hospitals. While the new jobs will displace some existing jobs, the net impact will remain positive.[13]

The full economic impact of the Kalamazoo Promise is shown in Table 6.3. At the end of the forecast period, it would be reasonable to expect that 2,221 new jobs had been created as a result of workers coming to the region because of the Kalamazoo Promise (this figure takes into account the displacement effect that comes from competition with the existing local workforce), as well as the creation of 41 new jobs supported by the spending of disposable income of Promise families, for total projected employment growth of 2,262. Similarly, by 2017, $133.4 million of personal income will have been generated through the earnings of new residents, along with an additional $8.4 million in disposable income due to the direct effect of the scholarships, for a total increase in personal income in the region of $141.2 million, or 1.4 percent. Although this is a small amount relative to aggregate personal income in the region ($10.8 billion in 2006), the results of the model illustrate the multiple dynamics through which the Kalamazoo Promise is likely to affect the regional economy. It is worth pointing out—especially to those outside KPS who wonder if and how the Kalamazoo Promise will benefit them—that the employment and income effects illustrated here are not confined to KPS or the city of Kalamazoo. While families moving to the region to take advantage of the Kalamazoo Promise will need to live within the district where the scholarship program is offered, they can work—and their disposable income can be spent—anywhere in the

Table 6.3 Projected Employment and Income Effects of the Kalamazoo Promise

	Employment			Personal income ($, millions)		
	New residents	New disposable income	Total	New residents	New disposable income	Total
2005	0	0	0	0	0	0
2006	471	11	481	16.08	1.33	17.41
2007	601	21	622	22.52	2.70	25.22
2008	788	31	818	31.43	4.13	35.56
2009	970	40	1,009	40.91	5.59	46.50
2010	1,092	41	1,133	48.81	6.04	54.85
2011	1,271	41	1,312	59.49	6.47	65.96
2012	1,392	41	1,433	68.48	6.84	75.32
2013	1,571	41	1,612	80.51	7.18	87.69
2014	1,751	41	1,792	93.46	7.48	100.94
2015	1,869	41	1,910	104.20	7.77	111.97
2016	2,045	41	2,086	118.30	8.08	126.38
2017	2,221	41	2,262	133.40	8.40	141.80

SOURCE: Forecast data from the W.E. Upjohn Institute.

region. Another effect not captured by the model but visible in the community is families who are moving to the region before their children reach school age. Ultimately, these children will show up in KPS enrollment figures, but in the meantime their parents are living, working, and spending their money irregardless of district boundaries.

ALIGNING THE COMMUNITY

For the potential economic gains of the Kalamazoo Promise to materialize—for the virtuous circle to take hold—community leaders must focus their efforts around a common set of goals. The critical players include regional economic development officials, city and county planners, downtown development leaders, the regional office of the statewide workforce development agency Michigan Works!, institutions of higher education, grassroots economic organizations, and the private sector. It was gratifying in this light to see the cover story of the *Kalamazoo Gazette* on the first Sunday in 2008, and the two-page spread that followed. After two years of covering the Kalamazoo Promise primarily as a scholarship program for district residents, the newspaper was putting the program's broader implications front and center, arguing that the region must leverage its plentiful educational assets in the interest of its economic future. A "to-do list" on the front page laid out four priorities:

1) to improve promotion and appreciation of the area's educational assets, particularly in the business community and in Lansing [the state capital];

2) to improve ties between local colleges and employers to keep more graduates in the area;

3) to improve coordination between educational institutions and community programs; and

4) to become a national leader in educating low-income and minority children.

The report went on to list the area's top 10 educational assets, including diverse institutions of higher education, strong K-12 school systems, workforce development organizations, and healthy nonprofit and philanthropic sectors. Especially uplifting was the message from Kitchens, the region's chief economic development official, placing education squarely at the center of Southwest Michigan First's business strategy.

Two other leaders offered more cautionary views. Kalamazoo Public Schools superintendent Michael Rice, a relative newcomer to the community, stressed the need to deploy the community's assets in a more organized fashion. "If someone said to me, what is the one thing we need most, it would be cohesion," said Rice in an interview. Kalamazoo Valley Community College president Marilyn Schlack, who has lived and worked in the region for several decades, took matters a step further, arguing for greater centralization of leadership: "The question is, where do we go from here, and how do we do it? Who takes the lead? I think we need someone who keeps this out in front of us, and says this is your job and that's your job" (*Kalamazoo Gazette* 2007b).

Echoing the interest of the Saturday Morning Group in charging an individual or small steering group with taking the lead, Schlack joins others in the community who believe that progress will not take place automatically—that if you want something to happen you need to make it someone's job to move it forward.

Adapting to the community's altered leadership paradigm—a challenge discussed in Chapter 4—is essential if the potential growth and employment benefits of the Kalamazoo Promise are to be realized, but the idea that a single individual or even a small group can in some sense drive the process is unrealistic. One of the truths revealed by the events of the 1990s is that Kalamazoo's days as a company town are over; no single firm will ever enjoy the same leadership role that the Upjohn Company did in its heyday. Another truth—and one that the Kalamazoo Promise holds the potential to change—is that the community's social divisions, especially those between a disproportionately large white middle class and a disproportionately large black and Hispanic low-income population, are so entrenched that leadership exercised in one part of town will meet almost reflexively with mistrust on the other side of the metaphorical and actual railroad tracks. The best medicine for what ails Kalamazoo, both economically and in terms of its class divide, is good jobs for workers at a variety of skill levels. Whether these can be generated with the spark of the Kalamazoo Promise depends in part on shifting economic winds that lie outside local control, but also on the wisdom and energy of a broad range of local actors.

Notes

1. Enrollment is not capped at either institution, so Promise students and their scholarship dollars do not displace students and dollars from other sources.
2. See, for example, Boudette (2006) and Associated Press (2006b).
3. Nonetheless, the median price of homes within KPS was still substantially lower than in the county, at $108,750 compared to $135,000.
4. Author's interview with John Jackson, Prudential Realtors, March 1, 2006.
5. Greater Kalamazoo Association of Realtors, Monthly Cumulative Sales Report, December 2007.
6. Figures from Downtown Kalamazoo Inc., reprinted in Liberty (2007).
7. In 2007, 49 percent of new private housing units authorized by building permits in Kalamazoo County were within the three municipalities that make up the bulk of

the KPS district, up from 39 percent in 2005 (W.E. Upjohn Institute for Employment Research 2008b).

8. Those eligible for the program are incoming juniors, seniors, or graduate students at WMU and Kalamazoo College, as well as students going into at least their second year at KVCC. Participants are paid a salary of at least minimum wage for 400 hours of work. Upon successful completion of the internship, each student receives two $500 bonuses, one from the employer and the other from the foundation. The student also receives a $2,500 scholarship at the end of each of the first and second semesters following the internship.

9. E-mail from Blaine Lam of Lam and Associates. For more on Share Kalamazoo, see http://www.sharekalamazoo.com.

10. Author's interview with Mattie Jordan-Woods, head of the Northside Association for Community Development.

11. My thanks to George Erickcek for lending his forecasting prowess to this chapter.

12. These estimates are based on the following assumptions: 1) The cost of tuition will increase annually, on average, by 4 percent above inflation. 2) The percent of eligible high school graduates taking advantage of the Promise will increase from 72.7 percent in 2006 to 85 percent in 2011 and then remain steady for the rest of the forecast period. 3) The retention rate for purposes of calculating tuition costs is estimated at 90 percent per year during the forecast period. (Note: This is higher than the student retention rate because students going to more expensive four-year universities are more likely to stay in college than students attending less expensive community colleges.) 4) On average, 68 percent of the tuition dollars awarded through the Promise go to families that had saved for their children's education. These savings are now available for consumption expenditures.

13. The annual addition of 158 workers will not be supported completely by sales to customers outside the area; instead employers will compete against existing firms in the county and hence there will be some displacement impacts. On average, each new worker is assumed to be supported by the industry's estimated nonlocal share of business; for example, if 10 percent of the county's insurance carriers' revenues come from nonlocal customers, then 10 percent of the new worker's income will come from nonlocal customers as well. The other 90 percent will come from other insurance companies in the county losing share. This is a measure of the displacement rate.

Part 3

Looking Forward

7
Assessing the Impact of the Kalamazoo Promise

It was a "perfect storm" of reasons that brought Gary and Katie Swartz to Kalamazoo in August 2006. Gary, a southwest Michigan native, and Katie, originally from the Chicago area, met at Michigan State University in the 1990s. Their jobs took them to Portland, Oregon, where Katie headed a nonprofit mentoring program and Gary taught special education in the public schools. Eight years later, when their twin girls were a year old, the couple started looking for a new house. "We lived in an 800-square foot house with one bathroom and there were now four of us," says Katie. But finding adequate, affordable housing was a daunting endeavor. As Katie bluntly puts it, "The housing market in Portland was outrageous."

Gary's parents came to visit in December 2005, and his mother mentioned the Kalamazoo Promise, which had been announced just a month earlier. "We looked it up online and thought it sounded interesting," recounts Katie, "then a couple of weeks later we started pulling up real estate ads just for fun, and we found these beautiful old homes for sale at really reasonable prices. It was when we started looking at houses that we made the decision to come." Gary flew to Michigan during his spring break in April 2006 to look for a job and a house, and found both. "It happened so fast," says Gary. "Free college tuition, reasonably priced housing, and our parents nearby. How could we not do it? If you took any one of those reasons out of the equation, we probably would have stayed in Portland."[1]

The Swartzes were fortunate in two respects—they were able to secure employment with relative ease, and they were moving from a high-priced to a lower-priced housing market. Gary had teaching experience and credentials, and readily found a position with KPS. In 2008, he began teaching at the district's new alternative middle school program, an ideal fit for someone who enjoys working with troubled teens. Katie brought her job with her, having worked for several years for an association management company based in Chicago. All of the firm's employees work remotely, so the move from Portland to Kalamazoo was of little consequence. The couple opted to live in the city of Kalamazoo despite its high property taxes because they value its unique housing stock, tight-knit neighborhoods, and proximity to downtown. With the proceeds from the sale of their West Coast home, Gary and Katie were able to buy a new house more than three times its size. "If we had stayed in Portland," says Katie, "we would have had to pay much more for something much smaller."

The twins will start kindergarten in fall 2009. Like other young children whose families moved to the community for the Kalamazoo Promise, they are part of the Promise-driven enrollment increase at KPS even though they may not be counted as such. It is impossible to estimate the size of the pipeline of families with children younger than school age who have already relocated to the area, but the existence of such a pipeline suggests that the enrollment impact of the scholarship program is stronger than current numbers suggest. Katie and Gary were drawn to KPS not just because of the Promise, but also because they want their children to be part of a school district that is diverse in terms of income, race, and ethnicity. Katie had attended a Catholic school system that sheltered her from such diversity (to her regret), but that also instilled in her high expectations about her educational goals. "I grew up with the understanding that going to college is what you do," she says, speaking of her prestigious high school that sends virtually every one of its graduates to higher education. "I wasn't a straight-A student, but being in those AP classes, I had a good GPA—it was an environment of high expectations, and I had to rise to them." Both parents plan to be deeply involved in their children's schools to make sure similar expectations are in place for the twins and their classmates.

Beyond the economic and educational implications of their move to Kalamazoo, Gary and Katie have enriched the social fabric of their neighborhood and the broader area. "It's important for us to feel part of our community. When we were in Portland, we did the same thing," says Katie, who was invited to join the board of the Volunteer Center of Greater Kalamazoo shortly after she relocated. "I was drawn to the Volunteer Center because it represents over 200 organizations in the community. It's a great chance to get the big picture about what's going on with nonprofits here." In 2008, as chair of the organization's largest annual fundraising event, she helped raise $20,000 for Volunteer Center programs and services.

Like the multiple reasons that drew them to Kalamazoo, the Swartzes' story illustrates the multiple avenues through which new residents can contribute to the health of the community. The purchase of a home, choice of employment, children's schooling, and volunteer activities affect not only the lives of those relocating, but also the community's stock of human, economic, and social assets. These contributions are especially strong and enduring when it is a young family moving to the region and putting down roots. Gary and Katie are emblematic of that thirty-something constituency at which the "Share Kalamazoo" campaign is aimed—the so-called "boomerang" generation that left the area for the big city, but now may be ready to return (see Chapter 6).

The Kalamazoo Promise sparked the Swartzes' decision to return, but it was not the sole reason. Similarly, the scholarship program alone is not a powerful enough tool to set the region on a trajectory of growth and renewal. But the Kalamazoo Promise is critically important as an organizing device for how the community sees itself and presents itself to others. By anchoring the region's economic development strategy in educational opportunity, the Kalamazoo Promise draws together the community's most valuable assets into a coherent framework and connects them to each other in a way that resonates with many different audiences. Yet none of this is automatic. It is easy to overlook the fact that Kalamazoo did not earn the donors' attention by virtue of some exceptional achievement or trait. To a large degree, the choice of Kalamazoo as the site of the donors' investment is a matter of geographic happenstance—this is where the donors live, and this is where they have chosen to invest. "We happen to be the community that received this gift," says Mayor Bobby Hopewell, "but we need to do the work so we can demonstrate success in areas where many communities struggle."[2]

In Chapter 1, I outlined three types of assets that could be affected positively by the Kalamazoo Promise: human capital, economic assets, and social capital. With three classes of Promise-eligible students now in college and three years of community alignment efforts around the broader goals of the Kalamazoo Promise, it is an opportune moment to assess the progress that has been made and the work that remains to be done.

HUMAN CAPITAL

Just as technological change in the nineteenth and twentieth centuries sparked an economic shift in the United States from agriculture
to manufacturing and gave rise to a new set of educational needs, so
has it brought about a subsequent shift to more knowledge-intensive
production and the higher level of skills and training associated with
it. As this shift has taken place, awareness has grown about the importance of investing in human capital—not only for individuals seeking
gainful employment and a decent income, but also for cities, regions,
and states eager to create or maintain a competitive edge in the global
economy. Many of the most recent innovations in educational and economic policy seek to build human capital, and the Kalamazoo Promise
is no exception.

Even in its first few years, the Kalamazoo Promise contributed to
the region's stock of human capital through several avenues. First, more
than a thousand scholarships have been awarded, covering the tuition
costs of students who might not otherwise have gone on to higher education and enabling those already on a college path to attend more selective (and sometimes more expensive) institutions. Second, the program
generated strong community awareness and engagement around the
goals of educational quality and student success for all. Third, almost
four decades of enrollment decline within KPS was reversed, with new
students coming not just from surrounding school districts but from
outside the county and state. Economic trends may work against the
powerful pull of the Kalamazoo Promise—those without jobs cannot
move to the region for the scholarship program alone—but the Promise
has undoubtedly minimized the ongoing contraction that would have
occurred in its absence. It has also generated the first construction of
new school buildings in 35 years, the first budget surpluses in decades,
and a larger pool of talent from which KPS can select its teachers and
administrators—all important factors in strengthening what had been
an urban school district in decline.

The longer-term potential for KPS is even more significant. Goals
that predated the announcement of the Promise—the fostering of a
college-going culture within the schools, strategies to reduce the achievement gap between higher- and lower-achieving students, and greater

student awareness of career opportunities and the training and education they require—have now been accelerated and made more urgent. The creation of a clear set of expectations for students, parents, teachers, and community members as the centerpiece of the school district's strategic plan moves these goals even further along. For lower-achieving students and those with behavioral issues, KPS has enhanced its alternative education offerings and in-school supports, while community organizations have stepped up with new mentoring, academic, and social support programs. Over the medium term, these developments should help lower dropout rates, increase graduation rates, and better prepare students for success in a postsecondary setting. At the same time, expanded opportunities for accelerated learning and dual enrollment, as well as efforts to curtail disruptive student behavior, make the district more attractive to the parents of higher-achieving students.

One of the critical factors needed to bring about these longer-term benefits is strong leadership of key educational institutions. From the beginning, the superintendents of school districts surrounding KPS, led by Craig Misner and later Ron Fuller at the intermediate school district, resisted the temptation to see the Kalamazoo Promise as a zero-sum game and promoted the program as something that could help strengthen educational offerings throughout the region. Marilyn Schlack, the president of KVCC and a key leader in economic development circles, has worked to ensure that the community college is responsive to the needs of its students as well as the regional economy. Western Michigan University President John Dunn, who took office in 2007, committed to reversing the school's enrollment decline and deepening its ties to the surrounding community. At KPS, Superintendent Michael Rice began his tenure in 2007 with a series of honest conversations about the district's strengths and weaknesses, and engaged the broader community in setting expectations for students and the adults who support them, as well as improving child and adult literacy.

A second critical factor already in place is a high level of community mobilization around the goal of student success. An upsurge in volunteering in the schools, the emergence of new tutoring and mentoring programs, ongoing communication among youth-serving organizations, foundation-funded initiatives addressing literacy and the prevention of youth violence, and support for school bond issues not only by KPS voters but by those in most of the surrounding districts are all evidence of a region that is willing to invest in its young people. Parents, too, have responded, with teachers reporting record attendance at parent-teacher conferences and greater parental interest in children's college options and preparedness.

The business community has been slower to engage with the schools, but this is beginning to change. Both educational and business leaders acknowledge that they need each other and are exploring avenues for closer collaboration through career awareness activities, job shadowing, mentoring, and adopt-a-school programs. Efforts to align the region's existing workforce development resources to connect them more closely with its educational system and business needs are also under way. Although it is a tall order, there is a new understanding that job creation and economic vitality in the region depend on the quality and interconnectedness of community institutions spanning the fields of early childhood development, K-12 and postsecondary education, workforce development, and economic development.

One area of critical need is a stronger system of early childhood development and education. The growing recognition that the twenty-first century workforce requires some kind of postsecondary education or training has been paralleled by an emerging consensus around the need for improved coverage and quality of early childhood interventions, including preschool. Ample research substantiating the relative cost-effectiveness of investing in children at an early age has led some states to implement universal preschool for their residents. Michigan's ongoing fiscal difficulties mean that it lags its neighbors in this area, but local actors are engaged in coordinating more closely the work of the region's early childhood health and education providers. Cooperative efforts include work through the countywide Great Start Collaborative (part of a statewide initiative), closer alignment of KPS programs with the county's federal Head Start preschool program for three- and four-year-olds, improvement in the district's state-funded Prekindergarten Early Education Program, and the implementation of full-day kindergarten at almost every KPS elementary school in fall 2008.

Another key factor in the accumulation of human capital is beyond the control of local actors. Without an upturn in the state economy, Michigan will continue to be a net exporter of jobs and people. Even if southwest Michigan outperforms the state, as it has in recent years, the level of economic dynamism needed to attract hundreds of new jobs and families may still remain out of reach. Continued corporate downsizing and slow economic growth resulting from the ongoing financial crisis also limit the net inflow of workers. The Kalamazoo Promise may enable the district to hold its own in terms of enrollment during any prolonged economic downturn, but without a large influx of working families from outside the region, KPS is unlikely to achieve the powerful boost to academic achievement that comes from greater socioeconomic integration of schools. In the first few years following the introduction of the Kalamazoo Promise, enrollment grew most quickly at those schools with the smallest proportion of low-income students, which also tend to be those with the lowest minority enrollment. Several of these schools are now at capacity, and families moving to the district will of necessity be looking at schools with more low-income and minority students. The investment of additional resources in the district's magnet schools, which are located in high-poverty areas, may also encourage some new families to choose these educational settings. But if, as research suggests, socioeconomic integration within individual schools is one of the strongest mechanisms for improving the academic performance of all students, limited enrollment growth with gains concentrated in the district's middle-income schools will slow progress toward better educational outcomes.

ECONOMIC ASSETS

As discussed in the previous chapter, the economic assets likely to be catalyzed by the Kalamazoo Promise will take years to materialize, and certainly, much depends on broader economic trends. For example, one of the most widely anticipated effects of the scholarship program was a rise in housing values within the public school district where median home prices lag the county average, but a slack real estate market has thus far outweighed any positive impact from the scholarship program, and without strong job growth, housing appreciation is not likely to occur in the short term.

On the brighter side, the Kalamazoo Promise has helped align the community around a plausible vision of its economic future as an "Education Community," where all parts of the whole are working together to invest in the success of the region's young people. For several years now, economic development entities such as Southwest Michigan First and the Southwest Michigan Innovation Center have sought to position Kalamazoo County as a home for high value-added, knowledge-intensive industry, primarily to capture spin-offs from the pharmaceuticals sector as well as businesses and entrepreneurs from outside the region. This strategy builds on some of the area's most important assets, including its life-science industries, research university, and hospitals, but it also brings Kalamazoo into direct competition with other regions seeking the same outcomes, including Greater Grand Rapids, and risks putting too many eggs in a single, life-sciences basket.[3] Even when the Upjohn Company played the key leadership role, the region's economy rested on a diverse mix of industries; since the economic shocks of the 1990s, when Kalamazoo lost its largest employer, it has become even clearer that today's regional economy must rest on a similarly diverse base—although, as is true everywhere, there will be little room for those lacking any postsecondary training or skills.[4]

The Kalamazoo Promise supports the current knowledge-intensive economic development strategy in several respects. Most directly, it puts skill-based training in reach of even the poorest residents of the community. Second, it raises the region's national profile more effectively than could any public relations campaign, no matter how well funded. Third, in an era in which investment decisions are often based on the availability of a skilled workforce and high-quality schools, the Kalamazoo Promise is a critical asset. Assuming it is leveraged effectively, in the medium term it will strengthen the public school system and over the longer term contribute to the creation of a better-educated workforce. And from day one, its very existence has signaled to outsiders that Kalamazoo is a community that values education. As the nation's older cities of the Northeast and Midwest seek to transform their identities from rust belt to new economy, the Kalamazoo Promise is already serving as an engine for this transformation, as well as a priceless marketing device.

Once again, leadership is a crucial variable in accomplishing this transformation. Mayor Bobby Hopewell, himself a business leader, points out the limitations of business leadership. "CEOs are wrestling with the worst economy we've had in years," says Hopewell, "so I think that they are not concentrating on this as much. But they should. Businesspeople have come together to work with Southwest Michigan First, downtown development, the Southwest Michigan Innovation Center, but not the Kalamazoo Promise. This is the biggest economic development tool we have, so why aren't we engaging?" Hopewell especially wants business leaders to engage with their own workers by providing employees' families and children with the support they need to benefit from the Kalamazoo Promise. "We have the folks who need us sitting right in our offices," he says. "It's a grand opportunity to have some sustained impact on your employees." City officials, too, are thinking creatively to ensure that the economic development benefits generated by the Kalamazoo Promise (in terms of new housing, population, or commercial development) do not accrue only to that part of the district that lies outside city boundaries. Intergovernmental cooperation among the region's municipalities in upgrading infrastructure and coordinating incentive packages for business is also crucial. Beyond their educational role, WMU and KVCC are valuable economic assets, and their activities must be integrated more fully with the economic development efforts of government and the private sector. The community college's career programs and training facility fill an important business need in tightening the workforce–employer connection. WMU's Business Technology and Research Park and many of the university's faculty members and programs are potential partners for private-sector development efforts in engineering, life sciences, and alternative fuels. Much greater effort needs to be exerted to entice college graduates, especially those with entrepreneurial skills, to remain in the region after graduation. Comprehensive support for start-up ventures in the form of financing, subsidized facilities, and business networks is available to those with high skills through the Southwest Michigan Innovation Center, but no one has yet developed a strategy to provide a similar system of support to younger entrepreneurs.

In terms of downtown development, the main impact of the Kalamazoo Promise may be psychological more than anything else. Downtown revitalization efforts have been under way for many years, but a new momentum is evident since the announcement of the scholarship program. The preservation of historic buildings and key renovations, such as that of the Radisson Plaza Hotel, were positive developments, but the progress of the commercial district had been intermittent, and there was a sense that improvement efforts were merely slowing an inevitable decline. By placing a bet on the improvement of the urban core through a scholarship program for graduates of the city's public school district, the donors signaled to others in the community that they believe in the city's future. In the afterglow that surrounded the announcement of the Kalamazoo Promise, many residents began to hope that the tipping point of urban decay had been avoided, with the urban core now set on a more promising trajectory. With new restaurants and entertainment options and the activities of a remarkably healthy arts and cultural scene (most of it located downtown), the central district is attracting younger residents and seeing the construction of new housing units. A rise in population density, albeit on a small scale, should lead to the creation of even more amenities and set in motion the virtuous circle described by urban experts as the best possible outcome for the nation's older cities.

A healthy downtown district also strengthens one of the more promising avenues for population growth: the anticipated return of that "boomerang" generation—young adults like Katie and Gary Swartz, who attended college or were raised in the area but left to pursue careers elsewhere. Now, with children in tow, these educated workers, some of them self-employed, are in the market for communities with reasonable housing prices and a high quality of life, including a vibrant urban core. With the added enticement of full college scholarships for their children, and grandparents nearby for child care purposes, this is a population ripe for recruitment.

The impact of the Kalamazoo Promise on the low-income neighborhoods that surround downtown is, as Mattie Jordan-Woods has recognized, a long way off (see p. 193). If, however, jobs for less-skilled workers materialize and the city and community organizations continue their focus on neighborhood safety and quality of life improvements, these areas could become more attractive to current and future residents. Low housing prices and proximity to downtown are enticements for those interested in urban neighborhoods. The gentrification scenario feared by some is unlikely—there is simply too much empty space and too many rental units to create the kind of demand accompanied by rapidly escalating prices. Instead, neighborhoods like Vine, Edison, and the Northside could see the renovation of existing properties, conversion of rentals into owner-occupied homes, construction of new homes on vacant lots, and more commercial activity. Over the long term and under the most optimistic conditions, the poverty rate in the city of Kalamazoo could fall, not just because of an influx of middle-class residents but also because poor residents, through the engine of education set in motion by the Kalamazoo Promise and ongoing neighborhood efforts, are becoming less poor.

SOCIAL CAPITAL

Kalamazoo's social fabric is a paradox. The community's exceptionally strong philanthropic and nonprofit sectors, as well as a high level of resident engagement in civic life, coexist with pronounced divisions along racial and income lines, an urban-suburban divide, and a lack of integration of the large student population into the life of the city. While the Kalamazoo Promise has already helped increase the community's stock of social capital, it is less certain if and when these longstanding divisions will be overcome.

The scholarship program has undoubtedly contributed to a heightened level of social and civic engagement. An outpouring of volunteer energy, the creation and expansion of community-based student support programs, and the approval of school bond issues demonstrate a growing understanding of education as pivotal to the region's health as well as a willingness to become personally involved. Diverse organizations, ranging from the symphony orchestra to local banks, have examined their missions in light of the Promise and begun to align their work with its goals. New avenues of communication have been created through a number of school-community task forces and meetings of organizational leaders convened in response to the Promise. Community-wide celebrations, such as Promise Week, as well as neighborhood events have united parents, teachers, grassroots leaders, and residents in new partnerships centered on supporting youth.

In all these efforts, the community has expanded upon a base of preexisting networks. Coordinating bodies such as Kalamazoo Communities In Schools, the Greater Kalamazoo United Way, KYDNET, and the Northside Ministerial Alliance provide centralized locales for people seeking to disseminate information or find partners. The uncertainty is, first, whether these partners can move beyond improved communication to forge a collaborative response to the challenges raised by the Kalamazoo Promise, and, second, whether such networks can be broadened to connect disparate populations and create the "bridging" of social networks necessary for transformative change. While these remain open questions, in contrast to the constraints on the creation of new economic assets imposed by the broader environment, the extent to which the Kalamazoo Promise strengthens the social fabric is well within local control.

Kalamazoo is often described as a community rich in resources but poor in coordination. In a world of limited resources, however, coordination is essential to direct resources where they are most needed and ensure maximum coverage and minimum overlap. Better communication among the community's many institutional actors is helpful, but true collaboration requires much more. One model from Kalamazoo's recent past is a joint initiative of the Department of Human Services, Goodwill Industries, and Housing Resources, Inc. that provides wraparound services to some of the area's poorest families. The "Making It Work" program addresses these families' housing and employment needs through a long-term case-management approach that has required new modes of operation on the part of all three agencies as well as supportive policy changes at the state level. The program is remarkable not only for the gains in self-sufficiency experienced by its clients, but for the extent of collaboration, described by one of its partners as, "Everyone puts their money on the table and removes their hands."[5] This degree of collective leadership is unusual, but strong partnerships are increasingly evident.

Two collaborations that have emerged since the announcement of the Kalamazoo Promise demonstrate a new attitude toward partnership and the benefits it can bring. One of these involves the Douglass Community Association, which has served the Northside since 1919, and the Boys and Girls Club of Kalamazoo, based in the Edison neighborhood since 1953. Historically, the two organizations worked independently, offering somewhat similar programs to young people in different neighborhoods while at the same time competing for funding from local foundations and the Greater Kalamazoo United Way. In 2007, the leadership of the two organizations, supported by the United Way, recognized that a more cooperative approach made sense and began discussing how best to fill the gaps in service to their constituents. The result was the opening of a unit of the Boys and Girls Club at the Douglass Community Association—the first collaboration of its kind for either organization. The partnership is significant in that it provides expanded programming for youth without the creation of a new organization or program. It also constitutes a bridge between two of the city's lowest income neighborhoods, opening up lines of communication that may help lessen the tension between Northside and Eastside youth that is at the center of some of the community's nascent gang activities. When asked what made the collaboration possible, the heads of the two organizations give strikingly similar answers. Tim Terrentine, executive director of the Douglass Community Association, says the most important element was selfless leadership. Rather than the usual response of nonprofit leaders and boards—"What are we going to lose and how much is it going to cost?"—management and boards of the Douglass Community Association and the Boys and Girls Club acknowledged that they had a better chance of positively affecting community youth through a partnership. "Kids are out in the street, and one organization can't bring them all in," says Terrentine.[6] "We did it by people leaving their egos at home and not feeling as though we had all the answers," says Bob Ezelle, executive director of the Boys and Girls Club of Kalamazoo.[7]

A second promising collaboration is a partnership between Big Brothers Big Sisters and area churches. A national trendsetter in partnering with religious institutions, the local Big Brothers Big Sisters organization has doubled the number of children it serves (to approximately 1,000) through partnerships being developed with close to a dozen area churches. The most extensive of these is a relationship with the Northside megachurch, Christian Life Center, and its outreach center, New Genesis. The church's preexisting mentoring efforts have been encompassed within an array of programs supported by Big Brothers Big Sisters, including matches between church members and local youth for community-based mentoring as well as matches between the church's high school students and local elementary school children for site-based work on academic, behavioral, and social skills. Big Brothers Big Sisters director Peter Tripp gives credit to Pastor Ervin Armstrong for his willingness to partner with an existing mentoring program rather than needing to "reinvent the wheel" at his own institution. The church now serves as a recruitment arm to identify mentors and a provider of space and materials. Big Brothers Big Sisters supports the church's programs through high-quality, proven mentoring models, the outcomes of which can be readily measured.

Both collaborations speak to the creation of bridging social capital—the first across neighborhoods and the second across generational and income lines. They also both reflect a growing understanding that Kalamazoo is not well served by the ongoing duplication of organizations and services, some of dubious quality. Better to build on best practices that have been refined and evaluated, and invest resources in spreading these more fully throughout the community.

Social capital has improved in other respects as well. While generally positive, the initial response to the Kalamazoo Promise also included some posturing around the issue of race and advocacy efforts designed mainly to score points with constituencies who felt marginalized or disenfranchised by existing decision-making structures. These negative reactions have for the most part abated and been replaced by painful but honest discussions of the racial and economic inequalities that hinder the success of the Kalamazoo Promise. "The Kalamazoo Promise dredged up a lot of issues that people didn't want to talk about," says Ezelle, "issues like race and economic self-sufficiency. What was under the surface is now out on the table. The idea that the program was not for everyone had to be attacked on a number of different fronts—teachers, kids, parents, media, businesses—they all had to buy in." Terrentine calls it a great dichotomy: a philanthropic community with poverty rates far in excess of the national average. "I see the Promise as this great lighthouse. It flashed on the light, and now everyone has to talk about the issues. The African American dropout rate, the child poverty rate—these are nothing new, but now everyone has to talk about them." A persistent minority achievement gap in the schools and the concentration of violent crime in the urban core interfere with the ability of the city's low-income, minority residents to benefit from the scholarship program. "At the end of the day," continues Terrentine, "when you're talking about the success of the Kalamazoo Promise, you're talking about opportunities for poor, disenfranchised children in the urban areas. If they're not successful, the Promise is not successful." Much of the initiative in addressing these issues is coming from these communities themselves, with an especially active role played by the churches, but progress will be hindered if the broader community cannot provide effective support for and participation in these efforts. Ezelle is hopeful:

"I've seen this community rise to the occasion in many different ways. Some of the people who are at the poverty level may not understand that the community has stepped forward through the United Way to get services to the people who need them. People do want to help even though they may not know how to do it."

Social gains will be maximized if community members set realistic goals and hold themselves and each other accountable for progress toward them. If leaders overpromise and underdeliver, the result will be an inevitable loss of momentum and disillusionment with the Promise. Clear performance measures that are reported publicly and at regular intervals can help the community confront and address unpleasant truths, rather than patting itself on the back for gains not actually made. In moving this goal-setting and alignment process forward, it is unlikely that a single leadership structure will emerge. A more plausible vision is one in which diverse sectors of the community coordinate their efforts with a common goal in mind. The multiple strategic priorities developed to guide community progress—educational excellence, student support, vitality of the urban core, and regional economic development—offer a rich agenda for engagement and plenty of work to go around. The breadth of this agenda virtually requires an alignment process and accountability mechanism that is horizontal and decentralized, rather than one that is engineered from the top down along command-and-control lines.

Ultimately, the critical question is whether the Kalamazoo Promise remains something marginal to the community, or whether it serves as a catalyst for deeper, transformative change. It is difficult to imagine how the program might affect the community negatively, and there are already signs that the net impact has been positive. The decline in enrollment within the region's largest school district has been halted, the growing concentration of poor students within that district has slowed, and funding is available to enable more students to attend college with lower levels of family hardship. In the absence of the Kalamazoo Promise, existing trends would most likely have worsened, especially given the increasingly negative economic climate, with continued enrollment decline in KPS, the stigmatization of the district as it is serves an even higher concentration of low-income students while receiving fewer state resources, and a weak school system exerting an economic and social drag on the core city. In this scenario, the divisions that exist within the region might have been exacerbated, with the urban core confronting the fate of declining relevance that already plagues many of the nation's older cities. But the Kalamazoo Promise has changed these dynamics. A negative outcome in this light means something quite different—a failure to achieve the full potential of the program and an inability to realize the transformative vision of the donors. As suggested throughout the pages of this book, the realization of the donors' vision is not in the least bit automatic. Their gift was a catalyst; the ongoing process of community change is the responsibility of everyone else.

One of the most powerful and least anticipated effects of the Kalamazoo Promise has been its emergence as a nationally recognized model for community transformation. Reportedly, the donors never considered what impact their gift might have outside their hometown, and the intense level of media scrutiny and emulation by other communities has taken many in Kalamazoo by surprise. But this effect should not be unexpected. The connection between investing in education and supporting economic development embodied in the Kalamazoo Promise makes immediate and intuitive sense to people in many different kinds of communities. Perhaps without intending to do so, the donors have created a new path for community transformation that speaks to two of the most pressing needs of the twenty-first century: higher educational attainment and greater economic competitiveness. Their generous and open-ended investment in the education of potentially every graduate of the Kalamazoo Public Schools, whether or not those students earn good grades and regardless of their family income, was designed to change the incentives of a broad range of actors in ways that would ultimately improve not just educational outcomes but also the economy. As other communities work to develop models that fit their needs and resources, it is essential that they keep the power and simplicity of this vision at the forefront of their planning (see "Lessons for Other Communities").

The anonymity of Kalamazoo's donors gave them the opportunity to do something in private that in a more public context is controversial; invest in the education of young people without regard to need or merit. The universality of this approach is critical to its potential success. Some of the communities that are developing programs under a public spotlight face pressure to limit scholarship recipients to those who are "deserving," or those whose success in college is foreordained; for example, the Pittsburgh Promise, the largest initiative to date, will increase

Lessons for Other Communities

1) To maximize a scholarship program's power as a catalyst for broader change, scholarships should not be limited by academic merit or financial need. It is the universality of the Kalamazoo Promise (in contrast to many other targeted scholarship programs) that has generated strong support for its goals among diverse populations and made it a tool for community transformation.

2) Scholarship funding alone, no matter how generous, will be insufficient to bring about the economic or social transformation of a community. It is through the process of engagement and alignment that scholarship resources can be leveraged for deeper change. The financial resources necessary for a universal, place-based scholarship program, and community alignment around the program's goals are both essential elements of a potentially transformative investment of this type.

3) Donor anonymity has had some important benefits for Kalamazoo in terms of putting power for implementing the program into the community's hands. While similar arrangements are unlikely, a scholarship program's effectiveness as a catalyst for change will be heightened if its donors and organizers create a leadership structure that is inclusive and represents "buy-in" by the broader community.

4) A community's response to scholarship funding will be maximized if it is able to build on existing institutional capacity to handle the challenges that will arise. While new resources will likely be needed, resources can be deployed most effectively if best practices piloted in other communities are adopted and existing organizations and networks relied upon for implementation.

5) Establishing a streamlined administrative process and minimal requirements for a scholarship program will have substantial benefits. In Kalamazoo, simple requirements, an easy application process, and strong database management have resulted in a program with low overhead that maximizes the funds available to students. Other communities with programs that initially had a more complex structure have already found the need to simplify it for administrative purposes.

6) Donors and organizers should consider including resources for evaluation in their program planning. Accurate and ongoing research-based assessments of a program's impact are essential both as feedback for the community and as an accountability measure for those charged with implementing change.

its high-school GPA requirement from 2.0 to 2.5 for the class of 2009 and impose high school attendance requirements for subsequent classes. If the goal of a Promise-type program is community transformation, high-school performance requirements may be a mistake. The purpose of the Kalamazoo Promise is not to reward achievement. If anything, it is most critical that such a program opens doors for those who run the greatest risk of receiving no post-secondary training. If a student who barely survived high school is able to acquire a marketable skill free of charge at the local community college, he or she is likely to become a productive, tax-paying member of society rather than a minimum-wage worker or someone who ultimately requires public resources in the form of public assistance or the criminal justice system. However, scholarship programs that focus on low-achieving and/or low-income students can be stigmatizing, as the early experience of Battle Creek's Legacy Scholars program suggests, and rarely enjoy broad-based support from other members of the community. A critical element of the Kalamazoo Promise is its ability to draw middle-class families into an urban school district, so it must offer something to the children of these families as well.

If a community's main concern is with the cost of a universal program, there are other, better ways to devise a program that is less expensive than the Kalamazoo Promise. The most obvious is to make scholarships last-dollar rather than first-dollar, building on the widespread availability of financial aid for low- and middle-income students (in Muskegon, Michigan, even in the absence of new funding, community groups came together to ensure that every student receives every dollar of financial aid to which he or she is entitled). Other options are to pay only for the first year or two of college (like the College for Everyone program in Greene County, North Carolina) or limit the range of schools that recipients can attend (as community college-based programs such as the Jackson Legacy and the Ventura Promise do). Innovative financing structures, such as the Michigan Promise Zone legislation, can also help. If the concern is with a student's personal values, then by all means institute a community service or work requirement (although from a purely logistical standpoint, the fewer criteria that need to be monitored in the implementation of the program, the better). Programs should also be guaranteed for a long enough period to provide predictability and a lasting framework within which students, families, and the broader community can make decisions.

The power of the Kalamazoo Promise rests in its place-based focus, universal coverage, flexibility, and commitment of funding in perpetuity. While the outcome is far from guaranteed, the dynamics set in motion by this simple gift may fundamentally change not just the lives of Kalamazoo's young people and the future of their community. It may also provide a new model by which communities throughout the nation choose to put educational opportunity at the heart of their economic development endeavors.

Notes

1. This and all subsequent quotes from Gary and Katie Swartz are from an interview with the author, July 31, 2008.
2. This and all subsequent quotes from Mayor Bobby Hopewell are from an interview with the author, August 8, 2008.
3. Battle Creek Unlimited, the economic development arm of neighboring Battle Creek, reports informally that 300 communities in 42 states tout themselves as centers for life sciences research.
4. The recruitment of and creation of support services for call centers is one area where Southwest Michigan First is working to support job-creation for workers with lower skills.
5. Sherry Thomas-Cloud, Kalamazoo director of the State of Michigan's Department of Human Services, as quoted by Ellen Kissinger Rothi in conversation with the author.
6. This and all subsequent quotes from Tim Terrentine, executive director of the Douglass Community Association, are from an interview with the author, July 31, 2008.
7. This and all subsequent quotes from Bob Ezelle, executive director of the Boys and Girls Club of Kalamazoo, are from an interview with the author, August 4, 2008.

References

Abernethy, Michael. 2006. "Edwards Extends College for Everyone." *Kinston Free Press,* May 20.

Associated Press. 2002. "Timber Firm Cuts Student Aid." *The Spokesman-Review.com.* September 28.

————. 2005. "Foundation Cuts Grants for Oregon State." March 9.

————. 2006a. "Kalamazoo School Officials Credit Promise with Enrollment Jump." September 29.

————. 2006b. "Home Sales Rise on Kalamazoo Promise." September 4.

Audia, Frank W., and Denise A. Buckley. 2003. *System Failure: Michigan's Broken Municipal Finance Model.* Report prepared by Plante & Moran to the Michigan Municipal League, Southfield, Michigan.

Bartik, Timothy J. 2006. *The Economic Development Benefits of Universal Preschool Education Compared to Traditional Economic Development Programs.* Report to the W.E. Upjohn Institute for Employment Research, Kalamazoo, MI.

Bartik, Timothy J., and Kevin Hollenbeck. 2006. "Graduation Requirements, Skills, Postsecondary Education, and the Michigan Economy." Testimony presented to Michigan Senate Education Committee, February 20. http://www.upjohninstitute.org/Bartik-Hollenbeck_testimony.pdf (accessed December 12, 2008).

Beeke, B. Candace. 2006. "Allen Edwin Changes Name and Expands." *Business Review*, December 21.

Bennett, Andrew. 1956. "The Development of the Kalamazoo Public Schools, 1900–1914." History Seminar of Kalamazoo College; no. 58. Kalamazoo, MI, January.

Bennett, Jeff. 2008. "Class Act—Kalamazoo's Lesson: Educate and They Will Come." *Wall Street Journal*, July 28, R:3.

Boren, Jeremy. 2007. "Pittsburgh Council Balks at Promise Qualifier." *Pittsburgh Tribune-Review*, December 19.

Boudette, Neal E. 2006. "Kalamazoo, Mich., Pegs Revitalization on a Tuition Plan." *Wall Street Journal*, March 10, A:1.

Boushey, Heather. 2005. *Student Debt: Bigger and Bigger.* Briefing paper. Washington, DC: Center for Economic and Policy Research, September.

Brown, Janice M., Britany Affolter-Caine, and Paul Dimond. Forthcoming. "Promise of Prosperity: Supporting Community Compacts for Human Capital and Economic Renewal." Policy brief. Washington, DC: Brookings Institution.

Bugler, Daniel T., Gary T. Henry, and Ross Rubenstein. 1999. *An Evaluation of*

Georgia's HOPE Scholarship Program. Council for School Performance, Atlanta. November 19.

Burchell, Robert W., Anthony Downs, Barbara McCann, and Sahan Mukherji. 2005. *Sprawl Costs: Economic Impacts of Unchecked Development.* Washington, DC: Island Press.

Bureau of Economic Analysis. 2007. "State Economic Growth Slowed in 2007." News release, June 5.

Campbell, Jerry. 2005. "Live from Kalamazoo..." *Kalamazoo Gazette,* November 12, A:3.

Center for Educational Performance and Information. 2008. *State of Michigan 2007 4-Year Cohort Graduation and Dropout Rate Report.* State of Michigan. August 23.

Cherry Commission. 2004. *Final Report of the Lt. Governor's Commission on Higher Education & Economic Growth.* Report prepared for Governor Jennifer Granholm, Lansing, MI.

Chourey, Sarita. 2005. "Neighboring Districts Ponder Implications for Enrollment." *Kalamazoo Gazette,* November 11, A:4.

———. 2006a. "Buzz Big after ABC Promise Report." *Kalamazoo Gazette,* September 9, A:1.

———. 2006b. "Kalamazoo-Portage Area Gets High Marks." *Kalamazoo Gazette,* August 23, A:12.

———. 2007. "Bond Issue Promoted as Promise Extension." *Kalamazoo Gazette,* February 21, A:3.

Citizens Research Council of Michigan (CRC). 2007a. *Regional Approaches to Economic Development, Part 1: The Challenge of Economic Development.* CRC Report 345-1, Lansing, MI.

———. 2007b. *Regional Approaches to Economic Development, Part 4: The Organizational Structure of Economic Development in Michigan.* CRC Report 345-4, Lansing, MI.

Clark, Terry N. 2003. *The City as Entertainment Machine.* New York: JAI Press.

College Board. 2007a. *Trends in College Pricing,* Trends in Higher Education Series. Washington, DC: The College Board.

———. 2007b. *Trends in Student Aid,* Trends in Higher Education Series. Washington, DC: The College Board.

———. 2008. *2008-09 College Prices.* Washington, DC: The College Board.

Committee for Economic Development. 2006. "The Economic Promise of Investing in High-Quality Preschool: Using Early Education to Improve Economic Growth and the Fiscal Sustainability of States and the Nation." Washington, DC: Committee for Economic Development.

Cornwell, Christopher M., David B. Mustard, and Deepa Sridhar. 2006. "The

Enrollment Effects of Merit-Based Financial Aid: Evidence from Georgia's HOPE Scholarship." *Journal of Labor Economics* 24: 761–786.

Cortright, Joseph. 2006. "Making Sense of Clusters: Regional Competitiveness and Economic Development." Washington, DC: The Brookings Institution. March.

Dickens, William T. Isabel Sawhill, and Jeffrey Tebbs. 2006. "The Effects of Investing in Early Education on Economic Growth." Policy brief no. 153. Washington, DC: The Brookings Institution, April.

Dowd, Alicia C. 2006. "Promises to Keep: Financial Aid, Equity, and the Case of the Kalamazoo Promise." Paper presented at ASHE Invited Presidential Symposium, the Association for the Study of Higher Education, held in Anaheim, CA, November 1–4.

Dreier, Peter, John Mollenkopf, and Todd Swanstrom. 2001. *Place Matters: Metropolitics for the Twenty-First Century*. Lawrence, KS: University Press of Kansas.

Dunbar, Willis F. 1955. *Michigan through the Centuries*. New York: Lewis Historical Publishing Company, Inc. Volume II, p. 308.

———. 1969. *Kalamazoo and How it Grew…and Grew…* Kalamazoo, MI: Western Michigan University Press.

Dynarski, Susan. 1999. "Does Aid Matter? Measuring the Effect of Student Aid on College Attendance and Completion." NBER working paper no. 7422. Cambridge, MA: National Bureau for Economic Research, November.

———. 2000. "Hope for Whom? Financial Aid for the Middle Class and Its Impact on College Attendance." NBER working paper no. 7756. Cambridge, MA: National Bureau for Economic Research, June.

———. Dynarski, Susan. 2002. "The New Merit Aid." NBER working paper no. 9400. Cambridge, MA: National Bureau for Economic Research, December.

———. 2005. "Building the Stock of College-Educated Labor." NBER working paper no. 11604. Cambridge, MA: National Bureau for Economic Research, September.

Economic Development Administration. 1997. "Cluster-Based Economic Development: A Key to Regional Competitiveness." Washington, DC: U.S. Department of Commerce, October.

Fast Company. 2007. "The 6th Annual Fast 50." March. http://www.fastcompany.com/fast50_07 (accessed December 12, 2008).

Federal Reserve Bank of Chicago. 2007. "Can Higher Education Foster Economic Growth? A Conference Summary." *Chicago Fed Letter*, no. 236a, March.

Files, John. 2006. "With Success of College Grant Program Comes Debate Over Its Rising Budget." *New York Times*, May 30.

228 Miller-Adams

Florida, Richard. 2005. *The Flight of the Creative Class*, New York: Harper-Collins.

Forbes.com. 2008. "Special Report: The World's Billionaires." March 5. http://www.forbes.com/lists/2007/10/07billionaires_The-Worlds-Billionaires_Rank.html (accessed December 12, 2008).

Fortune 500. 2008. "Our Annual Ranking of America's Largest Corporations." www.CNNMoney.com (accessed December 12, 2008).

Friedman, Thomas L. 2005. *The World Is Flat: A Brief History of the Twenty-First Century*. New York: Farrar, Straus, and Giroux.

Fulton, George, and Donald Grimes. 2006. "Michigan's Industrial Structure and Competitive Advantage: How Did We Get into This Pickle and Where Do We Go from Here?" Ann Arbor, MI: University of Michigan Press.

Glaeser, Edward L., and Christopher R. Berry. 2006. "Why Are Smart Places Getting Smarter?" Rappaport Institute/Taubman Center policy brief, PB-2006-2. Cambridge, MA: John F. Kennedy School of Government, Harvard University, March.

Glaeser, Edward L., and Albert Saiz. 2003. "The Rise of the Skilled City." Harvard Institute of Economic Research, discussion paper no. 2025. Cambridge, MA: Harvard University, December.

Goldin, Claudia, and Lawrence F. Katz. 1997. "Why the United States Led in Education: Lessons from Secondary School Expansion, 1910 to 1940." NBER working paper no. 6144. Cambridge, MA: National Bureau of Economic Research, August.

Goodman, Joshua. 2007. "Who Merits Financial Aid? Massachusetts' Adams Scholarship." Columbia University Economics discussion paper no. 0607-13. New York: Columbia University, July 18.

———. 2008. "Who Merits Financial Aid? Massachusetts Adams Scholarship." *Journal of Public Economics* 92(10): 2121–2131.

Granholm, Governor Jennifer. 2007. *Our Moment, Our Choice: Investing in Michigan's People*. State of the State Address, February 6, Lansing, MI.

Haveman, Robert, and Barbara Wolfe. 1995. "The Determinants of Children's Attainments: A Review of Methods and Findings." *Journal of Economic Literature*. 33(4): 1829–1878.

Heckman, James J., and Dimitriy V. Masterov. 2007. "The Productivity Argument for Investing in Young Children." NBER working paper no. W13016. Cambridge, MA: National Bureau for Economic Research, April.

Heller, Donald E. 2006a. "MCAS Scores and the Adams Scholarships: A Policy Failure." Policy brief for the Civil Rights Project at Harvard University, March 15. University Park, PA, Center for the Study of Higher Education at The Pennsylvania State University.

———. 2006b. "Merit Aid and College Access." Prepared for the "Symposium on the Consequences of Merit-Based Student Aid," held at the University of Wisconsin, Madison, March 1.

Heller Donald E., and Patricia Marin, eds. 2004. *State Merit Scholarship Programs and Racial Inequality.* Cambridge, MA: The Civil Rights Project at Harvard University.

Helliwell, John F., and Robert D. Putnam, 1999. "Education and Social Capital." NBER working paper no. 7121. Cambridge, MA: National Bureau for Economic Research, May.

Hirschman, Albert O. 1970. *Exit, Voice, and Loyalty: Responses to Decline in Firms, Organizations, and States.* Cambridge, MA: Harvard University Press.

Husock, Howard, and Wendell Cox. 1999. *Keeping Kalamazoo Competitive.* Report to the City of Portage, June. http://www.demographia.com/db-kzo.htm (accessed December 12, 2008).

Jessup, Kathy. 2005. "Let's Make Most of 'Incredible Opportunity,' New Mayor Says." *Kalamazoo Gazette*, November 15, A:1.

————. 2007. "Kalamazoo Rated among 100 Best Places for Kids." *Kalamazoo Gazette*, January 25, A:1.

————. 2008. "Area's Skill at Reinventing Itself Brings Jobs Growth." *Kalamazoo Gazette*, April 23, A:1.

Johnes, Geraint. 2006. "Education and Economic Growth." Eric John Hanson Memorial Lecture Series. University of Alberta, Edmonton, March 21.

Johnson, Gretchen. 2005. "Kalamazoo's Economic Revitalization." *Economic Development America* Spring: 14–17.

Jones, Al. 2005. "The Buzz: Who Could It Be?" *Kalamazoo Gazette*, November 12, A:1.

————. 2007. "Top 10 Local Business Stories of 2007." *Kalamazoo Gazette*, December 30, G:1.

Jones, Jeffrey N., Gary Miron, and Allison J. Kelaher Young. 2008. "The Impact of the Kalamazoo Promise on Teachers' Expectations for Students." Evaluation of the Kalamazoo Promise." Working paper no. 5. Western Michigan University College of Education. November.

Kahlenberg, Richard D. 2004. "Tuition Troubles." The Century Foundation, New York, October 21.

————. 2006a. "Cost Remains a Key Obstacle to College Access." *Chronicle of Higher Education* 52(27): B51.

————. 2006b. "A New Way on School Integration." Issue brief. New York: The Century Foundation, November 28.

————. 2007. *Rescuing* Brown v. Board of Education*: Profiles of Twelve School Districts Pursuing Socioeconomic School Integration.* Report from the Century Foundation, New York, June 28.

Kalamazoo County Health and Community Services. 2006. "Poverty in Kalamazoo County: 2006." June. http://www.kalcounty.com/hcs/pdf_files/poverty%20report%202006.pdf (accessed December 23, 2008).

Kalamazoo Gazette. 2006a. "Qualifying KPS Grads Seek the Promise." Editorial, July 26, A:10.

———. 2006b. "Keep Those Brains from Draining Away." Editorial, August 7, A:12.

———. 2007a. "The Promise Takes on KPS Dropout Rate." Editorial, June 6, A:12.

———. 2007b. "Kalamazoo Area Aims to be State, National Model." Editorial, January 6, A:1.

———. 2008a. "On Our Way to Becoming the Education City." Editorial, January 6, A:12.

———. 2008b. "'Yes' to KRESA Tax Renewal Says 'Yes' to Education." Editorial, April 27, A:16.

Kalamazoo Public Schools (KPS). 2007. "The Community Parent Task Force on Behavior and School Environment Report." Kalamazoo, MI, July 12.

———. 2008. *Strategic Planning Subcommittee Report: Expectations for Community, Educators, Parents, Students, and Support Staff.* KPS, Kalamazoo, MI.

Kane, Thomas J. 2007. "Evaluating the Impact of the D.C. Tuition Assistance Grant Program." *Journal of Human Resources* 42(3): 555–582. Summer.

Kane, Thomas J., and Cecilia Elena Rouse.1993. *Labor Market Returns to Two- and Four-Year Colleges: Is a Credit a Credit and Do Degrees Matter?* NBER working paper no. 4268. Cambridge, MA: National Bureau of Economic Research.

Katz, Bruce. 2006a. "The 2% Solution: Drawing a Critical Mass of Residents Downtown Is Key to Urban Revival." *Syracuse Post-Standard.* November 26. http://www.brookings.edu/opinions/2006/1126newyorkstate_katz.aspx (accessed December 12, 2008).

———. 2006b. "Transformative Investments: Unleashing the Potential of American Cities." Presentation at "Reinventing Older Communities: People, Places, Markets." Conference organized by the Federal Reserve Bank of Philadelphia, April 5.

Katz, Bruce. 2006c. "Six Ways Cities Can Reach Their Economic Potential." *Diverse Perspectives on Critical Issues, Living Cities Policy Series*, Vol. 1. Washington, DC: Living Cities, The National Community Development Initiative.

Kekic, Nick. 1984. *A Fine Place for a City: Titus Bronson and the Founding of Kalamazoo.* Kalamazoo, MI: Oak Opening Press.

Killian, Chris. 2005a. "KPS Family, But Not on Promised Land." *Kalamazoo Gazette*, November 21, G:1.

———. 2005b. "Residency Mandate Crucial to Growth." *Kalamazoo Gazette*, November 19, A:1.

———. 2006. "Home Sales up 6% This Year." *Kalamazoo Gazette*, June 22, A:1.

———. 2008. "New Homes in KPS Boost Tax Valuation." *Kalamazoo Gazette*, April 17, A:1.

King, Jacqueline E. 2000. *2000 Status Report on the Pell Grant Program*. Center for Policy Analysis, American Council on Education, Washington, DC.

Kitchens, Ron. 2008. "Support Economic Development in Region by Renewing Millage." *Kalamazoo Gazette*, April 27, A:19.

Letter to the Editor. 2005. *Kalamazoo Gazette*, November 24, A:21.

Liberty, John. 2007. "A New Tune Downtown." *Kalamazoo Gazette*, December 9, B:1.

Mack, Julie. 2005. "College Night Gets a New Twist." *Kalamazoo Gazette*, December 9, B:1.

———. 2006a. "88% of Eligible Students Taking KPS Promise." *Kalamazoo Gazette*, July 26, A:1.

———. 2006b. "Restrictions Eased on the Promise." *Kalamazoo Gazette*, April 24, A:1.

———. 2006c. "Black Women No. 1 for Promise." *Kalamazoo Gazette*, September 7, A:1.

———. 2006d. "National Panel Pans Details of Promise." *Kalamazoo Gazette*, November 4.

———. 2006e. "Kalamazoo Leaders Cast Off Promise Criticisms." *Kalamazoo Gazette*, November 13, A:3.

———. 2006f. "New Push to Prepare Minorities for College." *Kalamazoo Gazette*, January 2, A:1.

———. 2006g. "KPS Wants No Volunteer Left Behind." *Kalamazoo Gazette*, January 29, B:1.

———. 2006h. "Bank Offers 'Promise' Loans." *Kalamazoo Gazette*, March 31, A:3.

———. 2006i. "Promise Helps Reverse KPS Enrollment Decline." *Kalamazoo Gazette*, January 29, A:1.

———. 2006j. "Survey: School Voters May Back Tax Increase." *Kalamazoo Gazette*, January 24, B:1.

———. 2006k. "The Promise Nets Leadership Award for Kalamazoo." *Kalamazoo Gazette*, December 7, A:1.

———. 2007a. "Enrollment Increase at KPS Leads State." *Kalamazoo Gazette*, January 15, A:1.

———. 2007b. "KPS Foresees Small Increase in Enrollment." *Kalamazoo Gazette*, May 29, A:1.

———. 2007c. "Brown Ready to Turn Page." *Kalamazoo Gazette*, December 17, A:1.

———. 2007d. "Rice Stresses 'Hard Work' to Boost Kids' Educations." *Kalamazoo Gazette*, October 1, A:1.

———. 2007e. "Rice Wants to Detail KPS Expectations." *Kalamazoo Gazette*, September 9, B:1.

———. 2007f. "Rice Sets Initiatives to Lift KPS." *Kalamazoo Gazette*, December 31, A:1.

———. 2007g. "'Couldn't Do It Without Them' College Students Aiding Teachers in Kalamazoo Public Schools' Summer School." *Kalamazoo Gazette*, July 30, A:3.

———. 2007h. "KPS Seeking Right Balance on Discipline." *Kalamazoo Gazette*, March 11, B:1.

———. 2007i. "KPS Serious on Summer School—or Repeat Grade." *Kalamazoo Gazette*, June 13, A:3.

———. 2007j. "Parents Hot Over Proposed Class Sizes." *Kalamazoo Gazette*, March 15, A:1.

———. 2007k. "KPS' Class-Size Plan Highlights School Imbalance." *Kalamazoo Gazette*, March 18, A:1.

———. 2008a. "KPS Grads Flocking to U-M." *Kalamazoo Gazette*, June 14, A:1.

———. 2008b. "Kalamazoo Schools Outline Expectations." *Kalamazoo Gazette*, April 29, A:2.

———. 2008c. "KRESA Tax Passes with 57%." *Kalamazoo Gazette*, May 7, A:1.

———. 2008d. "Maybe Tax Question Came at the Right Time." *Kalamazoo Gazette*, May 10, A:2.

———. 2008e. "New Jobs Shift the Debate on Tax Vote." *Kalamazoo Gazette*, April 27, A:1.

Mackinder, Lisa. 2008. "Southwest Michigan Innovation Center." *MiBiz.com*, March 3. http://www.mibiz.com/absolutenm/templates/labworktemplate.aspx?articleid=13361&zoneid=162 (accessed December 12, 2008).

Massie, Larry B., and Peter J. Schmitt. 1998. *Kalamazoo: The Place behind the Products: An Illustrated History*. Sun Valley, CA: American Historical Press.

Mah, Linda S. 1991. "Desegregation, 20 years later." *Kalamazoo Gazette*, September 26, B:1.

McConkey, Karen. 2005. "GCHS Seniors to Pilot National Program." *Kinston Free Press*, September 29.

McLeod, Lynn. 2005. "Kalamazoo Promise Is Just a Gimmick Giveaway." *Kalamazoo Gazette*, December 11, Viewpoint, A:19.

Miller-Adams, Michelle. 2002. *Owning Up: Poverty, Assets, and the American Dream*. Washington, DC: Brookings Institution Press.

Miron, Gary, Jessaca Spybrook, and Stephanie Evergreen. 2008. "Key Findings from the 2007 Survey of High School Students." Evaluation of the Kalamazoo Promise, working paper no. 3. Kalamazoo, MI: The Evaluation Center, Western Michigan University, April.

Miron, Michelle. 2005. "Local Economists: Work to Retain Young, Educated." *Kalamazoo Gazette*, December 8, A:10.

———. 2006. "Looming Boom in Construction Has Some Excited, Others Cautious." *Kalamazoo Gazette*, February 20, A:1.

———. 2007a. "Local Sellers Wait Longer in a Tighter Housing Market." *Kalamazoo Gazette*, May 20, G:1.

———. 2007b. "Area Builders Revise Strategies for a Softer Housing Market." *Kalamazoo Gazette*, March 11, G:2.

———. 2007c. "Condo Boom." *Kalamazoo Gazette*, March 11, G:1.

———. 2007d. "Regional Development Group Wins National Real-Estate Award." *Kalamazoo Gazette*, May 3, A:9.

National Center for Education Statistics. 2005. *2003-04 National Postsecondary Student Aid Study (NPSAS:04)*. NCES no.: 2005164. February 11.

National Center for Higher Education Management Systems (NCHEMS). n.d. NCHEMS Information Center for State Higher Education Policymaking and Analysis. http://www.higheredinfo.org (accessed December 12, 2008).

National Center for Public Policy and Higher Education. 2006. "Measuring Up 2006: The State Report Card on Higher Education." San Jose, CA: The National Center for Public Policy and Higher Education.

Nixon, Alex. 2008a. "Troubled Homeowners Gain Allies." *Kalamazoo Gazette*, January 13, A:1.

———. 2008b. "Area Home Sales Fell 13% in '07." *Kalamazoo Gazette*, January 23, A:6.

Nyren, Ron. 2007. "Downtown Turnarounds." *Urban Land*. April.

O'Brien, Keith. 2006. "Wish You Were Here." *The Scientist*. 20(3): 38.

Orfield, Myron. 1997. *Metropolitics: A Regional Agenda for Community and Stability*. Washington, DC: Brookings Institution Press; Cambridge, MA: The Lincoln Institute of Land Policy.

Page-Adams, Deborah, and Michael Sherraden. 1996. "What We Know About Effects of Asset-Holding." Working paper no. 96-1. St. Louis, MO: Center for Social Development, Washington University.

Peppel, Fred. 2005. "Stalking the Celery City." Kalamazoo Public Library, Local History Collection.

Press News Service. 2007. "Kalamazoo to Add 200 Cameras in High Schools." December 14.

Project on Student Debt. 2007. "Quick Facts About Student Debt." September 4. Project on Student Debt, Berkeley, CA.

Putnam, Robert D. 2000. *Bowling Alone: The Collapse and Revival of American Community*. New York: Simon & Schuster.

Putnam, Robert D., and Lewis M. Feldstein. 2003. *Better Together: Restoring the American Community*. New York: Simon & Schuster.

Raabe, Steve. 2007 "Tim Marquez: Oil and Opportunity." *Denver Post*, February 3, K:1.

Ricks, Cedric. 2006. "KPS Gets Lower Interest Rate, Saving Millions." *Kalamazoo Gazette*, July 14, A:3.

Rose, Lowell C., and Alec M. Gallup. 2007. "The 39th Annual Phi Delta Kappa/Gallup Poll of the Public's Attitudes Toward the Public Schools." *Phi Delta Kappan* 89(1): 33–48.

Rusk, David. 1995. *Cities Without Suburbs*. Washington, DC: Woodrow Wilson Center Press, 2nd edition.

———. 1998. "The Kalamazoo County Compact," prepared for the Kalamazoo Consortium for Higher Education. presented October 7. http://www.visioncouncil.org/html/countycompact.htm (accessed December 12, 2008).

———. 1999. *Inside Game/Outside Game: Winning Strategies for Saving Urban America*. New York: The Century Foundation.

Rzepczynski, Kris. 1998. "You Called It WHAT? How Kalamazoo Got Its Name." Kalamazoo Public Library, Local History Collection.

Sabo, Matthew. 2002a. "Way Cleared to Change Scholarship Policy." *The Oregonian*, September 2.

———. 2002b. "Promise of Free College Ends Abruptly." *The Oregonian*, September 27.

Saguaro Seminar. 2001. "Social Capital Community Benchmark Survey." John F. Kennedy School of Government, Harvard University, March. Results available at http://www.bettertogether.org (accessed March 2, 2009).

Sawhill, Isabel V., and Jens Ludwig. 2007. "Success by Ten: Intervening Early, Often, and Effectively in the Education of Young Children." Hamilton Project discussion paper. Washington, DC: The Brookings Institution, February.

Selingo, Jeffrey. 2006. "John Edwards Talks About the Need for Greater Access to College." *Chronicle of Higher Education* 52(44): A23–A24.

Shapiro, Jesse M. 2006. "Smart Cities: Quality of Life, Productivity, and the Growth Effects of Human Capital." *Review of Economics and Statistics* 88(2): 324–335.

Smith, Adam. 1776. *Wealth of Nations*. Book I, Chapter 8. London: Methuen & Co.

Smith, Harold T. 1958. *The Position of the Paper Industry in the Economy of Kalamazoo County, Michigan, in 1954*. Kalamazoo: W.E. Upjohn Institute for Employment Research.

Southwest Michigan First. 2007. "Local College Students Begin Careers as Monroe-Brown Interns." Press release, May 7, Kalamazoo, MI.

Sugrue, Thomas J. 1996. *The Origins of the Urban Crisis: Race and Inequality in Postwar Detroit*. rev. ed. 2005. Princeton, NJ: Princeton University Press.

Summers-Coty, Kathryn. 2007. "School Aid Funding Formula: Further Closing of the School Aid Equity Gap." *State Notes: Topics of Legislative Interest*. State of Michigan Legislature. November/December.

The Segmentation Company (tsc). 2006. "Attracting the Young, College-Educated to Cities." Presentation to the CEOs for Cities National Meeting, held in Chicago, May 11.

Thompson, Edward P. n.d. "Desegregation, Kalamazoo Style." Unpublished manuscript of a speech to the Torch Club from the mid-1980s.

Thredgold, Jeff. 2007. "'Promise(d)' Land." *Tea Leaf*. Thredgold Economic Associates. January 17. www.thredgold.com (accessed December 12, 2008).

Tibor, Kristy. 2007. "Area Students Voice Concerns." *Kalamazoo Gazette*, February 10.

Timmerman, Elizabeth. 2000. "The Kalamazoo School Case: Supporting High School Education." Essay. Updated 2005. Kalamazoo Public Library, Local History Collection, Kalamazoo, MI.

Tribune-Chronicle (Warren, Ohio). 2007. "Chamber's School Plan Deserves Serious Study." Editorial, April 6.

U.S. Census Bureau. 2000. Fact Sheet: Greene County, North Carolina.

————. 2006. American Community Survey (ACS).

U.S. Commission on Civil Rights. 1977. *School Desegregation in Kalamazoo, Michigan*. Staff report, April.

U.S. Department of Education. *2005-2006 Federal Pell Grant Program End-of-Year Report*. Washington, DC: U.S. Department of Education Office of Postsecondary Education.

U.S. Department of Education, National Center for Education Statistics (NCES). 2007. *The Condition of Education 2007* (NCES 2007-064). Table 20-1. June.

University of Michigan, Office of the Registrar. n.d. "Cost of Attendance: Estimated Student Budgets." http://www.umich.edu/~regoff/tuition/ (accessed December 12, 2008).

W.E. Upjohn Institute for Employment Research. 2008a. *Business Outlook for West Michigan*. XXIV(2): 6.

————. 2008b. "New Private Housing Units Authorized by Building Permits, Kalamazoo County." Issued March 19. http://www.upjohninst.org/regional/ bldgpermits.pdf (accessed December 12, 2008).

Wayne, Leslie. 2007. "In Aiding Poor, Edwards Built Bridge to 2008." *New York Times*, June 22, A:1.

WMU News. 2005. "WMU Outlines Its Kalamazoo Promise Offer." December 1.

Western Michigan University Library Archives & Regional History Collections. n.d. http://www.wmich.edu/~ulib/archives/mlk/historical.html (accessed March 3, 2009).

Western Herald. 1963. XLVIII(27) December 20. Accessed through WMU Library archives.

World Bank. n.d. *A Brief History of LED* and *What Is LED?* Washington, DC: World Bank. Undated material from Web site, accessed through http://www .worldbank.org.

The Author

Dr. Michelle Miller-Adams has been a visiting scholar at the W.E. Upjohn Institute since January 2006. She is an expert on asset-building strategies and the author of *Owning Up: Poverty, Assets, and the American Dream* (Brookings Institution Press, 2002). She received a PhD in political science and a master's degree in international affairs from Columbia University, and a bachelor's degree in history (Phi Beta Kappa) from the University of California, Santa Barbara. Miller-Adams's professional career has spanned the fields of nonprofit management, finance, research, and academia; positions have included strategic planning consultant at the W.K. Kellogg Foundation, vice president of programs at the Twentieth Century Fund (now the Century Foundation), and vice president of research at Salomon Brothers. She was the principal investigator for a Ford Foundation–sponsored research project concerning asset-based strategies for fighting poverty, and is currently an assistant professor of political science at Grand Valley State University.

Index

The italic letters *f, n,* and *t* following a page number indicate that the subject information of the heading is within a figure, note, or table, respectively, on that page.

About the Institute

The W.E. Upjohn Institute for Employment Research is a nonprofit research organization devoted to finding and promoting solutions to employment-related problems at the national, state, and local levels. It is an activity of the W.E. Upjohn Unemployment Trustee Corporation, which was established in 1932 to administer a fund set aside by Dr. W.E. Upjohn, founder of The Upjohn Company, to seek ways to counteract the loss of employment income during economic downturns.

The Institute is funded largely by income from the W.E. Upjohn Unemployment Trust, supplemented by outside grants, contracts, and sales of publications. Activities of the Institute comprise the following elements: 1) a research program conducted by a resident staff of professional social scientists; 2) a competitive grant program, which expands and complements the internal research program by providing financial support to researchers outside the Institute; 3) a publications program, which provides the major vehicle for disseminating the research of staff and grantees, as well as other selected works in the field; and 4) an Employment Management Services division, which manages most of the publicly funded employment and training programs in the local area.

The broad objectives of the Institute's research, grant, and publication programs are to 1) promote scholarship and experimentation on issues of public and private employment and unemployment policy, and 2) make knowledge and scholarship relevant and useful to policymakers in their pursuit of solutions to employment and unemployment problems.

Current areas of concentration for these programs include causes, consequences, and measures to alleviate unemployment; social insurance and income maintenance programs; compensation; workforce quality; work arrangements; family labor issues; labor-management relations; and regional economic development and local labor markets.

CPSIA information can be obtained at www.ICGtesting.com
Printed in the USA
BVOW020456030212

282040BV00004B/3/P